Challenging Women
Since 1913

College of Saint Benedict Press

College and academy students in formal dress. Note the college/academy seal on the pillow.

Challenging Women

Since 1913

The College of Saint Benedict

For Ashleigh — It's Women such as you — and you —

Annette Atkins

Who make CSB proud!

Annette Atkins

College of Saint Benedict Press

2013

This project has been financed in part with funds provided by the State of Minnesota through the Minnesota Historical Society from the Arts and Cultural Heritage Fund.

MINNESOTA HISTORICAL & CULTURAL HERITAGE GRANTS

Published by College of Saint Benedict Press
College of Saint Benedict
37 South College Avenue
St. Joseph, Minnesota 56374

http://www.csbsju.edu/

Published in the United States of America.

ISBN 978-0-615-32026-7

Library of Congress Control Number: 2013938021

Cover design: Rachel Melis
Interior design: BookMobile Design & Digital Publisher Services
Photo credits: Photos of S. Claire Lynch and Bishop Peter Bartholome from the collections of the Stearns History Museum and Research Center, St. Cloud, Minn. Newspaper photos taken from *St. Cloud Times, Minneapolis Tribune,* and *Princeton Union,* with the assistance of the SHMRC and the Minnesota Historical Society. All other photos from the collections of the Saint Benedict's Monastery, College of Saint Benedict, and Saint John's University.

Contents

Foreword

by MaryAnn Baenninger

This book commemorates the centennial of the College of Saint Benedict, at the intersection of its first and second 100 years. Like the college itself, it is meant to be a lasting work, so I am compelled to start this foreword with the college's vision, which speaks to the enduring commitment the college has made to its students and its alumnae:

> Our history is characterized by a fierce belief in the power of liberal education, an engagement with the world around us, responsiveness to the needs of society, an enduring commitment to our Catholic and Benedictine heritage, and an unwavering focus on women's development as leaders, professionals, and scholars. We envision our future as grounded in these same commitments, and we embrace the changes and challenges impacting the world with the same courage, strength, and boldness of our foremothers.

The vision accurately describes who we were in 1913, who we are in 2013, and who we will be in 2113, but there is so much between the lines. The 100 years that have passed since the sisters began to teach students who wished to earn a college degree have been years of profound societal change for women, and years of deep and positive change for the College of Saint Benedict. The story for women is not a simple one, and neither is the story of the college.

As I write this foreword, the media are abuzz about a new book by

Sheryl Sandberg, the chief operating officer of Facebook. If you are reading this foreword in the early twenty-first century, you know what Facebook is, and you have probably heard about Sandberg's book. If you are reading this in the twenty-second century, it is my fervent hope that you do not need to read a book like Sandberg's. The book, *Lean In: Women, Work, and the Will to Lead,* is a look at why women do not yet hold 50 percent of the leadership roles in society. Sandberg encourages women to "lean in," rather than away, and broadly stated, not to assume that their brothers will always run the show.

The sisters of the Order of Saint Benedict "leaned in" 150 years ago when they came to central Minnesota, they "leaned in" in 1913 when they founded the College of Saint Benedict, and they "leaned in" scores of times when they took risks, made audacious gambles, and always strived for a better world, regardless of what they were building, literally and metaphorically. They taught the notion of "leaning in" to thousands of women before Sandberg used the phrase in her book.

They did this against the tide. In some ways, the pull of the water is no less strong today than it was in 1913. Women are still discovering how to make their way and how to bring coherence to their multiple roles. With each new freedom, responsibility, and hurdle comes more complication. For the entirety of the college's first 100 years—and into the second—Bennies have been like other women in that, as individuals, they have differing aspirations, they have various passions, and they make their own choices.

But Bennies share some distinct characteristics, and they can pick each other out in a crowd. (They can pick out Johnnies, too, but that is another story.) There is a grace, elegance, commitment, strength of character, intelligence, wisdom, and articulateness that defines Bennies. And a modesty, too.

I can say these complimentary things about Bennies because I am merely an honorary Bennie. Bennies almost never praise themselves. This thread of modesty runs through the history of the college. This is partly a "Minnesota thing" but it is more than that, and it is special. This honest humility is constant evidence of the high expectations Bennies hold for their own achievement and for the achievement of other Bennies. Excellence and continuous improvement are expected, and therefore, too often unacknowledged.

One of my jobs has been to help our students understand that the Benedictine value of humility can coexist with the acknowledgment of one's strengths, and with feeling a healthy sense of pride and accomplishment. In the "afterword" I will toot the college's and Bennies' horns a bit, but for now, back to what this book is about.

When we began to think about the college's centennial, I knew that we needed at least one book to tell the story of the college. At first I imagined that one of the sisters would write the book, as several sisters have written so ably about the college, in various forms, in the past. But, exemplifying who we are in our history, there were no sisters, for various reasons, who could take on this project at this time in their lives.

Our great good fortune is that we have a lay historian among us who is an expert on the exact kind of history this book demanded. Annette Atkins is a faculty member at CSB/SJU. She had recently written the history for Minnesota's sesquicentennial, *Creating Minnesota: A History from the Inside Out,* published by the Minnesota Historical Society. Annette is an historian, but really, she is a storyteller. I wanted the story to be told in a real way, more of an oral history than an exhaustive history.

Exceedingly worthy exhaustive histories of the college's early years can be found in the archives and in books written by sisters. The stories in this book complement the histories presented in *With Lamps Burning* by M. Grace McDonald, OSB (North Central Publishing Company, 1957), *Behind the Beginnings: Benedictine Women in America* by M. Incarnata Girgen, OSB (North Central Publishing Company, 1981), and *With Hearts Expanded: Transformations in the Lives of Benedictine Women, St. Joseph, MN* co-authored by Evin Rademacher, OSB, Emmanuel Renner, OSB, Olivia Forster, OSB, and Carol Berg, OSB (North Star Press, 2000). I invite those of you who want more detailed information on specific parts of the history of the college and Benedictine women in central Minnesota to consult these volumes. *With Lamps Burning* covers the journey of Benedictine sisters from Eichstätt in 1851 to central Minnesota in 1957, including the founding of the college. *Behind the Beginnings* focuses on the correspondence of Benedictines between 1840 and 1914, and *With Hearts Expanded* focuses on the transformation of the sisters of the Order of Saint Benedict community between 1857 and 2000.

College of Saint Benedict reached its 100th birthday by continually adapting to the changing needs of women and the changing needs for women's education. This book approaches the history of the college through the wide-angle lens of prevailing political, civic, and educational issues, including the suffragist movement (later the women's movement), the discourse on equal rights, the inception and trajectory of women's colleges, and, of course, the Catholic Church, and women's roles in the Church, and patriarchy. It allows us to see the story of the college in the context of the local diocese and bishops, and the "lifelong" relationship with Saint John's University, the sisters and the monks, the Bennies and the Johnnies.

The story is not always perfect or pretty, but it is real and vibrant. At its heart is the courage, strength, boldness, and persistence of our foremothers, and the legacy that stewards like me easily grow to love, value, embrace, and fiercely protect.

I hope you enjoy this book—including the sidebars and photo-essays—as much as I did. I hope, too, that the memories it conjures resonate with you, or that the spirit of Saint Ben's as you know it—past and present—shines though. I will return at the end of the book to tell you a little bit more about how some of the stories unfolded in the Saint Ben's of today.

I offer these words with deep gratitude to Annette Atkins.

MaryAnn Baenninger
President
College of Saint Benedict
St. Joseph, Minnesota
March 11, 2013

Preface and Acknowledgments

Mother Willibalda Scherbauer—a founder of Saint Benedict's Monastery in St. Joseph, Minn., in the mid-19th century—had a name that strikes the modern reader as difficult to say and nearly impossible to spell. The rolls of the monastery are full of similarly unfamiliar names—Walburga, Adelgundis, Clotilde, Mechtildis, for examples—that offer a lesson about meaning and context.

Those who know the history of Benedictinism may recognize that Willibalda's name commemorated St. Willibald, the eighth-century bishop of Eichstätt, where the sisters at Saint Ben's originated. St. Willibald's sister was St. Walburga, after whom the women's monastery

St. Walburga Monastery in Eichstätt

in Eichstätt was named. Willibald and Walburga were both related to St. Boniface, after whom Abbot Boniface Wimmer (the abbot who feuded for so long with Mother Benedicta Riepp) was named. The other names carry Benedictine and church history as well: Sisters Adelgundis and Mechtildis received the names of Benedictine abbesses and S. Clotilde was named for a holy Bergundian princess.

For the sisters who ventured from Eichstätt to Pennsylvania to central Minnesota, such names spoke of heritage and almost certainly inspired the women and armed them with courage. As S. M. Grace McDonald sets forth in *With Lamps Burning,* her 1957 history of her community, the sisters survived only because of their strong vocations, extraordinary effort, and a miracle or two.

Sister M. Grace McDonald, teacher, historian, and one of the college's founders

To the thousands of Germans who migrated to Minnesota, the sisters' names were like their own: Scherbauer, Richter, Marthaler, Philippi, Schmitt, and Schmittbauer, Terhaar, Eich, Knapp, and Koepp. Knowing that these Bavarian Catholics and their children would need the care in the new world they'd had in the old, the sisters came too. When life in America required that they abandon their cloisters and join the world, they did, taking care of orphans and of the sick, offering music and needlework lessons, teaching in Catholic schools, in the public school system, and on reservations. They started grade schools of their own and, in the 1880s, Saint Benedict's Academy, a high school for girls.[1]

Opening a school meant more than offering classes. Sisters ran the schools and taught the classes; they also ran the dormitories and dining rooms, the laundry, the farm, and the butcher shop. They did it within strict and tight budgets and kept strict books—this or that student bought an envelope ($.01), needed a veil ($.10), needed a scholarship ($25). They also kept an eye out for vocations.

Hundreds of children took what they learned from the sisters and grew into Catholic adults who built families and parishes and communities, better for their Benedictine grounding. Some of the young women—many still girls—knocked on the door of the convent, hoping to join. The community offered religious discipline and self-sacrifice, a life of prayer, devotion, and opportunities not generally open to women. The community of Benedictine women in St. Joseph, Minn., grew—from 7 to 70 to 700 to a peak of 1,246. The sisters ran their own community and schools in four states; they produced stunningly beautiful vestments and altar cloths, and they built hospitals and orphanages. As their number increased, they spun off new communities—to Duluth, Minn., to Atchison, Kan., and Eau Claire, Wisc., Saint Paul, Minn., Olympia, Wash., Ogden, Utah, also to Taiwan, Japan, Puerto Rico, and the Bahamas.

In 1913 the Benedictines had sister/teachers, sister/nurses, sister/leaders to educate and so added a college to their mission. While a high-school education may have been adequate for the young woman of the 19th century, the sisters saw that it would not be enough for the 20th. They also saw other communities of Catholic women opening colleges and seized the idea that so fit the sisters' own aspirations.

Education always awakens women's consciousness of their possibilities and introduces what for many women can be a profound dilemma: "how to live up to the promise of her education and at the same time fulfill her female role," as historian Barbara Solomon puts it. For Catholic women, this could be a "tri-lemma": how to live up to the promise of her education, her role as a woman, her life as a Catholic.[2]

Saint Benedict's College—as it was first known—started small, even timidly. But it didn't stay that way. Many Catholic women's colleges in the course of the last 100 years have risen and then fallen, have gone coed or out of existence, but the College of Saint Benedict has grown, strengthened, survived, and flourished. Its story is the focus of this book.

Readers will not learn here every player's name or every important date in the history of Saint Ben's. Far from it. Some will be disappointed or even shocked at what's *not* here. I've not included all the stories that could or even should be told—say, of the college's finances, academic profile, racial history, carbon footprint, or relation to other Minnesota colleges. Including everything would only turn a good story into an encyclopedia. For all of these omissions, I am sorry. I haven't found a way to include Joe O'Connell, S. Nancy Hynes, the student operas, details about the fine lay faculty, the work of the trustees, the student financial-aid people, the hundreds of other people and topics that I learned about in the course of this research.

This book does not, then, constitute a conventional institutional history. Instead, having spent wonderful days, months, years in college records and talking to college people, I've written a book that people might want to read, one that grapples with both the public face and the lived experience of being CSB, one that prompts discussion rather than offers definitive answers. I respect and regard CSB highly enough that I want not just to sing its praises but to think about it seriously, to raise serious issues, to speak to sometimes-unspoken-about topics. I've aimed to write a meaningful account. I hope I've succeeded.

Deciding what and what not to include is a challenge in putting together any story, and iterating the development of CSB over time was doubly so! Every time I sat down to write, my study filled up with the spirits of CSB people I want to remember and honor.

That's a well-populated category and includes people such as Ed Turley and Carolyn Finley, who make such fine music; S. Ann Marie Biermaier, a Saint Ben's high school and college graduate who guided many generations of teachers-in-training; Barbara Edwards Farley, another CSB grad who taught at Saint Ben's, then moved to Augsburg College, then to Illinois College as its president; Ozzie Mayers and Tom Darnall and Mike Opitz, who devoted all their careers to this women's college and its students; Phyllis Plantenberg, who as a junior at CSB played a barbarian in the pageant, became S. Dunstan, taught "killer" biology, and organized a community garden and the St. Joseph Farmers' Market; Norma Koetter, from a long line of St. Joe Losos who have worked for the Benedictines; S. Ingrid Anderson, who taught chemistry and called it home economics and who modeled elegance even in her habit; my colleagues Dave Bennetts and Ken Jones, Fr. Rene McGraw and the late Fr. Ray Pedrizetti and others who helped create a joint faculty and common curriculum for all of our students; and Bob Spaeth, "my" first dean here, a Johnnie grad married to a Bennie, who became parents of several Bennies.

The spirits of many beloved students hover around my desk, too: Katie Krolczyk, who volunteered in Costa Rica and D.C.; Katie Middleton, who studied abroad and has kept her passport handy ever since; Les Bendsten, a Johnnie who became a dedicated human rights campaigner; MaryAnn Leuthmer, who excelled at Spanish and cross-country skiing and music and then went to medical school; Jon McGee, who started at SJU about the time I did and has turned into a friend and colleague. There are other students too, frivolous or ambitious, who graduated or couldn't get out fast enough, who wanted to linger, who went to law or graduate school or happily took up an MRS degree.

As I have worked, I have felt a responsibility to all of these people. If they don't show up individually in these pages, they do show up in my approach. They have reminded me that the history of this community is complex and rich, multiple and varied, even contradictory. There's no single, straight line from 1913 to the present. The past is as messy and unkempt as life today, waiting to be pressed to order under the magnifying glass of the historian. As geographers know well, any attempt to turn a three-dimensional globe into a flat map distorts everything, one way or another.

Much in the history of women's colleges in general and CSB in particular speaks of struggle—with odds, obstacles, people—to succeed. This story, however, emphasizes opportunities and vision, aspirations and hopes. It explores the amazing ways in which the College of Saint Benedict has challenged women, opened worlds for them, and given them choices.

I have depended on the help of many more people than I can thank here. I'm grateful that President MaryAnn Baenninger asked me to write this story and then set me free to do it. She has not micromanaged or censored, but she has read it, did offer many helpful comments. The current prioress, S. Michaela Hedican, has been generous with her insight and access to records. The interpretations and the mistakes, however, are my own.

Provost Rita Knuesel and Vice Provost Joe DesJardins as well as, Dean Richard Ice, Associate Dean Dave Lyndgaard, Pam Reding, MaryJo Waggoner, and Shirley Kelly made it possible for me to take time from my teaching to write. My department chair and colleagues helped by filling in for the duration of the project.

I'm especially grateful to the worker bees in the Saint Benedict's Monastery Archives: Sisters Renee Rau, Evin Rademacher, Agatha Zwilling, Owen Lindblad, Stefanie Weisgram, and Clare Shadeg, plus John Parker (who helped mightily with photographs). The Thursday afternoon coffee breaks carried me along and made my archives work so much more fun.

The many sisters who have told me their stories and taught me about the monastery and college made this work both better and more pleasurable. I am especially grateful to have been welcomed into the daily life of the community for a time in 2012. Peggy Roske, archivist for the two colleges, and her student workers (especially Meghan Flanagan) went beyond their job descriptions to help me find and understand college records; they became valuable historical records in themselves. Brother David Klingeman, archivist at Saint John's, answered my many questions with remarkable speed and accuracy.

Sisters Ruth Nierengarten, Moira Wild, and Mariterese Woida and the whole staff of the Haehn Museum mounted thoughtful exhibits telling parts of this story and helping me to know and articulate the stories that matter. I am grieved that S. Ruth died just as this book was going to press.

S. Galen Martini and S. Kathleen Kalinowski were especially helpful, each in very special ways—Galen by asking so many questions and Kathleen by having so many answers—and both by offering lots of moral support and advice along the way.

Associate Prof. Rachel Melis designed a beautiful cover and in so many ways helped me see the college through her artist's eye.

Legions of students taking my CSB/SJU history class taught me through their research and questions. Among the most helpful were Leah Juster, Nicole Bach, and Andrew Gaydos, my "history entrepreneurs" Danika Lindquist, Megan Connolly, Margaret Free, Rob Hedberg, Alex Betley, and Rachel Mullin, and a generation of student workers. Thank you all.

I was grateful, too, to receive state funds to interview alumnae: This project has been financed in part with funds provided by the State of Minnesota through the Minnesota Historical Society from the Arts and Cultural Heritage Fund. Anne Juster did a superb job of transcribing the interviews. Mary Ann Haws—a CSB grad herself and related to literally dozens of CSB and SJU Mugglis and Haws—agreed to be interviewed and helped in this whole project (including getting the grant application in). I can't thank her enough.

My friends and family have heard too much about this book and for too long. They'll all be happy to move on to a new topic, I suspect. Thank you Kathy Paden, Patsy Murphy, Fr. Tim Backous, Fr. Rene McGraw, Marcia Anderson, Debbie Miller, Peg Meier, Jane Curry, Gretchen Kreuter, Bonnie Janda, Helen and Nick Holtam, Ali Lyon, Betsy and Tim Cartwright, Linda Peterson, Jeff and Ryan Cartwright, and most of all my husband, Tom Joyce (SJU '61).

Thanks to all of you who have taken the time to talk to me, to tell me of your experience, to teach me about the CSB you know, to show me the texture of your emotions and memories about this place, to help me understand.

In getting this book to press, my friend and the best copy editor ever—Ellen Green—improved the manuscript immeasurably and provided more support than an author could hope for. Mark Conway pushed the project uphill the last way; Hope Klocker, Glenda Burgeson, Julie Marthaler, BookMobile and Rachel Holscher (CSB '98) dragged it across the finish line.

Finally, I thank all of those connected with the College of Saint Benedict who support it in so many generous ways—time, talent, tithe—and whose love has made the whole enterprise worth doing and the writing of the book both a privilege and a joy.

Saint Joseph, Minnesota, January 2013

Notes on Terminology

Many people refer to Roman Catholic sisters as nuns and to the place of residence for religious communities as convents. Technically, the term "nun" refers to women who live cloistered or enclosed lives, as the nuns did in Eichstätt. The nuns from St. Walburg Abbey in Eichstätt, Germany, were not able to live an enclosed life so came to be called "sisters" as was the custom for all women religious in the United States.

Especially in response to the Second Vatican Council, Benedictine women have reclaimed the more accurate language of monastery for their place of residence. I have used the terms "sister" and "monastery" throughout this book. The only intentional exception is my use of "convent" to refer to the actual physical building when I'm talking about it prior to 1996 (when the term was changed to monastery. I've also used the abbreviation S. for sister.

The conventional way of referring to Benedictines (sisters and monks) includes the designation of OSB (Order of Saint Benedict): S. Carol Berg, OSB, for example. Since virtually all of the sisters (and monks) I refer to by name are Benedictines, I have omitted the OSB.

Even people familiar with Benedictine life are often vague on some common terms. "Prioress" or "Mother" are titles given to the head of a women's monastic community, so S. Louise Walz was the prioress and commonly called "Mother." Today the leader of the community would be identified as S. Michaela Hedican, Prioress of the Sisters of the Order of Saint Benedict.

An "abbot" is the head of a men's monastic community and all members are called "monk." A distinction in women's communities between "choir sisters" and "lay sisters" has disappeared. The similar distinction between priests and brothers remains significant. Priests—called Father—are ordained (can administer the sacraments). Brothers—called Brother—are not ordained.

All members of American Benedictine communities pledge themselves to be faithful to the Rule of Saint Benedict and profess vows of stability, conversion of life, and obedience (to the prioress/abbot), not the otherwise familiar apostolic vows of poverty, chastity, and obedience.

Challenging Women
Since 1913

ONE

$\sim$

We Are Bennies: CSB at 100

The College of Saint Benedict tells a remarkable story of remarkable success. In 1913 it stood among the first U.S. Catholic women's colleges—19 opened between 1899 and 1915. At its 50th birthday, it was one of about 250 women's colleges (116 Catholic); at its centennial it was one of 46 women's colleges (24 Catholic) in the United States. Of the four women's colleges founded in Minnesota (all Catholic), St. Teresa's has closed, St. Scholastica has gone coed, and St. Catherine's continues a strong single-sex undergraduate college and has added a large coed graduate program.* Saint Ben's is stronger than ever.[1]

The success of the college belongs first to the Benedictines. Mother Cecelia Kapsner and the founding faculty got the school up and running, constructed suitable academic spaces, reassured parents and pastors that Saint Ben's would be good for their girls, and provided steady hands for further development. The whole community of sisters provided economic support, committing themselves to a college that was theirs. They didn't ask the local bishop for funding. They didn't ask the abbot at Saint John's either. They funded it themselves—one student,

---

*CSB is one of only 12 Carnegie Classified women's national liberal arts colleges, the only one in Minnesota, and one of only two Catholic colleges of this type (with Saint Mary's in South Bend, Ind.) in the country. Six of the twelve are members of the original "Seven Sisters."

one music pupil, one grade-school teacher, one needlepoint project, one nurse at a time.[2]

Few of the founding sisters had much experience of higher education. That didn't deter them. They moved quickly and deftly to learn. For models they looked to the "Seven Sisters" and other women's colleges, to the normal schools where most teachers received their training, to the University of Minnesota, and to Catholic men's colleges. Then they came up with a version of a Catholic women's college all their own.

From its founding, Saint Ben's offered some vocation-specific courses in teaching, business, nutrition, and home economics to help women into the professions then open to them. It also taught its students to be good Catholics, parishioners, mothers, and citizens (even before women could vote). All coursework and degrees, however, were grounded in a strong liberal arts curriculum.

Such an education frees women to question, even to step out of the shadows of tradition and away from other people's expectations. Women's colleges, especially those run by orders of sisters, educated their students, too, by the example of women as faculty members, presidents, deans, business managers, by professional scientists and economists, historians, artists, and writers.

Saint Ben's presidents, too, get a large share of the credit for the college's success. Each one of them exercised her own (in one case, his own) brand of leadership, ambitions, and skills. Several deserve special mention: S. Claire Lynch held only a bachelor's degree when she made the leap from high school teacher to dean (president except in name) in 1932. In her nine years, she made sure the college received accreditation and sent faculty members away for advanced degrees. Under her leadership, the college was reorganized, its curriculum strengthened, its finances put on a firmer foundation, and its enormously helpful board of lay advisors recruited.

S. Remberta Westkaemper, president from 1957 to 1961, held a doctorate in biology. Her specialty was botany, what many 19th-century biologists considered a ladylike science. Like many "ladies" who practiced botany in the 20th century, she turned it into a highly developed profession. She certainly became the specialist in local flora, and she

Presidents S. Colman O'Connell, Carol Guardo, MaryAnn Baenninger, Stanley Idzerda, S. Emmanuel Renner, Mary Lyons

built the extensive, significant collection that is today the base of the CSB/SJU Bailey Herbarium. She was the college's first full-time president (the prioress/dean shared presidential responsibilities from 1913 to 1957), taking over just when needs mushroomed, issues multiplied, and conflict with the local bishop boiled over.

President Stanley Idzerda, appointed by the prioress in 1968, brought new perspectives to the office. Not only was he the first man but also the first layperson to serve in that role. He came full of admiration for the Benedictines and committed to the expansion and growth of the college. Saint Ben's was a gem, he decided, and too few students, faculty members, and administrators appreciated it. He took it as his job to convince them of their accomplishments and of their potential.

Presidents Emmanuel Renner (1979–1986) and Colman O'Connell (1986–1996) had long CSB experience. They had served as president and vice president respectively of their class; both had taught in high school and on the college faculty—S. Emmanuel in history and S. Colman in theater—for decades. They raised friends in the thousands and funds in the millions for the college. S. Emmanuel brought a quiet grace to the position—and strength to hold her own in negotiations with Saint John's.

*S. Remberta
Westkaemper,
president and
botanist*

S. Colman took to the job with a quick laugh, enormous energy, and a
love for change. Together they made one enormously significant institutional and psychological improvement for the college—a new library.
The college had since 1913 made do with a stunningly beautiful library
that was nevertheless painfully and finally embarrassingly small. A real
college needed a real library, and Presidents Renner and O'Connell saw
that CSB had one.

Most recently, MaryAnn Baenninger offers the college an expanded
vision of what it and its students can aspire to. Like all presidents, she
cannot dream alone or single-handedly put a vision into practice, but
she has brought to the campus a surge of new energy, indeed of determination. A few of the presidents get more attention in later chapters,
but President Baenninger remains at center stage here.

When MaryAnn—as she invites everyone to call her—took over as
president in 2004, she arrived with deep respect for the heritage of the
women-centered, sister-founded College of Saint Benedict. A laywoman

from Pennsylvania, a graduate of public, coed, Temple University, the holder of a doctorate in psychology and experience in higher-education accreditation, MaryAnn has made the college stronger, more vibrant, and more visible.

Saint Ben's has not generally sung of its own strengths. Minnesotans, after all, are known to be self-effacing, many identifying with the joke about the extroverted Finn, who looks at *your* shoes. Emotions—like wealth—should be hidden, so it goes, and "pretty good" is a pretty good compliment. So too the Benedictines have generally avoided "showing off," preferring to let their message and accomplishments speak for themselves. Fortunately for the college, two of its presidents, Presidents Idzerda and Baenninger—neither Benedictine nor Minnesotan—have broken from such restraint and trumpeted the college's quality. Stan worked to convince the faculty, students, and sisters that the college was better than it thought. MaryAnn works hard to make sure outsiders know it too.

In higher education, reputation counts for a lot, and CSB deserves a better one. It's growing: *U.S. News and World Report,* for example, has three times named Saint Ben's one of the "up and coming" liberal arts colleges in the nation, applauding its "commitment to arts and culture," its "compelling sense of place," and its "lively engagement of faith and reason."[3]

As president and public face of the college, MaryAnn models what it means to be a "Bennie" in her engagement with the community and her professional organizations, in being a national and international citizen, in balancing her professional and personal lives including motherhood and grandmotherhood, in her strong leadership. She chairs the Board of the Minnesota Private College Council and sits on the Minnesota Women's Economic Roundtable. She has served on the board of the Council of Independent Colleges and currently on the Executive Board of the Women's College Coalition and the Executive Committee of the Annapolis Group (an organization of selective liberal arts colleges). She's a trustee of the American University of Sharjah in the United Arab Emirates. She holds a seat on the Board of Minnesota Public Radio.

She has written about Saint Ben's in *Presidency,* a publication of the American Council on Education, in *University Business,* and most publicly, in *The Chronicle of Higher Education.* One *Chronicle* article highlights a "very MaryAnn" approach to one of her key issues: sustainability. A longtime SUV driver, MaryAnn asked CSB students to advise her on its replacement and since has driven a Smart Car and even a golf cart on campus.[4]

The college, under MaryAnn, has also put itself forward in important ways. It was one of the original signers of the American College and University Presidents' Climate Commitment to make "ecologically sound, socially just, and economically viable" decisions. After signing in 2007, CSB consciously attuned its perspective to the environmental impact of individual and collective actions both large and small, among other things setting double-sided copying as the default on campus printers, banning the sale of plain bottled water, and requiring that new buildings meet LEED silver requirements (or their equivalent). The college aims to be carbon neutral by 2035.

That MaryAnn asked students to recommend a car for her reflects another of the qualities that the trustees applaud: her connection with students. She identified strongly with the graduating class of 2008, calling its members "her" class. She started with them, grew with them. Every year at commencement, a graduating student is elected to address her class. When she finishes, she shakes MaryAnn's hand. It has become a tradition—and a tribute to MaryAnn's vision for the students—that the graduate whispers, "I'm going to have your job someday."

MaryAnn's 2011 article, "For Women on Campuses, Access Doesn't Equal Success," highlights one of her—and the college's—central and longtime passions: the empowerment of women. Saint Ben's has variously defined what it means to be a women's college—or a college for women—but challenging women has always been its guiding aspiration. Whether that meant training teachers and nurses and mothers-to-be or training for access to medical, graduate, and law schools or CEO and CFO positions, the college has taken seriously its job of educating women.

MaryAnn pushes beyond a surface postfeminist view of gender-free work and urges educators to see how gender-driven our students' lives continue to be. Women students in general, and CSB students in particular, show up with deeply gendered self-concepts. Women students on average, and traditionally at CSB, work harder and do better academically than men but underestimate their own abilities (and successes) relative to men. Graduates remain part of a culture that is not really postfeminist.

"Just look at the relatively low numbers of women in political office and men in nursing," points out MaryAnn.

Yes, change has occurred but not enough. "A gendered culture, mostly in unconscious ways, limits women's expectations for themselves and our expectations for them," she argues, and it similarly limits our expectations for men.

As a college for women, CSB has a special opportunity—and obligation—to address this issue. The first strategic plan that MaryAnn participated in crafting, *Strategic Directions 2010,* set goals for CSB and SJU separately and together to "be recognized nationally as institutions for student learning and faculty scholarship in gender education." This pushed both schools, faculty members in particular, to come to a better understanding of how gender affects students. The colleges expanded the Gender and Women's Studies program to a minor, then a major. Both women and men teach courses in the program; both women and men attend the courses, which take up what it means to be a woman and what it means to be a man.

CSB Strategic Directions 2015 has a sharper focus and is unique in recent years because there are both separate and coordinate plans within the overall plan. The CSB plan sets as its first goal providing "Unparalleled and Distinctive Opportunities for Women" and declares, "The College of Saint Benedict will offer to women unparalleled opportunities linking the liberal arts and sciences with professional preparation, civic engagement, leadership and global competence."

This, in brief, is MaryAnn's vision for the college. She pushes and prods and challenges all segments to work toward this aspiration. Some people chafe at her insistence on parity, on equal time, on CSB separateness. When she decreed that student employees working on the CSB campus not wear branded clothing that did not include CSB's name—CSB/SJU or CSB clothing was okay, SJU-only was not—some students of both schools thought the separateness had gone too far. As the president of a women's college that for so much of its history has lived in the shadow of the men's college nearby, MaryAnn saw the ban as CSB stepping into its own light.

For all of its history, Saint Ben's has been (unfairly) less known than Saint John's. Students complain that when they introduce themselves as from Saint Ben's, too many people ask, "Where?" It's MaryAnn's aspiration that Bennies routinely hear, instead, some version of "Wow!"

CSB lives with large social and financial deficits as a result of the history of women's roles in the United States. SJU does have a bigger graduate base (something that is changing as CSB graduates larger classes than SJU) and a wider, deeper network of alums who have had higher paying jobs and more disposable income to donate to their college. Yes, SJU gets more coverage in the regional press, particularly for sports. As long as women have earned 59 cents or 73 cents or even 89 cents to the dollar that men have made, women's colleges have been behind. The president of every women's college must work to overcome the tradition of those deficits.

CSB seeks, for one answer, to position the college in a bigger universe, not just in relation to SJU. MaryAnn's involvement in the Annapolis Group makes CSB a "player" among the nation's best liberal arts colleges, including the "Sisters" (the remaining members of the Seven Sisters group). The Council of Independent Colleges puts CSB in conversation with the nation's small independent colleges. Thus CSB sets itself in the 21st century not as the younger sister of another college but as the fully developed college it is.

What it means to Saint Ben's to be Catholic and Benedictine, just as what it means to be Catholic in the United States, has changed over time. Pope Pius X—now St. Pius X—in 1913 sought greater piety, less independence among the clergy (a "menace to ecclesiastical discipline"), more frequent Holy Communion, and the rejection of "Modernism." The Church knew what a Catholic college was supposed to be—a teacher of doctrine, a promulgator of the tenets of the faith, an enforcer of orthodoxy.[5]

The Catholic Church a century later is more fully characterized by living the questions, by the imperatives of Catholic social thought that propel action, by a post-Vatican II dependence on the primacy of conscience. CSB is proud to be Catholic. It's also proud to be Benedictine—even since the separate incorporation of the college and the monastery in the 1960s. Benedictinism and Catholicism provide the spirit and the context, a way of opening to the questions. Applicants for jobs at CSB often ask whether being non-Catholic is a problem, whether they can wear a yarmulke or headscarf on campus, what religious limitations they will face in their classrooms. Without hesitation CSB answers "no," "yes," "none."

Catholic colleges have agonized over whether to allow performances of Eve Ensler's *The Vagina Monologues* on campus. On the one hand, the play's explicit sanctioning of abortion, birth control, and lesbianism stand in opposition to the Catholic Church's teachings on all three. On the other, students know about, have feelings about, and need a place to raise and discuss such issues.

In the face of some internal and more external opposition, CSB supported the students who first proposed a public reading of the *Monologues*. The president and the provost asked only that the reading be nested in an academic context. Readers and their friends in the dozens have annually enrolled in faculty-directed, student-led discussions of the text. In this and multiple other ways, CSB balances its commitments to Catholicism and to the education of women.

The college under MaryAnn Baenninger takes seriously its "fierce belief in the power of a liberal arts education" to transform women into the leaders they can and should be, to inspire them to use their education to engage with their local communities, and to provide opportunities and challenge to become global citizens.

Students take a common, liberal arts, core curriculum that explicitly fosters this transformation. Saint Ben's does not uphold the false dichotomy between college and the "real world." A CSB education is about how to live in the world, whether on campus or off. Students meet requirements for both classwork and "experiential" learning. They take required ethics courses to think about how to live and work well. They take a "capstone" course in their major to integrate learning and doing. The specifically work-related majors—nursing, education, nutrition, and others—are grounded in the liberal arts. All students, whatever their majors, finish with a liberal arts education.

In nearly all of higher education, administrators and faculty and students are exploring ways to make their colleges' boundaries more porous and their campuses more welcoming. The rural/small town setting of CSB has long allowed students (and their parents) to feel safe and to view the college's isolation as a virtue.

Colleges and universities, secular and religious, coed and women only, for years kept women on campus as much as possible, kept tabs on them when they went off campus, kept them in (and men out of) their dormitories. The sense of the world as a dangerous place and college as a safe one persisted well into the 1960s. Since then, students have pushed back and out. They've sought, indeed insisted on, opportunities off campus to volunteer, work as interns, explore, and study abroad. The first group of students who studied abroad went to Luxembourg in 1969–70. A student in one of the first groups testifies that it took her, a farm girl from Benson, Minn., and made her "more daring, adventurous, and curious." Hundreds of other students have said similar things, especially that study abroad changed their lives in profound ways. Their behavior when they return demonstrates the changes, too.[6]

Students hunger for the wider world. Hundreds begin planning in their first year for the time when they can study abroad. Most students put at the center of their four-year plan a semester (or more) away. Athletic teams travel to Moorhead and to Brazil. The choir tours worldwide. Students take spring-break trips wherever they can—remarkably more of them in search of volunteer activities than of the spring breaks of mythology. All students know the language of a shrinking globe; they feel it and know that they're walking into it—not just when they graduate but every day.

MaryAnn hasn't needed to tune the campus to the outside world. But she and the staff of Academic Affairs at CSB/SJU, especially the Center for Global Education, have turned up its volume. The college has committed itself to developing "global citizens" and now requires that all students "demonstrate local and global intercultural competence" and become involved in a "global learning experience."[7]

Study abroad is one path to internationalization, and CSB students have taken advantage of opportunities to do so in large number. More than 60 percent now participate in study abroad programs. Members of the faculty lead almost all of these programs, which provide global learning opportunities for them too.

Getting students off campus is only one way to internationalize them. The Center for Global Education has developed a plan ("From Participation to Engagement") for "a more integrated and comprehensive approach to internationalization" incorporating study abroad, international students, faculty development, and international faculty and staff exchange and partnership. A ready supply of eager faculty members, too, has made the off-campus activities possible and enriching—and fostered longterm student-faculty friendships.

A few CSB alumnae in the 1930s met fierce and righteous anger from S. Claire Lynch when they objected to the college admitting women of color. Now Saint Ben's proudly counts women of many colors, from many places, among its students. Bahamian students have been some of the best CSB students for decades. Students of color do still report some resistance to their presence, some nervousness among students who aren't sure how to relate to them. They tell, too, of being followed in the local shopping mall, of being eyed suspiciously by police, of feeling "other."

In response, CSB has inaugurated many on-campus projects, one of the most beautiful is a photo series—*I Am a Bennie*—documenting the many faces of its student family, the faces of traditional and new students, Norwegian Americans and Bahamians, Chinese and Hispanics, Hmong and Haitians. Another photo project—*We Are Bennies*—depicts students in many settings and contexts. The "we" comes in all colors, sizes, personalities, faiths, and styles, from many places and going to many others. Both campaigns echo S. Claire's insistence upon and CSB's commitment to being the college of all of its students.

The "we" of CSB in its centennial year numbers just over 2,000 students—all women—a remarkable growth from the six students in 1913. Those first six, Catholic, students came from three states. Four were laywomen, two sisters. The profile of the 21st-century student body is alike in some key ways—all female, most from intact nuclear families and from the region, many from modest financial circumstances. But

CSB women have changed demographically in more ways than they have stayed the same. Entering classes are only about 60–65 percent Catholic, 16 percent of the most recent first year class are American students of color, and another 7 percent international students. Twenty-five percent of CSB students come from outside Minnesota, and of those the largest number are from Los Angeles.

Only a few women's colleges and even fewer Catholic women's colleges survived the American educational and church upheaval of the 1960s and 1970s. Some women's colleges tried to make various accommodations to "brother" schools and either didn't survive or were absorbed. The College of Saint Benedict took a different path, working out a cooperative relationship with Saint John's University. While the reality sometimes meant more clash than cooperation, the two colleges have made it work and have the satisfaction of seeing both colleges thrive.

At a recent SJU football game, the parents of an out-of-state CSB student were overheard to ask, "When exactly did CSB and SJU merge?"

The answer is "never," but the two schools have so seamlessly connected their admission offices, curricula, course offerings, and campuses that the mistake is not surprising. Still, the campus culture of CSB is distinct from that of SJU. CSB students live in women-only dorms; they elect their own representatives to the CSB Student Senate; they have their own traditions and celebrations and their own habits of worship and leisure. Their residence halls are superintended by career student-development professionals.

Busloads of Johnnies and Bennies flock to social events on opposite campuses—whatever the closing hours. But Bennies play their own sports. CSB's award-winning Dance Team performs at Johnnie football games (and Blazer events), but SJU supplies its own cheerleaders (the "Rat Pack"). Other than the Posture Queen, CSB has no history of college "royalty" or beauty contests.

The faculty in 2013 includes only a few Benedictine women and many of them are near retirement. Until the 1960s, many young women in every entering class of students hoped or expected to go into religious life. The Second Vatican Council and the women's movement changed

Sisters and students connect through the Benedictine Friends program.

that. CSB once drew much of its faculty from its graduates—especially the Benedictines—so the number of religious faculty has also plummeted. Students have "Benedictine friends" among the Sisters of Saint Benedict's Monastery, but only rarely do they have Benedictine teachers.

Today laypeople make up the faculty; the laypeople include CSB alumnae, who sometimes become administrators as well. CSB student Rita Knuesel—like others before and after—went away to graduate school, then returned to teach at CSB. Since 2007, she has led both CSB and SJU as provost. Other CSB graduates, too, have happily returned to work at their alma mater. They bring their memories of their student days. They are also at the forefront of the charge to make Saint Ben's even better. The founding sisters must be smiling at what their efforts have wrought.

Lay faculty members have also come from all over the world to CSB. Professor Madhu Mitra's flowing saris are wonderfully reminiscent of the sisters' graceful habits; her rigor reminiscent of theirs,

Prof. Madhu Mitra in sari

too. Many faculty members—male and female—came primarily for a job but stay because they made a life at the college, a life of commitment, also reminiscent of the sisters'.

The first layman, hired in the 1930s, taught music, a second (Emerson Hynes, a recent SJU graduate) taught economics. Women teach in every department on campus—as they always have here and as they have done so much less often at other colleges. Now, more than 150 women and men hold CSB contracts, slightly more than half of the combined CSB/SJU faculty.

Emerson Hynes, Economics Department

The other "we" of CSB is those who have attended and graduated from the college, a remarkably loyal band. They help keep the college moving forward with gifts of talent, time, and tithe. They serve and have served in multiple ways—as trustees, mentors, employers, and role models. The Alumnae Association has been strong for nearly all of the college's 100 years. The "Old Girls," as many alumnae used to refer to themselves, by the 1930s founded chapters of former students in Minneapolis, St. Paul, St. Cloud, and Los Angeles. And for a long time now there have been chapters all over the country and the world. They published first the *Handshake* and then *The Benet* newsletters reporting on alumnae doings and college life. Their members returned to campus for lectures and retreats and to show off husbands and babies. Class after class of CSB women recount how closely they've kept in touch with other "Bennies," as they call themselves now.

The community feeling fostered by the college and the friendships forged by students with each other—and the college—are strong. Some renew those bonds at the annual June reunion, where they live together again in the residence halls. Others take vacations with each other, meet up for coffee, stay in contact at least through email and Facebook. And they support the college financially, contributing to raise and equip new buildings, to fund scholarships and fellowships,

THE BENET

| 1809 | 1865 | | 1732 | 1799 |

Silhouette by H. Diemert — Official Student and Alumnae Publication of the College of St. Benedict — Silhouette by H. Diemert

VOL. XII No 3 · College of St. Benedict, St. Joseph, Minnesota · February 21, 1947

Members of the Student Council plan a Wednesday noon donation drive for CARE parcels to be sent to Europe.

W.A.A. Sponsors Students' Recreation With Mixers, Tournaments and Contests

Laurels go to the Women's Athletic Association for the many varied recreational activities it sponsors between studies and exams, and for the well-rounded leisure time program it offers all year round, under the direction of Connie Spain, president, and Miss Grace Donovan, adviser.

So successful was the first combination skating party and mixer, that more such parties were arranged by the W.A.A. and St. John's Monogram Club. Between the dance floor and the skating rink, the crowds, easily accommodated, enjoyed these events.

Nearly everyone comes out for the occasional Friday evening sleigh rides. Touring the campus and country side, sleigh races and sing-

Musical Convocation Features Orchestra, Pianists and Singers

Music students will entertain the faculty and students in concert and recital at the regular convocation hour Thursday, February 27.

Under direction of Sister Firmin, the college orchestra will play Williams' Concerto in A minor, featuring Ann Rose

First it was The Handshake, *then* The Benet, *then* Saint Benedict's Magazine *(this one featuring Judge Elizabeth Hayden).*

James Manley (here with his wife and student, Mary Willette, now Mary Hughes) taught music at CSB from the 1930s.

to ease operating expenses, and to check the cost of tuition. These are the "sisters" of the college's second century, the women upon whom the college will depend for its survival.

In 1913 the college—classrooms and living spaces, library, gym, and art museum—fit into one building, attached to the convent and the academy. For decades the sisters far outnumbered the college students, as did the Academy students. In 2013 the 500 incoming students (out of a total CSB enrollment of 2,000) outnumber the sisters and the faculty and the staff together. Where once the students occupied a small part of St. Joe, they now account for a majority of the population and have turned St. Joseph into one of the only towns in the state that has a female majority.

These students live in many buildings—residence halls and apartments that many Saint John's students envy. In 2012, 124 of the students moved into the college's newest student housing, Centennial Commons. Named in honor of the college's 100th anniversary, of course, the Commons embodies both the tradition and the aspirations of the college.

Like the Rotunda in Teresa, the Commons was designed to foster community. In the Rotunda, two floors of student rooms opened onto a central gathering place where the students and the college held multiple formal and informal gatherings. They held teas and Christmas parties in that space, listened to the communal phonograph and then radio, put on skits and concerts, sometimes they even studied there. In the Commons, students live four to an apartment, each with a kitchen, living room, and front porch. The porch invites students to interact with their neighbors. The central building offers an event room, a kitchen, study spaces, and computers, encouraging connections among the students.

Rotunda students may have chafed at the rules that governed their nights out and their visitors in, and those rules loosened only in the early 1970s, when women simply refused to sign in and sign out and, so the stories go, the number of students who sneaked in male and female visitors made enforcement nearly impossible. The students determine

Sisters Emmanuel and Colman taking a walk through Centennial Commons

View of St. Joseph, looking west, sometime in the 1930s

their own hours and, generally, their own guest rules. Roommates might know when each other is coming and going, but the college doesn't keep track.

Sisters no longer live in each dorm; instead a professional student-development staff now supervises the living areas. Generations of Rotunda students remember saying compline—evening prayer—all together. That's no longer an active tradition. Even so, the students live on a campus with an intertwined geography that is still home to more than 200 Benedictine sisters. The Benedictine Friends program pairs students and sisters for meals and meetups. The Companions on a Journey groups and the active Campus Ministry program keep students alert to their own spirituality and to the campus legacy of Benedictinism. Small groups find community in other contexts: in study groups, on sports teams, on the student senate, in their volunteer work. Community remains one of the central characteristics that students identify as part of their CSB life.

The contemporary College of Saint Benedict shares many traits with its earlier self. It honors its Benedictine past and the vibrancy of Benedictine values in the present. It seeks to keep enduring connections between the sisters and the students and among the alumnae. It fosters community. It continues to be run and staffed by remarkable women and men. The college takes into the 21st century a strong understanding of itself and its purpose and graduates who can take on the world.

The cityscape of St. Joe

Mother Benedicta Riepp and
Abbot Boniface Wimmer

Mother Benedicta Riepp (1825–1862) and Abbot Boniface Wimmer (1809–1887)—what a duo! These two towering figures in the history of the Minnesota Benedictines have cast long shadows over the College of Saint Benedict and Saint John's University. The Benedicta Arts Center at CSB carries her name; Wimmer Hall at Saint John's carries his. More than that, the story of their feud has infiltrated the collective memory of the two places and shaped their relationship. Their feud—to call it anything less would be a distorting understatement—centered on power. (Isn't that what feuds are usually about?)

In the middle 1850s, Abbot Boniface and Mother Benedicta clashed over several aspects of this one issue: was he in charge of the sisters? Did she need his permission to act? Could he forbid her to act? Who should make decisions for the sisters and about their work? Who should have the ear of the king—Ludwig of Bavaria—whose kingdom they had both recently left?

As Mother Benedicta saw herself and the world, God called her to work in Pennsylvania and then in Minnesota. She was charged with the care of many souls. She sought neither personal gain nor advancement. She didn't set out to overthrow the traditional hierarchy of the church in which she had taken her vows. She made enormous sacrifices in order to live out her vocation and to serve as she felt called to do. She felt a calling and determined to follow it.

As Abbot Boniface Wimmer saw the world, he was her superior, not simply because he was a priest and a man (though those were contributing reasons in his eyes and theirs) but also because, as he argued "the sisters were invited by and were sent to me; I provided a place for a convent for them, gave them the necessary buildings, made many long and expensive trips, spent very much money for them . . . and am also, in many respects, the head of the Order as founder or co-founder, as advocate, as promoter of vocations for the sisters."

He also worried that if he didn't keep a hold on Mother Benedicta and her sister renegades, "the sisters could bring prejudice, disgrace, and scandal upon my priests and brothers, the children of my parishes, the sisters themselves, and the Order, and in the end I would have to support a crowd of womenfolk, who would be good-for-nothing and would be for me a means of annoyance without my being able to remedy matters."[1]

So, he believed that, whatever her calling, she must answer to him. He had responsibility for the Benedictines in the United States—that included her. He was accustomed to being obeyed and had a church structure that upheld a particular chain of command. She was ignoring it.

They jousted with each other and then took their disagreements to anyone who would listen—up to and including Pope Pius IX. Benedicta accused Boniface of the arbitrary use of power. He accused her of the arbitrary rejection of his legitimate authority. She resented his demeaning of her; he, her demeaning of him. She went outside the traditional lines of authority to have his judgments and decisions reversed. He pushed the traditional lines to have his positions upheld.

Suggesting the tenor of their disagreements: Benedicta wrote: "I readily agree that [Abbot Boniface] in every respect understands better than I do now how to direct our whole order. In respect to our sisters, however . . . much and especially what concerns the internal direction of the convent, should not always be left to men." Boniface replied: "each of my priests is naturally better schooled in monastic life than Sister Benedicta. . . . She thought herself smarter than I and all my brothers."[2] Even from the distance of more than 150 years it's hard to tell which one was the more stubborn, the stronger, the more determined!

The part of their battle that has made its way most deeply into the lore and life of the two colleges centers around money. Against Boniface's directives, Benedicta and a small group of sisters went to Minnesota where they did not have enough money to survive. She appealed to King Ludwig of Bavaria for financial support. He sent some funding to her via Boniface. Instead of forwarding the florins to Benedicta, Boniface sent them to Prior Benedict Haindl (also in Minnesota) to buy land. That land, called "Indianbush" is the site on which Saint John's Abbey and University have stood since 1857.

That Boniface "stole" this money from Benedicta has inspired a century and a half of feeling among some at Saint Ben's that they'd been victimized not just by Boniface but by the monks of Saint John's. When students and others rave about the extraordinary beauty of the Saint John's campus, people who know the story of Boniface and Benedicta have felt a new surge of resentment.

A careful reading of letters to, from, and about Benedicta and Boniface reveals that Benedicta was anything but a victim. In fact, she might have been even more successful at getting her way than Boniface was. She founded a convent in Erie, Penn., against his wishes, and it survived. She founded another community in Minnesota against his specific orders.

In appealing to King Ludwig she reported that Boniface had stolen her money. The king's chaplain scolded Boniface telling him he had no "right to take what was allotted to others, no matter how honestly you mean it." But then, after a flurry of exchanges the chaplain ordered Boniface not to repay the sisters. After another set Boniface agreed to repay, but didn't. Another flurry, the King said no payment was necessary. Only a careful—and patient—lawyer would be able to sort it all out; even then two lawyers might reasonably disagree.

It was also the case that while Saint John's Abbey and University have benefited from the land that the money bought, Boniface was not actually at Saint John's—except for an occasional visit—but living full time in Pennsylvania. The Saint John's monks who had closer dealings with the sisters tried to make amends by providing an architect, building materials, and manpower for the construction of the Main Building. They also helped the sisters pay off some debts. Other, less formal, paybacks have taken place, too. In terms of the actual debt, then, the books have long since been cleared. What they couldn't and can't repay are the advantages that the church and society have conferred on Saint John's over time. The battle between Benedicta and Boniface serves as a metaphor for the legacy of inequality under which the sisters, and by extension the college, developed.[3]

As a final note to this story: Yes Boniface redirected the money, and yes Saint John's has all that land. But Boniface was never able to exercise over Benedicta the power he believed was his. Benedicta founded not only the community in Saint Joseph but also, as is reported on the Saint Benedict's Monastery website, "At the time of her death [in 1862—at the age of 36] after only ten years in the United States, six independent communities of Benedictine women were established and thriving. One hundred fifty years later, 46 monasteries in the United States, Canada, Mexico, Puerto Rico, Bahamas, Taiwan, and Japan trace their roots to Mother Benedicta Riepp." The College of Saint Benedict does, too.

In the end, then, Benedicta seems to have won overall in her battles with Boniface. She certainly got the last word. When a pontifical order instructed Benedicta to return to Eichstätt, Boniface must have felt the victor. But she did not return. She died in St. Joseph and was buried in the sisters' cemetery near the monastery and college.

A simple story of bad monks mistreating innocent sisters pales when lined up next to the truer, more interesting, more compelling story of this fiercely stubborn, righteous, powerful duo. They both deserve their due.

TWO

~

Here We Come, Ready or Not!

In the fall of 1913, six young women arrived at the new Saint Benedict's College in St. Joseph, Minn. Esther Mueller had traveled only a short distance, from her family's farm just outside St. Joe. Josephine Misho, another German-American, came from Sauk Rapids, a bit farther away. Helen McDonald, neither German nor local but at age 21 the oldest of the entering students, traveled from Eau Claire, Wisc., where St. Joseph Benedictines ran a grade school and high school. Her father worked as a cook in a lumber camp and so lived away from home for months at a time. Her mother kept a boardinghouse.

Margaret McKeon, from a "mixed" marriage—Irish-American and Moravian—traveled from Montgomery, south of Minneapolis. Her father was a physician. Josephine Skluzacek, the oldest, came from a big Bohemian family near Northfield, Minn. She had worked as a bank assistant before going off to college.

The College/Academy seal in use until the mid-1920s

Minnesota Street, St. Joseph, Minn., around 1920

*Three Bennies
around 1920*

Margaret Grant, the youngest, took college classes while still enrolled as a high school senior at Saint Benedict's Academy.[1]

Each of these young women had made a decision about going to college that reflected both her personal aspirations and family circumstances. They could make these choices because of forces larger than themselves—particularly because of developments in American Catholicism and changing ideas about the roles of women.

Saint Benedict's College, like most women's colleges of the 19th and early 20th centuries, grew out of a high school started by an order of sisters. The Benedictines had founded Saint Benedict's Academy in the 1880s to educate Catholic girls in the region, including many who would join the religious community. The sisters staffed and ran the academy as one of many educational and nursing "missions" in central Minnesota.

The community of sisters was predominantly but not exclusively German and German-American, like the people they served. The founding sisters, all from the motherhouse in Eichstätt, Germany, settled in Stearns County in 1858. Seventeen women (plus four "scholars" and one servant) comprised the community by 1870, nearly 50 in 1880, and 80 by 1900. By 1910, just before the opening of the college, more than 150 sisters and another 60 "aspirants," as the sisters called young women in the early stages of joining the community, belonged to the monastery in St. Joseph.

The students of the academy lived something of a monastic life themselves—in close proximity to the sisters, their days organized by work and prayer. The buildings of the convent and the school adjoined seamlessly. The rapid growth in the number of sisters put pressure on the space. The steady growth in the number of students meant that the monastery had a hard time housing all of the sisters and students.

Students in uniform

The American Catholic Church grew dramatically too from the mid-19th century, largely due to immigration. The church wanted to serve and protect Catholic immigrants from the forces of Protestantism—and secularism—so strong in the United States.[2] To this end, the American Catholic bishops, in council in Baltimore in 1884, created a standardized catechism to provide for a uniformity of understanding. They also founded Catholic University of America to provide Catholic and American graduate programs for priests. And they mandated that every Catholic parish establish its own school.

All of these actions had a profound impact on the Catholic sisters in the United States—including the sisters of Saint Benedict in Saint Joseph—though perhaps not entirely in the way anticipated by the bishops in council. First, what came to be known as *The Baltimore Catechism* became the basic teaching tool for Catholics for nearly a century. Any Catholic over the age of 50 can still recite the answer to "Who made you?" the first Catechism question and its follow-up "Why did God make you?"[3] Second, the Catholic men's colleges created generations of educated Catholic lay and religious men in the United States, excluding lay and religious women. And third, the parish schools employed thousands of Catholic women—primarily sisters—for 75 years.

The bishops ordered the founding of parochial schools but did not fund them. No parish had enough priests to staff the schools or enough money to hire lay teachers, so bishops and priests and parishes turned to the sisters—to teach as part of their vocations. They did so. The sisters' contributions to American education in general and Catholic education in particular are incalculable. By 1920 Catholic sisters ran nearly 7,000 elementary schools and were teaching 1.7 million students in the United States.[4]

The push for Catholic education grew at the high school level, too. In 1900 sisters ran about a hundred high schools in the United States; by 1920, there were well over 1,500. The womanpower required to support this teaching was huge: by one estimate, 50,000 sisters taught in Catholic schools in the United States before 1920. And they did it for a fraction of what priests or lay teachers would have been paid. Parishes provided the sisters with housing and a small stipend (as late as the 1940s, the stipend was only $25 per month per teacher). Parishioners held food fairs, made donations, and otherwise did what they could to support the sisters, who could earn a bit more by cleaning the church, providing flowers, laundering altar cloths, and pressing vestments. Only a vocation could have commanded such a life.

The pressure on all communities of religious women was great as bishops, parish priests, parents, schools clamored for more and more and then still a few more teachers. The young women who joined the Benedictines in St. Joseph barely had time to learn how to pray before they were sent to Cold Spring or Mandan or Eau Claire or any of the 85 other places where Benedictines built and staffed parish schools.

Fortunately—or not—the states of the 1880s and 1890s required little more than that teachers read faster than their pupils. Some teachers had the equivalent of a high school education, a few had a bit more, and some had less. Sisters often turned up for teaching assignments armed primarily with faith and dedication. They learned how to teach from each other, on the job. Then, early in the 20th century, the states increased their expectations for teachers. Minnesota required a high school diploma for elementary teaching and two years beyond for high school teachers.[5]

If they were to continue staffing their schools, the sisters/teachers had to get more education themselves—a big problem for religious women. Laywomen in central Minnesota who wanted to be teachers could attend St. Cloud Normal School or the University of Minnesota. Or they could go to one of many private colleges in the state: Hamline, Macalester, Carleton, Gustavus Adolphus, or St. Olaf, Concordia, or Augsburg. Any of those, however, constituted a problem for the sisters of Saint Benedict. The church hierarchy frowned even on Catholic laywomen attending these "non-Catholic" colleges. For sisters, such attendance was prohibited. So how were they to get the education to carry out their mission? Find a Catholic college—or found one.

Catch-22. The Catholic colleges founded by the bishops enrolled male students only, as did virtually every Catholic college in the United States, including Saint John's University, run by the Benedictines just a few miles from St. Joseph, and St. Thomas, the diocesan college in St. Paul. More and more colleges in the United States became co-educational after Oberlin admitted women in the 1830s, but Catholics did not believe in co-education beyond grade school. A number of women's seminaries and academies—like Saint Benedict's Academy— enrolled high-school-aged girls. Saint Mary's in Notre Dame, Ind., for example, admitted students from the 1840s and called itself a college. But the first Catholic college for women—the College of Notre Dame in Maryland—was not founded until 1895.

Between 1905 and 1915, as many as 14 Catholic women's colleges opened in the United States, four of them in Minnesota: The College of St. Catherine in 1905, the College of St. Teresa in 1907, the College of St. Scholastica in 1912, and the College of Saint Benedict in 1913. This wealth of colleges for women is a credit to John Ireland, archbishop of St. Paul.

American Catholic bishops generally opposed higher education for both lay and religious women—fearing rightly that it might radicalize and encourage them to question religious teachers and teaching. John Ireland opposed woman suffrage for the same reason; nevertheless, he was one of only two American bishops actively supporting women's education. Born in Ireland, he caught the eye of the Catholic hierarchy after he moved to St. Paul. Sent to France for seminary, he returned to Minnesota and became the state's first bishop, then archbishop. He attended the council at which the bishops called for parish parochial schools, and he no doubt sought advice and counsel from his sibling Seraphine Ireland CSJ, who led the Sisters of Saint Joseph of Carondelet in St. Paul. She had strong and clear ideas and a passion to carry out her religious work. She and her sisters could do that better if they were educated. Fr. and S. Ireland spent holidays together; he was a regular visitor in her community; they remained close confidants throughout their lives. He understood through her what it would take for the sisters to educate Catholic children—education for themselves as well as for other Catholic women. Perhaps it was an accident that he was such a strong advocate among the American Catholic bishops for women's education. Perhaps it was the result of Mother Seraphine and her sisters' persuasive powers!

While other bishops fought the opening of Catholic women's colleges, Ireland actively supported his sister's community by assigning the royalties of his book *The Church and Modern Society* to the sisters. Historians of the College of Saint Catherine (now St. Catherine University or "St. Kate's") tell of sisters going door to door in the diocese, peddling copies of Ireland's book to increase those royalties. They did a good job of it, too, earning nearly $60,000. That plus a major donation of land provided foundational funding for the college.

While other bishops actively fought against religious women attending secular colleges, Ireland supported it. "His" sisters regularly attended the University of Minnesota and the University of Chicago. Fr. Thomas Shields, one of Ireland's "brightest young priests" trained in St. Paul, carried Ireland's passion for women's education with him when he joined the faculty of Catholic University in 1902. He devoted energy and time to the "more perfect training of our Catholic sisterhoods," founded at CU in 1911 a summer school for Catholic sisters (CU still excluded them), and became the first dean of the Catholic Sisters College in 1914. The sisters could not hope to run a college without a college education themselves. Ireland made that possible, and Shields put it into effect.

Bishop John Ireland

Just as with their grade schools and high schools, the Benedictine sisters knew that to staff their own college they had to do advanced work themselves. Graduating from the academy, even doing well there, was not enough; they needed college degrees. And so they turned to friends and relatives—many families had both daughters and sons among the Benedictines—at Saint John's. Mother Cecelia, for example, no doubt talked with her brother at Saint John's to see what might be done. The early paperwork for Saint Ben's reports that—with the exception of one lay faculty woman who earned a bachelor's degree in home economics at the University of Minnesota and of Fr. Henry Borgerding, the chaplain and theology teacher—the earliest members of the faculty, all sisters, held bachelor of art degrees from Saint John's University. No one remembers, and neither the Saint John's nor the Saint Benedict's archives reveals, how this was accomplished, but it was. No doubt the dozens of sibling connections at Saint Ben's and Saint John's helped this project along.

With their bachelor's degrees in hand, the sisters could and did embark on postgraduate work. Most of them took courses at the University of Minnesota or at Dubuque (now Loras) College, authorized

The Kapsner Family (Mother Cecelia, back row, second from left)

S. Adelgundis Bergman

by Catholic University and also under the supervision of Fr. Shields. The sisters completed their master's degrees through summer study at Catholic University's Sisters College in Washington, D.C.

Duly certified by their own degrees, the sisters could start their own college. They had two purposes and served both through what was first Saint Benedict's College and later the College of Saint Benedict—one college for lay students and one for sisters. By design, the lay students attended the college during the traditional academic year, from September to May. They took a full array of courses, taught by the newly trained and capable teachers in college classrooms and laboratories, and had access to a growing library. They paid tuition and room and board, of course, at a going and reasonable rate and with a fair amount of scholarship and work-study assistance. These classes always included many women who after their first or second year entered religious life.

During the summers, when the "regular" students went home—there was no summer school for CSB students—the "regular" faculty members taught the same college classes to sister/teachers returning to the monastery for summer school. From 1913 until at least the mid-1960s, the summer program enrolled at least as many "students" as did the academic year program. Initially, all of them were Benedictines. Eventually, sisters from other religious communities enrolled as well. Those who took enough summer courses could earn a college degree. The regular students graduated in May, the summer students in August. Usually a young woman took a year or two of classes, joined the Benedictine community, and began to teach, returning to the college for several summers to complete her degree. The teaching sisters did all they could to make the summer college as "real" a college experience as possible, including programs of speakers and concerts and putting the sisters up in the dorms (no other room for all of them!).

*Sisters' college,
summer studying*

The sisters always dealt with limited and complicated finances, and the summer program was a brilliant solution to how to educate their hundreds of elementary- and secondary-school teachers at a cost the community could bear. They might have hoped that the undergraduate college for lay students would support the sisters' college. It did not. They invited sisters of other orders also to attend the summer school. Their tuition helped a bit. The salaries earned by the elementary and secondary school sister/teachers supported both.[6]

The first lay students of CSB likely knew little of the relationship of the summer college to their own or of how important it was in shaping their college. They probably knew little, either, of the sisters' work inside the church to expand their own opportunities, no doubt pushing the hierarchical limits placed on living out their vocations. All young Catholic women did know, however, that the Catholic sisters were to be reckoned with! They did not say mass, and "Sister" was never equal to "Father," but to every Catholic child (and many adults), the sisters were commanding figures.

They were holy, too, of course, but by renouncing the ways of the world, the sisters also renounced many of the rules and roles governing other women. Any young woman joining a monastery knew she would not live a "conventional" life. The monastery long attracted young women seeing opportunity there that they didn't see elsewhere.

In the 19th century, laywomen in the United States began to demand and to take new opportunities, without all the demands of religious vows (though celibacy was a price that many women paid for their ambition). From the 1830s to the 1850s, when the first women's "colleges"—Mount Holyoke and Vassar and Wellesley and Smith, among the most prominent—appeared, women assumed active and vocal roles in American reform movements, especially those for temperance and the abolition of slavery. The limits on a woman's ability to speak in public and to work actively for reform sparked too a movement for women's rights, a chorus of calls for woman suffrage. The movement spurred many American women to learn and speak the language of women's rights—and opportunities.

Other factors, too, worked to open doors for women. The most recent scholarship estimates that about 750,000 men lost their lives in the American Civil War. Even more powerfully than the prewar women's rights movements, this catastrophe propelled many women from home and family by removing the possibility of marriage. The jobs they sought and held and the opportunities they pursued increased. The number of women in women's religious orders went up, as did the number of women in teaching generally, in the professions, and in factories and shops. The effects of this expansion echoed through several generations and found profound and public expression in the first two decades of the 20th century—the Progressive Era.

Even a casual reading of the newspaper in 1913 would have encouraged young women to think big. A 1913 story in the *Minneapolis Morning Tribune* called Jane Addams "the best known and most loved woman in America." Addams had attended Rockford Female Seminary in Illinois, hoping to become a doctor. Her own health prevented that, but after a time in Europe, she and her friend Ellen Gates Starr opened a settlement house in Chicago, to work with children, immigrants, and the poor. If they had been Catholic, Addams and Starr would have fit well into religious life. They were pathbreaking in that they did this work as laywomen.

The newspaper also reported that more and more women—especially college-educated women—"desire or are obliged to become self-supporting." Many of them were going into teaching. A University of Minnesota bulletin aimed at liberal arts graduates reported women in insurance and real estate and as buyers for department stores, though it admitted "no assurance of making a comfortable livelihood can be given to women" in those fields. Others? Yes. Among the fields reported as easily entered were commercial photography, probation, charity or newspaper work, domestic science, interior decoration, municipal research, YWCA work, and librarianship. "Miss" Gratia Countryman had already headed the Minneapolis Public Library for nearly a decade, for example. Minneapolis and St. Paul were opening their own settlement houses. Women both married and single were showing up outside of the home in large number.

A newspaper short story—"Should a Girl Continue to Work after Marriage?"—told of newlyweds Mr. and Mrs. Wright, who discovered that "the independence of both man and woman is what makes the perfect unit in marriage." As Mrs. Wright so adroitly asserted, forcing an educated woman to stay home against her wishes was "like trying to put an elephant in a mouse trap." The newspaper reinforced traditional roles for women and men but was nonetheless replete with stories of women taking on new roles and jobs and ambitions.[7]

Women across Minnesota were increasingly engaged in the woman suffrage movement, in organizations promoting better cities and roads, parks, schools, labor legislation, and temperance. Women formed study clubs, opened and ran local libraries, took part in their churches' social action programs. They formed the Political Equality League, the Minneapolis League of Catholic Women, and hundreds of other organizations with educational and service aims. Clearly, women were hungry for education, and they were pushing at the boundaries that constrained them.[8]

Not that the roles for women and men were different for Catholics than for others—or that Catholicism allowed wider latitude to women. Quite the contrary! Women religious sidestepped many of the limits imposed by traditional roles, and membership in religious communities offered Catholic women a respectable, indeed holy, role in public life. Their religious commitments exempted them from many of the societal fears and expectations confining unmarried women, especially educated unmarried women, namely that education would masculinize them or condemn them to a single life.

Those first six students at Saint Ben's, then, entered college in the midst of great societal change. They moved into rooms in the Rotunda—the "Ro" as generations called it—where nearly a half-century of Bennies would live. Just think of it—*rotunda!* Churches have rotundas. The nation's capitol has a rotunda. So does the Minnesota capitol, and Thomas Jefferson's University of Virginia. Putting young women in a building with a roof or even a skylight has a whole different feel from putting them in a *rotunda*. Big dreams, indeed.

This new Teresa Hall was attached physically to the older convent and Academy buildings, but was designated as a separate, distinct college space. Great care went into the planning and execution of Teresa Hall. The Ro was its centerpiece. Everything seemed to happen there. Student rooms opened on to either the Ro's main floor or its gallery. Each room—the catalogs proudly reported—came with its own sink (quite a luxury), with sufficient bathrooms nearby. For some students, from farms especially, having indoor facilities at all was a treat. Off the Ro was a large dormitory space shared eventually by a couple dozen students, with cubicles divided off with curtains and storage lockers out

The Ro

A student room in the Ro

in the hall. The greater amenities of the Ro rooms were offset, the dorm students remembered, by the sisterhood and late-night, after-lights-out whispered conversations.

If the Ro called up a classical aura, the library was designed in a modern art deco style. The dark woodwork of the shelving and the desks, the hardwood floors all announced that this was a library that took its students' aspirations seriously. No finishing school subjects would be mastered in this space, but history and economics for sure. At the heart of the library were a fireplace and alcove decorated with hand-made tiles—real showpieces. There was nothing inexpensive about this space and there was everything ambitious.

The art room, a kind of museum showplace, near the library inspired students to locate themselves in a long fine-arts tradition. Yes, they could and did take sewing and dressmaking and embroidery lessons and knew how to make beautiful things. The room said that they were to know and appreciate the most beautiful things, too.

The lovely woodwork of these two rooms was repeated downstairs in the dining rooms where the students sat "family style" for meals. Also downstairs, the building's planners had included a gymnasium. Perhaps, as another chapter will take up in more detail, the ceiling was a little low and the space a bit awkward for modern sports, but it offered a place where students would be able to exercise and play and dance and stretch. It was more than enough for its day and more than many colleges—especially coed ones—offered for women.

Classrooms and lab spaces, too, proved sufficient and comfortable enough to teach and learn in, lovely enough to enjoy. A stage and auditorium offered performance and convocation spaces. Teresa supported the college's life for nearly 50 years. The library was moved out. The student rooms, the dining rooms, the theater, the gymnasium—they all have their own buildings. Now Teresa is part of what's called The Main; it accommodates faculty offices, financial aid, communication and marketing, and the business office. Its functions have changed completely; its loveliness hasn't. It's still a showplace.

The sisters had also commissioned to coincide with the opening of their college the grand Sacred Heart Chapel. While *chapel* is the ecclesiastically correct word for the building—a place of worship that is not part of a parish—ordinarily one thinks of a chapel as a small building or as part of a larger one. The Sacred Heart Chapel is a grand building—big enough to hold the sisters of the community, the sisters they expected to join them, and the students they planned to educate! The chapel as much as the college symbolized the sisters' aspirations for their enterprise. Perhaps its towering presence would also reassure parents or pastors worrying about the secularizing tendency of a college education for their girls.

The new buildings grew up on the south side of the village of St. Joseph, home to about 450. Another 250—sisters, staff, and charges— lived on the Benedictine side of town. The Catholic Church of St. Joseph faced a robust Main Street full of useful businesses—the St. Joseph Meat Market, Loso's and Linnemann's general stores, and a bank. The town supported its own doctor, tailor, shoemaker, and one public school teacher—though no public school. Two blacksmiths, one teamster, and one saddler serviced the horses that were still in 1910 a common sight in town. The railroad employed another couple dozen

The new campus

Chapel under construction

St. Joseph

people. A few residents were comfortable enough to employ servants and men who did odd jobs. And of course the predominantly German-American St. Joe boasted of at least two saloons and three bartenders. Only three people in 1910 reported that they worked for the convent—young women, doing laundry. The sisters, with a handful of live-in helpers, handled their own work.

The college students of the first and following years may have hoped for an ivory tower. Instead they found themselves in a community of women running a college, a high school, and a primary school for boys and girls. The sisters taught music and needlework to a steady stream of children. At the insistence of Mother Benedicta Riepp, they had abandoned the cloistered life of their Eichstätt, Bavaria, motherhouse, to meet the demand for their services in America.

They had not abandoned the hope of self-sufficiency, or self-containment, at least. They operated a farm, raising crops and cows, hogs and chickens. They grew flax for spinning and fields of potatoes to feed themselves and their students. Every sister contributed to the community's spiritual and economic well-being.

Chronically short of funds, the monastery needed whatever the sisters could earn. The talented S. Justina Knapp and others added substantially to income by making extraordinary embroidered vestments and altar cloths, real works of art. Other sisters made candy, raised chickens, and grew flowers to sell. Still others made candles for the many altars they

*Detail from an embroidery of
St. George, one of the sisters'
masterpieces*

cared for in the diocese.
They had little cash but
almost endless woman-
power. And they did as
much as they could do
themselves.

The sisters taught virtu-
ally all of the classes at the
college. If a sister wasn't
trained to fill a need, she
received training, some-
times just enough to get
her into the classroom with a promise that she'd get more later. Many
a talented math teacher was put to teaching English because that was
needed instead. One priest lived in a small, brick house (standing on
the campus to this day), and various monks from Saint John's Abbey
taught a course or two, usually in theology.

The sounds of construction must have interrupted the concentration of the first students on campus. Teresa Hall—where they lived,
attended classes, and studied in the library—was complete when they
arrived, but the chapel was not. Costing twice what Teresa Hall did,
the chapel was much more elaborate, with polished Rockville granite and Carrera marble, finely worked pillars, and a huge dome rising
above the St. Joseph skyline.

Mother Cecelia Kapsner—head of this congregation of Benedictines
from 1901 to 1919—had a load of brains and talent! Little in her back-
ground would have prepared her for the responsibilities of her position.
While she was prioress, she oversaw and directed enormous changes

in the size, missions, and physical plant of the community, the last of which included a new hospital in Bismarck, a new power plant on the campus, 24 new Catholic schools, an infirmary, new barns, and the purchase of land for a hospital in St. Cloud.[9]

Born in Germany in 1859, Cecelia was age 15 when her family came to America, 17 when she joined the Benedictines. Her family—she was the second-born and oldest girl in a family of 11—settled in nearby Pierz, Minn. She and three of her sisters and one of her brothers became Benedictines. Since 1886, when S. Cecelia joined the community, there has always been at least one Kapsner on the faculty or staff of the college.

The Saint Ben's students certainly knew of S. Cecelia—they would have seen her at mass and prayers—but their lives revolved more directly around S. Dominica Borgerding, S. Jeanette Roesch, S. Adelgundis Bergman, S. Grace McDonald, S. Irma Schumacher, and Fr. Henry Borgerding—the college's founding faculty.

The sisters in that hardy band had prepared for years for the arrival of their students, but they also made up a lot as they went along.

Another generation of Kapsners

Like the college itself, the sisters grew out of Saint Benedict's Academy, where most had both studied and taught. The academy offered multiple programs to suit many students' needs—a "normal" course for prospective teachers, a commercial course, a pre-collegiate course, and a music program. The college's first catalog took up one page at the beginning of the academy catalog. College and high school students shared classrooms (sequentially), lived by the same rules, and wore the same uniforms. The records of the college and academy for many years—as well as of the alumnae associations—are so intertwined as to make sorting one from the other impossible.

Even so, it is clear the sisters set for the college a separate and ambitious curriculum "in conformity with the best educational standards," as they trumpeted proudly in the early college catalogs. All students took one course in "domestic science," but no one would have mistaken the college for a "finishing school." First-year requirements included Latin, German or French, as well as history, philosophy, and chemistry or physics; second-year requirements included psychology, trigonometry, and biology. The sisters were completely clear in wanting their college to be a lot like their academy, only a lot better.

OUR UNIFORM

In searching for ideas for their college, the sisters took some cues from the Seven Sisters, those Ivy League colleges that from the 1830s had been inventing women's higher education. All women's colleges debated the purposes, and experimented with the design, of women's education. American higher education had long seesawed in its understanding of appropriate goals for

The academy and the college students looked a lot alike.

Students wore uniforms and customized them with collars.

college learning for women and for men. The first men's colleges were long on philosophy and theology, as they served the practical purpose of training clergymen. When "civilizing" the sons of the well-to-do became part of their brief, the colleges added a wider array of courses to prepare students for the public world of law, medicine, and business.[10]

In a culture generally consigning middle- and upper-class women (whatever their economic circumstances) to the "separate sphere" of home and family, what purpose should the education of women serve? The women's colleges wanted to offer education *equal* to that of men's, but they wondered if it should be the *same*? Oberlin, the first private college to admit women, segregated them in a separate program, as did several of the state universities early admitting women.

Mount Holyoke, Smith, and other women's colleges may have been developed because men's colleges excluded women, but the women's colleges made a virtue of single-gender education in that women taught alone could excel without intimidation or sexual distraction (usually). They offered courses speaking to women's conventional roles, but more

College and academy graduation in 1919

importantly they designed curricula that equaled the men's without simply copying them. Moreover, the women-only environment muffled the drum roll of conformity beating outside their walls. The women's colleges—most of them founded by talented, able women—hired other talented, able women to teach there and admitted talented girls who would become able, given the right circumstances and encouragement.

Saint Benedict's College grew dramatically in its first five years—in both students and definition. The 1913 college/academy catalog that had devoted only one page to the college program morphed to 43 pages for the college program alone in the 1919–1920 edition. A banner headline announced that the college was "affiliated with the Catholic University of America" and the two-year program of the University of Minnesota. Students could earn a bachelor of arts or bachelor of science degree or a bachelor of arts in music. They could major in philosophy, psychology, Greek, French/Spanish, German, English, rhetoric and public speaking, botany, zoology, geology, chemistry, physics, mathematics, political and social science, history, or music.

The number of graduates in 1919 was still small—three laywomen and S. Remberta Westkaemper, who later earned her doctorate, created the college biology department, taught in the college for 40 years, and served as the college's first full-time president.

The prospect of teaching at the college must have provided incentive for some women called to the religious life of the Benedictines. They might have envisioned a teaching life for themselves sans religious community, but the chances for teaching through their working lifetimes, perhaps even in the college, were good. The community watched for its brightest and smartest and sent them to college, then put them into positions of responsibility and leadership that few laywomen held.

In 1919 Mother Cecelia stepped down and S. Louise Walz became prioress of the community and president of Saint Benedict's College. It took her a few years to develop her own vision for the school and to find in S. Claire Lynch a woman ready and able to make the new college anew.

The Curriculum—a strong and ambitious curriculum from the college's beginnings

1916

In 1916 the CSB catalog spelled out the religion courses for Catholic students.

> RELIGION AND CHURCH HISTORY
> (Required of all Catholic Students.)
>
> COURSE I.
> *Dogma*: Credentials of Christian Revelation. Existence of God. Nature and Perfections of God. Errors concerning God. Creation. The Messiah; promised and prepared for. The Messiah; prefigured and foretold. The Incarnation. The Hidden and Public Life of Jesus Christ. The Redemption. The Church. The Work of Sanctification. Comparison of Jewish and Christian Religion. Persecutions of the Early Church.
> Two hours a week, both semesters.
>
> COURSE II.
> *Moral Law*: General Principles of Morality. Virtue and Sin. Commandments of God and of the Church. The Evangelical Counsels and Beatitudes. Christ's Influence on the World's Religious and Moral Progress. Monasticism. Crusades. Scholasticism. General Councils. Renaissance.
> Two hours a week, both semesters.
>
> COURSE III.
> *Worship*: Grace. Prayer. The Sacraments. Sacramentals. Liturgy and Ritual of the Church. The so-called Reformation; its causes and results. The Jesuits. Napoleon and the Church in France. Religious revival in England. Bismarck and the Church in Germany. Modernism. Agnosticism.
> Two hours a week, both semesters.
>
> 19

> COURSE IV.
> *Critical Analysis of Controverted Dogmas and Tenets of the Sects*: Organization of the Church. The Church and Civilization. The Influence of the Church in Social Organization. The Church, an Educational Factor. Distinguished Catholic Artists and Scientists. The Papacy in the 19th and 20th Centuries.
> Two hours a week, both semesters.

That same catalog showed how the founding sisters had also established a strong liberal arts curriculum. Because of the times and the opportunities available to women in the United States in the college's early years, most students did not plan to finish at all, and so took mostly the basic (liberal-arts core) courses. Whatever goals the students held for themselves, the college pushed them to think better and to broaden themselves.

REQUIREMENTS FOR DEGREES IN ANY DEPARTMENT

English 2 (8 points); Mathematics 1 (3 points); History 1 (3 points); Science 1 (4 points); Philosophy 2 (6 points); Classical Language 1 (4 points); Modern Language 1 (4 points); Electives (30 points) may be chosen by the student under the direction of the Dean. The electives must be continued throughout the entire year. A total of sixty-two points is required for college graduation.

The college offered additional courses in many fields, even in Greek:

GREEK

COURSE I.

Introduction to Greek Grammar: Syntax and Exercises. Elementary Prose Composition.　　Three hours a week.

COURSE II.

Xenophon: Anabasis, first four books. Selections from New Testament.　　Three hours a week.

COURSE III.

Homer: Iliad, first three books. Selections from Greek Fathers, Saint Basil and St. Chrysostom.　　Three hours a week.

COURSE IV.

Herodotus: Selections. Lysias: Several Orations. Demosthenes: De Corona. Sophocles: Antigone. Oedipus Tyrannus.　　Three hours a week.

COURSE V.

Plato: The Republic. Aristotle: Ethics. History of Greek Literature.　　Three hours a week.

Home Economics (a hybrid of nutrition, biology, and chemistry) was important, too.

DEPARTMENT OF HOME ECONOMICS.

Students who wish to become teachers of Home Economics must pursue the course leading to the Degree of Bachelor of Science. The Electives of this course consist of studies in Cooking, Dietetics, Food Study, Household Chemistry, Bacteriology, Home Nursing, Physiology, Household Management, Textiles and Domestic Art. At least fifteen educational credits are required for the completion of this course.

COOKING.

COURSE I.

Theory of Composition of Foods. Nutritive Value. Selection of Foods. Marketing. Care of the Kitchen and Kitchen Equipment. Practice in the Preparation of Meats and Vegetables, Bread, Eggs, Soups.

COURSE II.

Theory of Planning, Preparing and Serving of Meals. Fancy

30

Cooking. Practice in the making of Salads, Entrees, Fancy Desserts, Ices, Candies, Frozen Creams. Canning and Preserving.

COURSE III.

Dietetics: Uses, Composition and Classification of Foods, Digestion and the Absorption of Food. Milk and Milk Derivatives. Eggs. Fish. Meat. Plant Foods. Dietaries. Feeding of Infants and Children. Diet in Disease. Practice in Dietaries for Children. The Aged. Invalid Cooking.

COURSE IV.

Biology. (See Science Course.)

COURSE V.

General Chemistry. (See College Chemistry.)

COURSE VI.

Bacteriology: Brief History of Bacteriology. Relation of Bacteria to Disease. Bacteria in Processes of Nature. Description of the most important Bacteria. Methods of Multiplication. Bacterial Invasion. Common Communicable Diseases. Bacteria in Surgery. Solutions—their Preparation and Uses. Fumigation. Home Sanitation. Household Bacteriology: Dust. Molds. Yeast. Butter Making and Cheese. Vinegar. Preserving Food.

COURSE VII.

Food Study: General Composition of Foods. Changes during Cooking and Preparation. Vegetable Foods. Flavoring Extracts. Milk and Dairy Products. Meats. Vinegar. Spices and Condiments. Beverages. Digestibility of Foods. Comparative Cost and Value of Foods. Aniline Dyes and other Food Colors.

COURSE VIII.

Chemistry of the Household: Chemistry of Water, Air, Fuels and Carbo-hydrates. Digestion. Effects of Cooking. Decay. Chemistry of the Laundry. Bleaching. Home Soap Making. Chemicals and their use in the Household. Antiseptics, Disinfectants, and Insecticides. Chemistry of Baking Powder and Bread Making.

COURSE IX.

Chemistry of Food and Nutrition: The Organic Foodstuffs. General Composition of Foods and Action of Ferments. Fate of

31

1946

Thirty years later, in 1946, Religion had become Theology and was co-ordinated with Philosophy.

Division of Theology, Philosophy, and Education

Courses in theology and philosopy are coordinated so that the student may have a firm foundation for his faith, as well as a knowledge of Catholic doctrines and of Scripture. Sufficient emphasis is put upon apologetics to enable the student to meet the pseudo-scientific attacks upon faith.

The plan of the division is essentially liberal in that the emphasis is on intellectual development. The relationship of the truths of religion and philosophy to life problems is emphasized. High standards of personal conduct and holiness are encouraged. An effort is made to have the students use and appreciate the means of grace which the Church places at their disposal in her sacramental and liturgical life.

The theories of education taught are in accord with the basic truths of Catholicism. Care is taken to help the student recognize false principles of education.

The requirements had expanded to include the social and natural sciences, as well as physical education.

LOWER DIVISION

Group requirements in the lower division for the degree of Bachelor of Arts:

1.	English	13 credits
2.	Social science	9 credits
*3	Natural science or mathematics	8 credits
4.	Foreign language	0 to 14 credits
5.	Philosophy	6 credits
**6.	Theology	8 credits
7.	Physical education without credit	2 years
8.	Electives to make a total of 60 credits	

For requirements for a degree of Bachelor of Science in home economics and in business education see the respective departments.

* Not required of those with a major in music.
** Not required of non-Catholic students.

The college offered these majors:

> Major sequences are offered by the following departments: Biology, Chemistry, Business Education, English, French, German, History, Home Economics, Latin, Mathematics, Music, Sociology. The courses constituting a major sequence are announced in this bulletin at the beginning of each department. The student must maintain an average of C or above in the major sequence.

1962

The curricular language of the college grew more confident.

AIMS

The College of St. Benedict is primarily a liberal arts college. It places major emphasis on those branches of learning which discipline the mind and which give the richest and most complete view of truth. Its chief aim, therefore, is to help students know the best that science, literature, and the arts have to offer and to help them integrate this knowledge around the core of their Faith. Since students neither achieve a complete training nor arrive at a full view of truth by means of an exclusively intellectual concentration, a reasonable amount of attention is paid to moral, social, and physical development.

GENERAL COURSE REQUIREMENTS

For the degree of Bachelor of Arts (see page 12 for list of major fields) the general course requirements are:

	credits	
Theology	14	not required of non-Catholics
Philosophy	14	
English	12	
Social Sciences	9	
Foreign Language	0 to 14	see page 13 & 14 for explanation
Natural Sciences or Mathematics	8	not required of music majors
Art, Music, or Theatre	1	
Music 9-10	1	
Physical Education (4 semesters)		

For the degree of Bachelor of Science (see page 12 for list of major fields) the general course requirements are:

	credits
Theology	14 not required of non-Catholics
Philosophy	14
English	9
Social Sciences	6
Natural Sciences or Mathematics	8
Art, Music, or Theatre	1
Music 9-10	1
Physical Education (4 semesters)	

The courses in English, social sciences, foreign languages, natural sciences, mathematics, and physical education must be in the lower division (courses numbered 1-29) and are usually completed during the first two years of the program. Philosophy courses required are 9, 12, 35, 36 and 45. Theology courses required are 13-14, 21-22, 31-34, and 36.

The majors had been reconfigured again.

EDUCATIONAL PLAN

THE EDUCATIONAL PLAN

The College of St. Benedict offers a four-year course of study in the liberal arts and sciences leading to the degrees of Bachelor of Arts and Bachelor of Science.

Bachelor of Arts degrees are offered in

Art	Latin
Biology	Mathematics
Chemistry	Medical Technology
Elementary Education	Music
English	Philosophy
French	Social Science
German	Sociology
History	

Bachelor of Science degrees are offered in
Business Education*
Dietetics
Home Economics
* not conferred after 1964

The educational objective of the first two years of college is to give you as broad an experience as possible in the content, discipline, and values of the various general fields of knowledge — the natural and social sciences, the humanities, and theology. Thus, the college requires a certain pattern of courses for a degree; this pattern, together with other degree requirements, is given on page 28. You should become familiar with this pattern since it is the foundation on which you will build your college program. Most of the general college requirements listed there are satisfied during the freshman and sophomore years.

1979–1980

General Education

At the College of Saint Benedict, the general education component (that part of the curriculum required of all students) is an outcomes-oriented program. Rather than specifying particular courses which every student must take, this program specifies outcomes which every student must be able to demonstrate. Students who have already attained some of these outcomes will be given opportunities to demonstrate this attainment by exams or through other assessment procedures. Each student will be assisted in selecting course work which will help her achieve the required outcomes.
The areas of competence are:

Level I — Basic Skills
Writing
Interpersonal Communications

Level II — Disciplinary Perspectives
Fine Arts (Art, Music or Theater)
History
Literature
Natural Science
Philosophy
Social Science
Theology

Level III — Integrative Learning
An examination of human values and global concerns, discovering relationships among seemingly disparate concepts, propositions, skills and beliefs.

COLLEGE OF SAINT BENEDICT

Degrees Conferred 1979

	BA	BS
Accounting	4	1
Art	14	
Biology	3	1
Bus. Adm.	20.5	
Consumer Homemaking	6	
Dietetics		2.5
Early Child Devel.	6	
Elem. Education	81	
English	11	
Family Life Ed.	1.5	
Family Studies	7	
Gen. Home Ec.	.5	
German	3	
Government	5.5	
History	2.5	
Home Ec. Education	.5	
Housing/Interior Design	1	
Humanities	4	
Indiv. Major	3.5	
Interior Design	5	
Liberal Studies	1	
Mathematics	3	
Medical Technology		1
Music	13	
Natural Science	3	1.5
Nursing		46.5
Nutrition Science		.5
Philosophy	1	
Psychology	12	
Religious Education	.5	
Social Science	5	
Social Work	27	
Sociology	3	
Spanish	3	
Textiles/Merchandising	3	
Theater	7	
Theology	8	
Totals	269	54

The 1920s at CSB

~

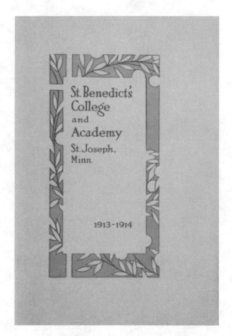

*Cover of
the college's
first catalog*

The Minneapolis Morning Tribune *showed the new, postwar fashions, July 30, 1920.*

Editorial staff of College Days

*One of the stars of the early 1920s,
Genevieve Lynch (not to be confused
with her contemporary S. Claire Lynch)*

*Many students in every class
became "Brides of Christ."*

Mary Ellen Chase visited CSB in the winter of 1929 and talked about "How to Become Really Important." Chase, an author of novels, children's books, and an autobiography, earned her doctorate at the University of Minnesota in 1922. She taught at the U of M, then at Smith College from 1926 to 1955.

From the report on her visit in the *Saint Benedict's Quarterly*, Feb. 1930:

> After giving us the popular idea of what importance is, she told us . . . that being really important is being humble and simple. We must be natural, seeing ourselves in perspective with other people and not imagining that we are the only worthwhile people in the world.

> She urged the students to read and think: "In this fast-moving age few of us take time to do our own thinking. We leave that to someone else."

WHAT ABOUT IT?

We admit that you, our alumnae sisters, perhaps had less adequate preparation in the line of home training and parish activity when you were in school than the girls are now receiving at St. Benedict's. Not necessarily, but probably that implies a deficiency in your activities today. What have you done, or what are you doing about it?

Surely you realize the ultimate purpose of every girl's life, whether she is college bred or not, is marriage and a home with children. In recognition of this truth St. Benedict's has inculcated this principle as a main guide into her extra-curricular activities. The associated clubs of the home economics department have centralized their attentions around home-making, thus affording girls in other major fields an opportunity to widen their interests to home management, decoration and care.

The second phase under stress is training for intelligent initiative in parish work. The Sodality fosters all types of parish interests from study clubs to altar preparation.

Just because you missed such preparation gives you no excuse to sit back on your heels in complaiscent criticism of others' efforts Begin at home on your own children, instilling in them principles of Christianity in home life. To make you further appreciate these standards, join an officially directed study club, master what it offers, and then volunteer to pass on your knowledge. You dare not shirk the responsibility that college education has prepared you for. Take over some of the work unthinking Catholics have unceremoniously dumped upon their parish priests. Show your Catholic spirit through these two means, resolving to surpass all your previous successes, and this undertaking can have but gloriously happy results.

From College Days

The sisters had been educating nurses since 1907 at their St. Cloud Hospital—St. Raphael's. Two students from that class: Helen Kramer and Lydia Kost

Oh, who are these students! Does anyone know?

The interior of the Sacred Heart chapel

An all-female cast for a production of H.M.S. Pinafore

*From 1923 sisters raised bees and provided
honey for the monastery, the students, and
for sale. Those responsible: Sisters Isabel
McDonnell (1923–1928), Marciana
Horn (1926–1938), and Annina Zierden
(1941–1959). In the 2000s, S. Phyllis
Plantenberg revived the beekeeping (and)
helped found a farmers' market in St. Joe.*

*As late as the 1960s sisters routinely dug potatoes on that farm. Here they are pictured
with several of the paid farm workers and, likely, the farm manager.*

S. Adelgundis, as dean, wrote to Isabel Revier, Aug. 19, 1930, to encourage her to attend CSB, where she would find "every educational advantage." Among those advantages: "Our courses are thorough and extensive. Our equipment is of the best; our building modern; our teachers well qualified."

The college was also more affordable than many: "Few colleges have so large a farm in connection with the institution as we have. It is because of this fact that we can give lower rates on board than many other colleges."

(Ms. Revier did not pick CSB. Instead she attended one year of teacher's college, then the Mankato Beauty School. She ran her own hair salon for more than 50 years.)

Several of the college's founding sisters and friends. Back row: (l to r) Mr. Nangle, S. Adelgundis Bergman, S. Josephine Carlin, S. Digna Wieland, S. Eugenia O'Neill, S. Jeanette Roesch, John Reilly, S. Vivia Nangle; front: Mary Merickel, S. Olivia Egan, Rose Reilly, Bill Reilly, S. Amanda Muggli

THREE

~

A Force of Nature

The College of Saint Benedict from its founding has benefited from the leadership of talented, able, and ambitious women. Few of those who were Benedictines would have called themselves ambitious. If pressed, they would have talked of doing God's work. But every surviving Catholic women's college—or women's religious community—exists because of the vision and determination of a series of strong leaders. Fortunately for CSB, Mother Louise Walz and S. Claire Lynch, armed with courage and imagination, took charge of its future in the 1930s.

Mother Louise Walz

Mother Louise, after serving two decades as subprioress under the tutelage of Mother Cecelia, was prioress from 1919 to 1937. Born in Germany, she moved with her family to Minnesota in 1872. She had an eighth-grade education and a storehouse of vigor and drive. Serving three terms as leader of her community and college, she built new buildings to house the flood of new aspirants, to accommodate the expanding religious needlework department, and to update the campus. She worked in close association with the bishop and parish priests to staff elementary and high schools, and in cooperation with her dean to run and staff the college. She oversaw the development of St. Cloud Hospital and a program of nurses' training.

One of Mother Louise's most ambitious and visionary moves was the opening of a Benedictine mission in China. In 1930, after careful deliberation and consultation within the community, she sent six sisters (of the hundred who volunteered) to China to open a college for young women (they thought). These sisters, from Minnesota, Wisconsin, and North and South Dakota, were trained and experienced in teaching home economics, math, and English. They had no international experience and not a word of Chinese. They were armed for their religious and educational mission with a crash course in Chinese culture, history, and geography. With the blessing of their community, the six sisters set off for Beijing.

Nothing—not the teaching, the needs of the people, or the Chinese political situation—turned out to be what they expected. After a time of learning Chinese and teaching briefly in Beijing, the teacher/sisters moved to Kaifeng, where they cared for the poor and nursed the sick. From 1937 and the start of the Second Sino-Japanese War, they cared for refugees and soldiers, often dodging bullets themselves. It was not the work they'd signed on for, but as S. Grace McDonald wrote, "They said a prayer and kept on working."

News report from the Sisters in China

Benedictine Nun Sends Mission News

Because news of the Benedictine Sisters in Kaifeng, China, is enjoyed by such a large number of the alumnae, a portion of one of Sister Francetta's letters is quoted:

"We are more busy than ever; it seems there are so many poor to take care of and Sister Annelda is rushed in the dispensary. Our Catechumenate is a bee hive—so many come to study Catechism. There are more than sixty who come to recite prayers every day.

"For a New Year gift we had a wee premature baby left on our doorstep—a pitiful thing partly black and blue from exposure. We knew she had no chance to live—and so the little girl was baptised Dominica; and with her passport signed and sealed, she slipped into heaven a few days after we found her.

"Our house is not finished, but fast getting there. We need more prayers that funds will continue to come in for our other many needs."

With the Japanese bombing of Pearl Harbor and the U.S. entry into World War II, the sisters became the enemies of the invading Japanese, who interned the sisters in Beijing. At the conclusion of the war, the sisters, caught up in the communist revolution, were forced to flee to Formosa and Japan. They kept praying, and they kept working. In Japan they offered lessons in Chinese and American cooking. It wasn't college work, but it paid.[1]

The St. Joseph community supported the women and their work for decades and helped the college forge a longstanding tie to Asia. This constituted a huge financial commitment that strained resources and thus affected the college, especially on the heels of the opening of the St. Cloud Hospital, but no one at the monastery or the college expressed any regrets.

The connection to China went two ways. When Saint Ben's sent its first missionaries to China, China sent it first "missionaries" to CSB. Two young Chinese women enrolled in the fall of 1930. Together they and the other students created an example of what an international campus could be.

Mother Louise, as prioress and president, oversaw the development of the college. She cared deeply about the education of Catholic young women and about CSB's success. And like the leaders of other women's religious communities, she knew that the presence of a college inspired vocations, drawing smart and ambitious women to sisterhood.

With many irons in many fires, Mother Louise delegated to the dean most of the responsibilities for the college. In 1925, Mother Louise appointed as dean S. Inez Hilger, a young (34 years old), dynamic, smart academic—the first of the deans not to be one of the college's founders. After completing a bachelor's degree at Saint Ben's— and some grade and high school teaching—she earned her master's degree at Catholic University, where the faculty identified her as a brilliant scholar.

S. Inez, however, put her scholarly interests aside at the request of Mother Louise. As dean, Inez took steps to uncouple the college from the academy, specifically making sure that their catalogs, graduations, and deans were separate and distinct. She oversaw the name change from Saint Benedict's College and Academy to the College of Saint Benedict and Saint Benedict's Academy. She had further aspirations for the college, but after two years she left the position. She returned to Catholic University as the first woman religious admitted to the regular doctoral program and became one of CSB's most important scholars and teachers. S. Adelgundis, one of the college's founders then stepped in for four years. She did a conscientious job, but the college needed something more and someone else.

Mother Louise's choice of S. Claire Lynch was just the bolt of energy the college needed for the 1930s. Her task: stabilize the college's

finances, improve its reputation, raise its visibility, get bigger and get better. This would have been a big enough job at any time, but taking control in the darkest year of the Great Depression made the job harder. Doing it just after the monastery had committed itself to the hospital and China made it urgent. She used the circumstances of her appointment as a spur for quick and dramatic action.

Born Clare Lynch, S. Claire was the youngest of the 10 children of James and Rose Boyle Lynch. Just two years beyond a bachelor's degree at the time she was named dean at Saint Ben's, she most recently had been teaching at

The Force of Nature herself –
S. Claire Lynch

St. Patrick's High School in Eau Claire. She had no administrative experience. But she was smart, and she had the right instincts for the job. Her first action reflected her powerful belief in formal education: She canceled her enrollment in a graduate history course at Marquette University in Milwaukee and signed up, instead, for a course in college administration offered by the dean of its graduate school, Edward Fitzpatrick. She learned a great deal from that Irish-American professor and mentor, who was also president of Mount Mary College—a Catholic women's college not unlike Saint Ben's.

CSB faced three major problems: competition for students, a depressed economy, and public attitudes (read *fears*) about women's colleges. S. Claire addressed them in that order, immediately setting about change. She did not leave records enough—personal or professional—to reveal how she defined obstacles or reached decisions, but the number of changes and the velocity with which she made them indicate that she knew everything about speed and little about deliberation.

In her first year, the college formulated and adopted a set of statutes for the administration of the college. It revised, clarified, and expanded its bulletin. It introduced new administrative forms. It relocated and expanded the registrar's office. And it expanded the library's study space.

S. Claire had a way of getting things done. One eulogist at her funeral remembered, "S. Claire was full of ideas . . . not always played out in an orderly fashion." In one story recalling her methods, she called S. Firmin Escher into her office and told her to start a student orchestra. S. Firmin protested that they had no instruments, no space, no resources. "Take care of that," S. Claire instructed. And in fact, she did.

S. Mariella Gable, in the English department, reported being cornered and asked by S. Claire why her students had not won any national prizes. The question infuriated Mariella, but before long, two of

An early college orchestra

her students won prizes from *The Atlantic Magazine,* including a summer stay for student and teacher at the Bread Loaf Writers' Conference.

More than one person described S. Claire as *mulier fortis,* a term from Proverbs translated literally as *strong woman* but suggesting something more like a force of nature. Hear the force in this line from one of her dean's reports: "There is still a great need of preventing the dissipation of student energy in worthless extra-curricular activities." See the force in the changes wrought during her nine years as dean.

S. Claire's transformation of Saint Ben's began with the faculty and the curriculum. CSB faced increasing and sharper competition for students. The number of women's colleges had increased dramatically in the 1920s. The new *and* the older colleges—women's and coed—increased their recruiting energy, too. And the Ivies drew more and more students.

In any case, four Catholic colleges for women, wrote S. Adelgundis to Aloysius Malloy OSF at the College of St. Teresa in Winona, were "too many for the state of Minnesota." Each community of religious running a college, however, had strong financial motive—educating its sisters for less cost at home than away. St. Teresa's trained Franciscans, St. Scholastica trained Benedictines in Duluth; St. Catherine's trained Sisters of St. Joseph of Carondelet in St. Paul. There was cachet in running a college, and as Adelgundis wrote, in "the privilege of granting degrees to our own sisters." Friendly with each other, the four colleges nonetheless competed for students (and sister aspirants).[2]

The College of St. Catherine had several key advantages in the college-girl sweepstakes. It was the largest of the four women's colleges, in 1930–31 enrolling more than 400 students and graduating 59. It had built bigger earlier, and its dormitories could accommodate more students. Because of its location in the heart of Irish-Catholic St. Paul it served more day students more easily than could the colleges in smaller towns.[3]

Saint Ben's was in fact the smallest of the four women's colleges, indeed the smallest of all the four-year colleges in Minnesota. When S. Claire took charge in 1932–33, the college enrolled 133 students and graduated fewer than 20 per year. The catalog promised the curriculum of a much larger college—more aspiration than fact, with many courses enrolling fewer than five students, though several enrolled more than 50. Saint Ben's was so completely a residential college that it had not recruited day students, fewer than a dozen in 1932. Unlike St. Paul, St. Joseph had few college-age women. Potential students in St. Cloud, 12 miles away, had no easy transportation. Furthermore, the CSB campus could accommodate only about 150 students total. The college needed more than that to survive!

St. Kate's second advantage was Antonia McHugh CSJ. While Saint Ben's was going through two presidents and four deans, S. Antonia ran St. Kate's. She had the strong support of both Mother Seraphine Ireland and Archbishop John Ireland. S. Antonia had a University of Chicago education that steeled her intellectual ambitions and connected her to influential laypersons. She determined, for example, that St. Kate's should become a member of Phi Beta Kappa and made it so eventually through dogged effort. She used her Chicago connections to raise money from the Carnegie Foundation.

S. Antonia also brought to the St. Kate's campus women of national and international stature. Writers Willa Cather, Edna St. Vincent Millay, and Mary Ellen Chase, for example, considered Antonia a friend and the college a second home. Her vision inspired her to push students to see themselves on a national stage. St. Kate's students consistently did well in *The Atlantic* poetry contests. Such results inspired, or more likely, prodded S. Claire.

Another advantage was St. Kate's urban location. Not only did many of its students come from the neighborhood, but many of its graduates remained in the Twin Cities, maintaining connections with their alma mater. The college had many alums such as Abigail Quigley, who graduated in 1936. She earned a master's degree at the University of Minnesota and did graduate work at the University of Chicago before returning to St. Paul and marrying (later U.S. Senator) Eugene McCarthy. And she played an active role at St. Kate's for the rest of her life.

Saint Ben's, especially under S. Claire, put a lot of energy into its alumnae association and into creating an annual campus reunion. It had (and has) exceptionally loyal alums, but only a few remained in St. Joe, St. Cloud, or Stearns County.

Reunion of Classes of '33 and before

St. Teresa's also had much to offer potential students—especially in the person of Mary Malloy. With a doctorate from Cornell, Mary went to Winona in 1907 to help launch the college there. She served as a lay dean until 1923, when she joined the Franciscans as S. Mary Aloysius. She became president of St. Teresa's in 1928 and held the position until 1946. She and S. Antonia were active on the national stage, serving on the Conference of Women's Colleges of the National Catholic Educational Association. S. Mary Aloysius was its secretary.

St. Kate's and St. Teresa's and St. Scholastica all enjoyed accreditation by the North Central Association before Saint Ben's. When CSB under S. Adelgundis applied for NCA accreditation, the evaluator declared it "not quite ready." In fact because the college was so small it barely qualified. The NCA visitors declared that the college had unacceptable staffing and curriculum issues, including too much overlap with the academy. The denial of accreditation worried S. Adelgundis. "Unless we get this acknowledgement by the North Central," she wrote, "we cannot hope to keep our boarders in college."[4]

So when S. Claire took over, there were mountains to climb, path breakers to follow, a North Central map for a guide. She had no experience in leading a college—or anything else. Neither did she have the doctorate she would push faculty members to pursue. She did have big ideas, a strong will, and a talent for moving others in the direction she thought best.

S. Claire focused first on securing accreditation. As she prepared the college's reapplication, she peppered the secretary of the North Central Association with questions: What did NCA mean in 1931 when it wrote this? Would X satisfy that? How was she to interpret Y? Peppered, indeed.

The new dean took the North Central report as her to-do list. Did North Central want the faculty more involved in administrative affairs? She scheduled monthly faculty meetings (usually on Sunday mornings, possible only with a faculty mostly Benedictine) and set up several faculty committees: Registration, Class Schedule; Curriculum; Library; Student Scholarship and Delinquency; Recreation and Discipline. "These committees meet regularly," she reported, "to discuss new methods of procedure, problems of administration, and modification of the curriculum." Check. Did North Central want each department led by someone with a doctorate? She reorganized the departments, decreasing their number to almost exactly the same number of her faculty members who had the Ph.D. Check.[5]

Did North Central want the faculty to have more education? The competition required it, and S. Claire believed in it, too. So she advocated. Only 7 of 44 of the current faculty members had doctorates (from Catholic University or the University of Minnesota); 23 had only bachelor's degrees. This was a longer-term project, so she started right away. She moved the "bachelors" out and pushed for their return to graduate school. Sisters had generally done graduate work only in summer, between teaching assignments. Under S. Claire, more of them took classes year round, in part to speed up the conferral of degrees. By the end of her term as dean, CSB had 9 faculty members with doctorates, an increase of 22 with masters' degrees (up from 13), and a significant decrease in those with bachelor's degrees only (mainly in the library and physical education). She pushed them all to write and publish more, to attend professional meetings, and to make more public presentations. Check that off the list, too.

To S. Claire change was a good thing, and she may not have been

Faculty Have Diversified Summer Destinations

If you call at the College during the summer, don't be surprised to find the faculty—that is, most of the faculty members not at home. Just glancing down the list of names we find that plans for the summer include the following:

Sisters Grace, Glenore, and Alacoque will be on the staff of the Diocesan Teachers' College in St. Paul. At Mount St. Scholastica College, Atchison, Kansas, Sister Remberta will be busily employed teaching botany in the regular summer school session of the College. Sister Mary, who spent the year at the University of St. Louis, decided that it might be more comfortable to spend the summer in Minnesota. She will be on the summer-school staff at the College of St. Benedict. That's one you will find "at home." Others teaching at St. Benedict's summer session are Sister Claudette, Sister Cecile, Sister Irma, and Sister Magna.

Sister Rogatia will teach chemistry at the Bismarck Hospital, and Sister Jeanette will go farther west, to Montana, where she will teach vacation school at Forsyth.

Among those studying is Sister Luanne, who will be at the University of Chicago, where she plans to finish her work for a Ph. D. in Latin before September. Sister Urban will also be in Chicago attending the Chicago Musical College, and Sister Stella at MacPhail in Minneapolis. Sister Jane will attend summer school at Marquette, and Sisters Maglore and Prudentia at Notre Dame. Sister Aloysia is courageous—she is going to brave the heat at the University of St. Louis. Attending the University of Minnesota will be Sisters Marcine, Jeroma, Jameen, and Thomas.

We have saved the biggest news until last. Sister Uruline is sailing for China —perhaps sometime in August. She will join the small band of our sisters in Kaifeng and, of course, her visit will be much more than a vacation trip. Rather, it is a dedication for life—and, of course, we all wish Sister much happiness and God's blessing upon her great undertaking.

S. Claire made sure that the sisters' plans got attention.

fully patient with her sisters who preferred tradition and a slower pace. The college secured accreditation provisionally in March 1933 and fully in 1934. Then Claire turned her attention to making the college more demanding and intellectually challenging.

She set the faculty to the task of studying and discussing grades (she was afraid of grade inflation, even then). They resisted her implication that they graded too easily, arguing that the nature of the college itself— "the intimate association with the faculty, the small-sized classes, the individual help, the close supervision of their study time and study habits"—would, of course, mean high grades for their students.[6]

Another year the faculty meetings focused on Newman's *Essays on a University,* which S. Claire hoped would help the faculty understand "the true nature of a Liberal Arts college." For the beginning of each school year she organized faculty institutes, each of which raised an issue she thought compelling to faculty growth. And she instituted a program bringing speakers to the campus. Certainly she intended them for the students, but she also saw the lecturers as part of her education plan for her sisters, perhaps even for herself.

North Central had been concerned about the size of Saint Ben's, so S. Claire devised strategies to increase enrollment. The first was to bring in more day students, those who lived at home but attended classes during the day. St. Joe was too small to provide many more, but there were many potential students in St. Cloud, should a way for daily travel to the college be found. S. Claire hired taxis to shuttle them. The next year she bought the first small "Bennie Bus." When that could not meet the demand, she bought a used Greyhound. By 1940, 80 day students were making the trip from St. Cloud to St. Joe.

S. Claire led other significant efforts to increase enrollment: To get the names of potential recruits, the college canvassed students and friends, scoured the lists of Catholic students who took the Minnesota College Aptitude test, and paid close attention to newspaper stories about high school students. It made contact with each of these students by letter; and one of the sisters visited anyone showing interest. The sisters proved to be good sellers of the college.

From its start, the college had offered scholarships and subsidies to its students: one went home on weekends for a reduction in fees, another worked in the kitchen, another received a 30 percent reduction, and another got 50 percent off. Clearly the college dealt with each student individually, making what accommodation it could to clear her path.

During the depression of the 1930s, students requested even more financial aid. S. Claire tapped into a New Deal program designed to keep young people out of the job market. The college also devised what we'd now call work-study and found funds to offer merit scholarships.

The college recruited so many new students that it couldn't accommodate all of them. S. Claire went door to door in St. Joe trying to rent rooms. By 1940 enrollment had more than doubled since 1930.

Simultaneously, S. Claire asked what kind of education those students needed. That the college offered courses in china painting and that many students actively sought practical majors in home economics and nutrition was to be accepted (and respected, too). But to S. Claire, china painting was the kind of course that kept the college from the

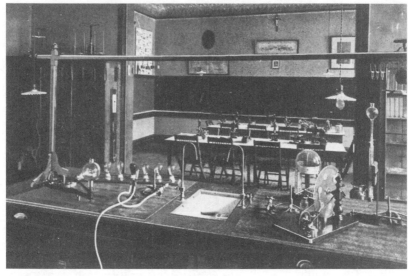

A CSB science lab

reputation she wanted it to deserve. Moreover, students in the practical majors needed a liberal education, too. Biology, physics, chemistry, and math offerings more than doubled, history courses quadrupled. Everyone took more philosophy classes by order of the faculty, as well as religion courses that were theology rather than catechism.[7]

The college also taught the students how to be serious students: mandatory twice-weekly study halls for first-year students with mini-lectures on "How to Study;" twice-weekly lectures on "What Constitutes a College Education." First-year orientation was peppered with academic how-tos. S. Claire required students to attend a lecture series that included performances of music and lectures on art, architecture, history, science, literature. Each year the program was more ambitious, eventually including the *Catholic Worker's* Dorothy Day and writer Carl Sandburg. The series always included one woman from another women's college and another from a Catholic women's college.

She was a factory of ideas and ambitions and perhaps not an entirely reliable narrator of student attitudes when she insisted that "both faculty and students feel that there has been a tendency to overemphasize the extra-curricular activities at the expense of scholarly pursuits." The

THE HANDSHAKE

VOLUME 1 ——ST. JOSEPH—— FEBRUARY 1936 ——MINNESOTA—— NUMBER 1

OFFICIAL ALUMNAE PUBLICATION OF THE COLLEGE OF ST. BENEDICT

Symposium for Alumnae Members is Outstanding Event at St. Benedicts

College Presents Elaborate Two-day Program for Delegates from Alumnae Chapter.

An outstanding service to alumnae members was the symposium recently held at the College of St. Benedict. It was attended by ten delegates from the St. Cloud, St. Paul, and Minneapolis Chapters. It had a double purpose: first, to acquaint the alumnae with the activities of the college as they are worked out by the system of clubs; secondly, to bring this information on the proper use of leisure time to their respective chapters to be put into practical use. The college clubs and faculty cooperated in the two-day session, November 23 and 24, by giving demonstrations and lectures.

CLUB DEMONSTRATIONS

The senior class under direction of Hazel Huber, Montana, gave a demonstration of what a chapter meeting should not be in contrast to the model meeting following it with Idelia Loso, St. Joseph, as chairman.

The League of Women Voters, with Mary Pottner as chairman, held a panel meeting, the freshmen taking the stand, "The United States Should Adhere to the World Court." The stand was presented by Betty Schneider and objections from the floor were refuted by other members.

The announcement of just one of S. Claire's alumnae symposia

Carl Sandburg

POET PRESENTS GIFT TO COLLEGE

Carl Sandburg, one of America's outstanding poets, presented the College of St. Benedict two personally autographed volumes for Christmas.

They were his collection of poems, "Good Morning America" and his study "Abraham Lincoln: The Prairie Years."

Carl Sandburg was a guest at the College a day and half at the opening of the college term when he read his poems to a delighted audience. His presentation of his volumes personally autographed, is but one more indication of a genuinely warm friendship formed at that time.

Important speakers, indeed

students manufactured some of their own plans: teas, sporting events, boys. Lenore Lucking was praised in the student/alumnae newsletter for keeping "the Johnnies coming Joeward." Students got themselves to Saint John's for football games and to St. Cloud, they dated whenever possible, some didn't study as much as they might have (!).

S. Claire no doubt had two goals in mind in rejuvenating the alumnae association: continuing education and fundraising. Faculty members regularly were volunteered to speak to alumnae groups. The May homecoming drew alums back to campus for fun; a fall alumnae symposium tackled weighty subjects such as "The Responsibility of the Catholic Woman in the Present Crisis" and "Women in Public Life." These events kept alumnae engaged, and the alumnae association encouraged a habit of giving to the college with organized fundraising events.

Throughout her time as dean, Claire worried and worked most, however, on the college's finances. When she took over, the sisters were carrying a debt of nearly $1 million for the hospital. Educating the Benedictine sisters to bachelor's degrees was expensive. Sending them away to graduate school was as costly as it was essential. Higher ambitions cost the community, too. Instead of summers at the University of Minnesota or in Dubuque, for example, more sisters spent whole academic years in Washington, New York City, or Chicago.

In addition, the community's income fell when parishioners hurt by depression and drought could not give to their local churches, and then parishes could not pay the teachers. The sisters did not stop teaching when the pay stopped. They just tightened their belts and made do. Mother Louise urged even more economies on the already frugal sisters—please make your shoes, your habit, your eyeglasses last one more year. She even started a "Self Denial Fund," asking the sisters to contribute what they could. These were very lean years in the community.

As to college finances, S. Claire had an excellent teacher in her Marquette mentor Edward Fitzpatrick. In his 1931 article, "Financial Stewardship," published in the *Journal of Higher Education,* he looked at why Catholic colleges were so poor and so poor at raising money. He argued that they did a bad job of demonstrating their need and of making evident their responsible use of contributions. The power

---

February, 1941

Dean Appeals To You

Dear Alumnae:

During the past few days I spent some time checking alumnae files. It was indeed gratifying to see how faithful most of the alumnae have been in the payment of annual dues, particularly the response of the college graduates to the personal letter sent them last March. It was an over-sight, I am sure, on the part of a few who did not respond to that personal letter.

Some alumnae have the erroneous idea that dues are to be paid only by the active chapter members. Although it is true that because of the circumstances of organized chapters the active chapter members have more opportunities to share the advantages of the alumnae association, on the other hand, active chapter members are giving a great deal more in money, time, and energy than the payment of annual dues.

Furthermore, the annual dues should signify not only a recognition of the benefits received as alumnae but should likewise be an expression of gratitude to the institution for the benefits received as students.

Some of you may not be aware of the purposes for which the money is being used. In one of the next issues of the HANDSHAKE the financial statement of the Executive Board will be published. When you see how very worthwhile are the projects being sponsored by the association, I am sure that all of you will want to cooperate and do the minimum by sending your check of one dollar and fifty cents—fifty cents for the HANDSHAKE and a dollar for your annual dues.

Sincerely yours,
Sister Claire,
Dean of the College.

S. Claire didn't hesitate to ask for money.

and majesty of the Church led many to believe that the religious communities were wealthy or had access to the church's bounty. And the tendency of Catholic institutions to be secretive about the disposition of funds further discouraged contributions.

S. Claire's mentor recommended first that Catholic colleges embark on a "campaign of education" to make a case for outside funding. Then they should demonstrate "present funds are being used with utmost economy . . . and efficiency." They should show that they spend donated funds carefully and according to donors' wishes.

He also suggested the appointment of a board of lay advisors, saying women's colleges would especially benefit. A carefully chosen board of prominent businessmen could reassure outsiders of the economic management of the institution. (That the members of such a board would be male reflected the fact of fewer women in business at the time.) Such a plan, he said, would also open the private world of the church to outsiders and reassure donors, though he did not

Advisors to S. Claire and the college: Rose Reilly, Joseph Gaida, Edward Callahan

specify as to how a primarily male board might reassure the donors of a women's college.[8]

In 1934 S. Claire appointed just such a board. Minneapolis lawyer Edward J. Callahan served as chair. Both Irish-American and about the same age, Lynch and Callahan forged a close and friendly working relationship. The lawyer spent many hours on campus and explicitly and implicitly supported the dean's vision. Other advisors included Francis Gross, president of the German National Bank in Minneapolis; Frank Mulcahy, president of the Northwest Mortgage Company, also in Minneapolis; and Joseph Matt, publisher of the Catholic-German newspaper *Der Wanderer,* in St. Paul. Joseph Gaida, a St. Cloud physician, and Rose Reilly, president of the alumnae association, joined them before long.

The board played more than a symbolic role. It met quarterly, and between meetings its chair often communicated with S. Claire. The board helped with financial advice directly. It also helped with recruitment policy and recruitment and with the placement of graduates. This system of advisors stayed in place until the 1960s. The advisors attended major public events of the college and dressed in cap and gown for graduation ceremonies. Ed Callahan spoke on campus to groups of students and presented as part of the convocation series on "Opportunities for College Women." The advisors became part of the public face of the college.[9]

Saint Ben's had been explicit in its first two decades in its mission as a college for women. It continued to enroll only women, but its public documents took a decided shift in emphasizing its Catholicism. For many years the college catalog announced, "The purpose of Saint Benedict's College is the higher education of women." Under S. Claire the aims of the college were expressed differently:

> The justification of a Catholic college is two-fold: in addition to secular studies it offers that further instruction in the science of religion, which will make for intelligent Catholic leadership. It surrounds the student with the means of grace, which will develop and protect personal virtue and integrity. Without this strong life of grace in the individual, leadership and social action, properly understood, are not possible. To promote the individual development of high character and its best influence on society through intelligent leadership is a double objective that St. Benedict's enjoys with every other Catholic college.

Finally, two paragraphs later, the word *woman* appears: "Frequent attendance at Mass and Holy Communion is felt to be necessary for that development of grace and virtue which is the sine qua non of the true Catholic woman." That's it.

Hmmm. Nothing in the college record accounts for this shift—no discussion in the faculty or among the sisters, no committee or faculty meeting action, no minutes of the advisory committee advising such. The Catholicism of the college had been part of its fabric from the beginning and was reinforced explicitly and implicitly by the presence of so many sisters on the faculty, the integration of mass and prayer as regular parts of the daily schedule, the presence of religion in the curriculum. There seem to have been no obvious threats to the college's Catholicism, no danger it would be considered other than Catholic. Were the sisters getting some heat from parents or priests, bishop or archbishop? Not impossible. In any case, S. Claire repositioned the college as primarily Catholic as opposed to its previous emphasis as a place for the education of women.

Another shift in practice seems related. S. Claire wanted a closer relationship with Saint John's University. Saint Ben's had long hired monks from Saint John's to teach theology. The two monasteries handled this cooperation formally and in writing: "Please, Abbot Alcuin, could you supply us with XX to teach YY," the letter would go.

Students at the two schools had long socialized with each other. Many counterparts came from the same families, neighborhoods, towns, and schools. Many likely shared rides, even names! From 1903 to 1918, 18 students named Borgerding attended CSB and SJU (9 each). They came from Belgrade, Melrose, and Freeport, Minn. Some were directly related to S. Dominica Borgerding, a college founder; the rest were relatives. The list doesn't include cousins at the two schools with different last names.

In those same years and later, many Gertkens, Luetmers, Terhaars, Losos and Linnemanns, Bitzans and Mugglis, attended Saint Ben's and Saint John's. The young women and men who already knew each other could introduce their classmates; they could and did oil the social networks of both places; they double-dated. Brothers could visit their sisters at Saint Ben's and meet their classmates and roommates, and so forth.

Many students knew each other, but the opportunities—formal and informal—for them to get together were limited. The social life of each institution circled on its own campus, with its own social and athletic activities, among its own students. This inward focus was part of what had afforded the students of each college such close-knit communities. The students had always found ways to socialize across campus, but the colleges didn't make it easy for them.

S. Claire remembered a conversation of one of the monks with Abbot Alcuin Deutsch: "Father Abbot," the monk asked, "how can we ever hope to have Catholic marriages if our boys do not meet Catholic girls while attending college?" The abbot replied: "See here, young man, Saint John's was not founded primarily as a matrimonial bureau."[10] And so generations of Johnnies talk about Saint Ben's as a no-man's-land, figuratively and literally.

S. Claire worked to moderate the separation. The first steps included cross-campus musical performances. Both colleges continued to mount plays and dramatic performances with single-sex casts, but from the mid-1930s at least one play a year included both Saint John's and Saint Ben's students. Their performances necessarily required rehearsals and late nights; no doubt they invited friendships and dating.

Clubs at the two colleges, even if they didn't go coed—and they didn't—could arrange occasional joint meetings. The International Relations Clubs of the two campuses, for example, met for a debate on the power of the presidency in April 1934. Afterwards, the CSB juniors hosted a dance for Johnnies and Bennies decorated with "myriads of balloons, red hearts . . . and soft red lighting effects." Both CSB and the SJU faculty members served as chaperones. Students from both colleges participated with others in a statewide model League of Nations.[11] More and more men appeared in Saint Ben's student publications and on the campus. More and more women showed up in the *St. John's Record,* at football games, in Collegeville.

Why in the 1930s did S. Claire take these steps? During Saint Ben's first 20 years and during the century of women's higher education in the United States, there had been much concern about the danger of coeducation, the danger of men and women distracting each other from the work of college. Single-sex education was the solution. The oldest of the private colleges—many of the most prestigious—and virtually all of the Catholic colleges were single sex. Even so, in the 20th century coeducation gained in popularity and numbers. "In the past half century, after a halting start," the *New York Times* reported in 1933, "coeducation has literally swept most of our territory and captured most of our students." Eunice Fuller Barnard, the *Times* reporter who in 1933 wrote a series of articles on the 100th anniversary of higher education for women in the United States, reported that coeducation was the wave of the future. By the end of the 1920s, 75 percent of college students were attending coed schools. In the 1930s, women's colleges were closing; men's colleges were going coed.

The presidents of coed colleges were wont to argue the superiority of the mixed college in providing "the normal life environment" and a context both more pleasant and more intellectually stimulating than the single-sex institution. They claimed the opportunity for "better social adjustment and . . . balanced attitude toward the other sex." Indeed, they implied, such opportunity made for better marriage choices.[12]

If this *New York Times* reporter accurately represented the larger landscape, S. Claire's effort to connect Saint Ben's with Saint John's may have been part of her work to ensure CSB's competitiveness. If more and more students were choosing coeducational colleges, Saint Ben's had to present a more "normal" environment. Especially during the depression, when lower costs combined with coeducation to increase the appeal of the state schools, CSB had to acknowledge student interest in dating, in "boys." Introducing joint club meetings, concerts, and hayrides, she countered, acknowledged the trend without jeopardizing the benefits of a women's college.

Another 1930s idea about women's colleges may well have played a role in S. Claire's actions. The fears of some people that college made women unsuitable for, or uninterested in, marriage had long dogged women's education. Eugenicists, fearing that college-educated women would not marry at the rate of women with less education, warned of "race suicide" caused by educated women not having children. The deeper social anxiety was that women's colleges both harbored and encouraged lesbianism.

Women faculty members at women's colleges—single as a usual requirement of employment—had long been the subject of gossip, but critics in the 1930s accused colleges of making "out-and-out homosexuality" into "something of a fad" and of being "breeding places for Sapphism."[13]

Women's colleges certainly were largely women-only communities. Until the mid-1930s, the only men on the Saint Ben's campus were the farm workers, a couple of monks, and an occasional music teacher (the long-serving Mr. Manley). The entire on-campus community—administration, faculty, student bodies of the college and the high school—was female. And single.

At virtually every college—including those for women—marriage disqualified a woman from employment. If one was already married, she would not be hired; if she was already employed, she had to resign when she wed. Some part of this situation reflected cultural ideas about (middle-class) women's place in the home; some part, the expectation that women teachers live among the students, as prefects in the dorms. Regardless, CSB and other Catholic colleges did not hire married women.

Not surprisingly, then, many women formed strong bonds with other women. Whether their relationships were actively sexual is unclear—and irrelevant here—but the commitment of many women to each other was a standard feature of the Seven Sisters. Their lifelong relationships were often called "Boston marriage."

In the late 19th century, coed schools were seen as sexually dangerous. In the 20th century, the notion of danger was reconfigured to present women's colleges so. No doubt this fear was less acute in central Minnesota, where Catholics and non-Catholics were long familiar with women's religious communities and few were reading *Well of Loneliness,* Radclyffe Hall's novel of women loving women. Neither was there much attention to Gertrude Stein and Alice B. Toklas in Paris or even to Edna St. Vincent Millay's friendships with women. Still, the specter of the "lesbian menace" haunted women's colleges in the 1930s (and still does).

This fear took a painful toll, and women's colleges worked hard in the 1930s to get more men on campus. The Seven Sisters hired more male faculty members and administrators. Miss Mary Woolley (she was always called Miss, as women faculty members were and were routinely known) served as president of Mount Holyoke from 1901 to 1937. She and her friend Jeannette Marks appeared together regularly; they traveled and lived together as well. For years they lived in the college president's residence. When Miss Woolley retired, Mount Holyoke hired Roswell G. Ham, its first male president, against her opposition and that of many faculty members, students, and alums. The appointment stood. Roswell was, the *Boston Globe* reported, a "he man," and a "family man" would be "a fine tonic for the spinster management of Mount Holyoke" and get it out of its "feminine rut." The college's board (mostly made up of men) thought a male president would "set a proper tone." Ham's presence helped "masculinize" the campus, as did his pointed efforts to hire more men to the faculty.[14]

S. Claire apparently made no public statement about the fear of lesbianism, but she increased the formal and informal contact of CSB with SJU students substantially. She also hired male faculty members.

College administration gave S. Claire an avenue for her ideas, idealism, and energy. In the first few years of her term, she focused on local

Johnnies Give Sweetheart Dance

With red hearts and cupids' bows, paper lace and mottoes, the Johnnies will present their annual pre-Lenten dance as a Sweetheart Dance on Valentine's Day. It will be held at the Knights of Columbus Hall in St. Cloud, from ten until one, as the St. John's-Gustavus Adolphus basketball game will be played earlier in the evening.

The dance is being sponsored by the St. John's Student Council. The committee chairmen include: George LePage, general chairman; Randall Murphy, tickets; George Grace, decorations; Benny Lorenz, refreshments; and James Lamb, transportation.

Announcement of a dance at SJU

Bennies and Johnnies dancing

issues. After plugging major holes in the dike, she moved to a larger playing field. She attended meetings and conferences and quickly became active in the National Catholic Educational Association (NCEA). In 1936 she accepted appointment to its accreditation committee (under the chairmanship of her friend Edward Fitzpatrick). In 1940–41 she attended meetings of the Minnesota Educational Association, American Catholic Philosophical Association, Midwest Catholic Educational Association, North Central Association, and the National Catholic Education Association (no one on the faculty traveled to more meetings than she).

S. Claire resigned in 1941 to return to graduate school. She earned a doctorate in history from Catholic University, then joined the CSB faculty. In 1948 she volunteered to be among sisters founding a new community in Eau Claire. This move is one of the puzzles of her life—there was no college in Eau Claire, no realistic hope for one. Why did she go where elementary or secondary teaching would almost certainly constitute her work?

A few years later S. Claire volunteered again, to leave Eau Claire and participate in the opening of the St. Paul Priory—another Benedictine community providing teachers for Benedictine grade school and high schools. She lived in the Twin Cities until her death at age 86 in 1984. She returned to St. Joseph on many occasions, including the dedication of Claire Lynch Hall. She agreed to the naming (who could resist S. Emmanuel Renner's persuasive talents!). She might have preferred that an academic building carry her name, but she didn't turn down the honor of any building in her name.

The College of Saint Benedict in 1932 was a small, isolated, inward looking, safe, small college with limited goals and a constrained horizon. A decade later the college was still small, but its horizons had broadened dramatically. Its connections to Saint John's had deepened, as had its contact with the other Catholic women's colleges in the state. More outsiders came in and more students went out—to conferences, to competitions, to volunteer. They saw themselves as part of larger Catholic movements as well—Rural Life, Catholic Worker, Liturgical Movement. Through its day students the campus had a

Graduation 1938

stronger connection to St. Cloud and St. Cloud to the college. The sister-teachers were better educated, better connected to others in their fields, more public in their work. The board of advisors brought outsiders into the administration of the college and created bonds between the sisters and the business/professional communities in St. Cloud and the Twin Cities. Most of this was S. Claire Lynch's doing, supported by her community, the two prioresses under whom she worked, and a faculty willing to be inspired and ready to make a better college.

The 1940s at CSB

~

These students, from St. Joseph and St. Cloud, planned the 1941 Big Sister-Little Sister Party: Front row: (l to r) Josephine Kohler, Catherine Pribyl, Katherine Broker; back: Mary Louise Reilly, Dorothy Holland, Ruth Linnemann.

From *Bulletin of the College of St. Benedict 1944–1945:*

The first aim of the College of Saint Benedict is to make you think.

That is what liberal means; Saint Benedict's is a liberal arts college.

You will study the best that has been known and thought in the world. You will integrate this mass of information. You will form generalizations. You will think.

Since man's intellect is his highest gift, its development is the greatest human good man can possess.

But you do not develop intellectually in a physical, social, and religious vacuum.

Through games and sports you will increase health, vigor, beauty of body. This physical development is, moreover, a source of joyous recreation.

Poise, charm, and the pleasure of fine human contacts are yours if you enter whole-heartedly into the social program.

Religion is not just something that you study in class. It is something that permeates your whole life. All that you think, speak, do, dream is fragrant with spirituality. Catholic principles bear blossoms where, without your opportunities, materialism would go to bitter seed.

A liberal education does not train you for a profession.

But you will be enormously benefited for any profession you choose.

You must always live with yourself. A liberal education gives you the privilege of living with your best self.

Saint Benedict's is dedicated to helping you develop your best self intellectually, physically, socially, and spiritually.

Catherine Van Buren (and her accompanist) appeared at CSB in 1940. She later taught some of the world's great sopranos, including Leontyne Price.

In 1942 these students' uniforms expressed their individuality. Back row: (l to r) Isabella Latourneau, Josephine Kohler, Jeannette Klassen, Charlene Gaffney, Imelda Schuster; front: Mary Flaherty, Kathleen Yanes, Dorothy Peffer, Frances Schwartz, Rita Lenard

S. Incarnata Girgen, dean, consulted with Joseph Matt, editor of the Catholic newspaper Der Wanderer *and member of the college's board of advisors.*

Saturday Pageant practice

Cadet nurses preparing
for war

From The Benet, *1942: Four seniors and one junior have recently been chosen in a faculty and student poll as members of the Who's Who among Students in American Universities & Colleges. Character, leadership, scholarship, and potentialities of future usefulness to society formed the basis upon which the selection was made. The girls chosen are Harriet Hunstiger [St. Cloud], Genevieve Powers [LaMoure, ND], Consuelo Romero [New York], Irene Staniszewski [Milwaukee], Jeanette Thielman [St. Cloud], and Lois Malloy [later S. Kristen, Bismarck, N.D.].*

We know you'll be as interested as Therese Kashmitter, Anna Lou Ellenbecker, and Eileen Opaatz are in FANDEL blouses, a big item in any coed's wardrobe. For every variety in color and style visit the blouse department on second floor at FANDEL'S.

Fandel's Department Store in St. Cloud hired CSB students to pose for its ads in CSB publications.

Herberger's also went after the CSB business.

When a "Benny" thinks of fashion She thinks of

Herberger's

● California Sportswear!
● Suits with the 1947 Look!
● Dresses in tune with Spring!
● Full swinging Coats!

All this at prices to fit your budget!

Do your Easter Shopping at Herberger's and you'll be "Fashion-right"

Students switched from a piano, to a Victrola, then to a common radio in the 1940s.

Margaret Mollner, Edith Lagundo,
Maxine Bradford, Dolores Borman,
and Katherine Raths in physical
education class in 1942

COLLEGIANA

1. McDonald, Anderson, and Connolly participate in the All-College Day discussion held at St. Benedict's.
2. Farewell—Young, Prickril and Rausch on an informal visit.
3. Tschida was happy to pose for this.
4. Katie and Juan.
5. A card game in the rotunda at St. Benedict's.
6. Desmond and other All-College Day participants.
7. Dietz wins a bond as Johnson draws his number. Laubach and Heille directed the bond drive.
8. One day as Bruts was passing through St. Joe . . .
9. Two neckties and Reardon and Kelley.

From Sagatagan, *Saint John's 1945 yearbook*

S. Mariella Gable's writing students submitted regularly to *The Atlantic Monthly* writing contest. Nancy Hynes, OSB, listed the winners in her introduction to Mariella's book, *The Literature of Spiritual Values and Catholic Fiction:*

The *Atlantic Monthly* first prizes were for short story, "The Hanky and the Sins" by Bernadette Loosbroek (1942) and essay, "These Gentle Communists," by Mary Thomes (1944). Other honorable mentions: top twenty essays, "Emily Post to the Contrary Notwithstanding" by Betty Wahl and "That One Talent" by Genevieve Powers (1942); third honorable mention, short story, "Novice in the Cellar," and story of merit, "They Also Serve," both by Elizabeth Zwilling (1944); honorable mention, essay, "Dante Loves Beatrice," by Betty Wahl and top twenty essays, "My Father and Eric Gill," by Mary Martin (1945).

1952 reunion of the class of 1947

So, Let Your Light Shine on 1957

The Pageant dominated the opening weeks of the 1957 fall semester at the College of Saint Benedict, as it had for 22 years. CSB initiated new students by enacting the story of how Benedictines for 1,400 years had played a central role in the preservation and transmission of Christian wisdom.[1] S. Mariella Gable, a professor in the English Department and the author and director of the Pageant, wanted every CSB student to know this inspiring and amazing story.

She herself had not learned about this Benedictine heritage as a Saint Ben's student, not even as a Benedictine novice, or even in her first decade in the monastery, but as a graduate student at Columbia University when she was in her thirties. The story so moved her and her ignorance of it so embarrassed her that she vowed students would "never, never, never" (her emphasis) again leave CSB without knowing this Benedictine history.

The idea for the form of the pageant also grew out of S. Mariella's Columbia time when she would have known about—and perhaps even have seen—the spring Greek festival performed at Barnard. Barnard and other women's colleges regularly held spring games in a manner explicitly reminiscent of ancient Greece: flowing gowns, discus throwing, and torches. For more than 30 years Barnard and other women's colleges organized Greek-style spring flings, often called pageants.

When Mariella returned

The passing of the torch was the Pageant's central image and every student wanted to be a "flame" (and to have a photo as beautiful as this one!).

The torch had come from St. Benedict and St. Scholastica, through other Benedictines, saints, popes, thinkers.

from graduate school, she invented "So Let Your Light Shine: A Pageant Honoring the Freshmen." It wasn't a reenactment of Greek athletics; no games or trials as the Barnard pageant was, and it was held in

The wisdom of the ages passed to barbarians (enacted but not pictured here) and to noblemen.

the fall rather than the spring. It dropped the pagan aura of the ancients, but it did adopt the flowing gowns, and the torch was its centerpiece—the torch of learning passed from those ancient Greeks to the lawn of the College of Saint Benedict.

"So Let Your Light Shine" was for almost 30 years a signature event of every student's experience at CSB. In every one of those years, the college shortened the class day by two hours for the first two weeks of the fall semester to free up the whole college community to participate. Not

Peasants, too

optional! Constance Zierden, S. Marcine Schirber, S. Firmin Escher, an orchestra from St. Cloud State University, the campus electricians who worked with Northern States Power to bring in extra electricity for the event, sisters who drilled the students, and virtually the entire faculty and student body took part. The Pageant called on everyone to do something: making costumes and invitations; playing the roles of the Benedictines, barbarians, saints, flames; reciting, singing, handling the chairs and ushering the guests. It was a miracle that any studying got

The Benedictines, through their commitments to Ora (Prayer) and Labora (Work) guided the transmission of knowledge and wisdom (students played all the parts in the Pageant, including those of the Benedictine sisters).

The flames reached even to current students who, in turn, passed the torches on to the incoming students.

done in those first few weeks. No wonder CSB never developed a tradition of autumn homecoming. The college focused instead on teaching the first-years about this remarkable and profound history of which they were the heirs.

The centerpiece and central image of the pageant was fire—the flame of knowledge and Christianity.[2] "Behold the light/Behold the light of 14 centuries," the chorus chanted in unison, "Behold the light that gave us princes and scholars, laborers and saints, the light that preserved western civilization, the light that illumines the pavement of the Way."[3] The Pageant always took place at night, better to see "the gentle flames of Christianity weaving gracefully around a bright night fire." At the Pageant's climax, after St. Benedict handed each new student her cap and gown, the Benedictine saints passed lighted torches to the new students. Holding the torches aloft, the students "in a burst of song" pledged their loyalty to the traditions that the flames represented.

The pageant expressed the sacredness of that received knowledge and the responsibilities that Christianity conferred. It taught, too, about discipline and fitting in. No one "girl" was to call attention to herself, and every girl was to do her part to create the overall effect. The director issued firm rules and strict rebukes: "STOP CHEWING GUM"; the saints were ordered to stop "dilly dallying" and the chorus to "Keep perfect silence when lining up, marching, performing, AND WHILE MARCHING

OFF." Everyone was ordered to "Look alert and happy, and walk with one foot in front of the other instead of plodding, swaying, and lounging like awkward adolescents." When you pledge your loyalty your voices "ought to rise like a wonderful and thrilling outburst—not like a little song of schoolgirls."

For nearly 30 years the pageant defined Saint Ben's. Lay and religious alumnae alike can still recite lines from memory (and in chorus):

> We are the Franks and the Teutons,
> The Huns and the terrible Gauls,
> We are the Picts and the Britons,
> The Wild to our wild blood calls.
> And never a nation shall change
> Our wandering feet from wandering.
> Where wild tribes range.[4]

The pageant reached its apex in 1957—big crowds, newspaper coverage, all-campus involvement. Then everything changed. Not quite, but almost, overnight.

Taken at a rehearsal, this photo shows the central circle around which the pageant revolved plus the stands (upper right) where the students received and passed on the torches. The "Ora" tableau stood to the left of the student section and the "Labora" to the right (out of the photo). At a performance the saints would have been lined up to the left of the Ora and then moved into place at the bottom of the bleachers to hand the torches on.

By the end of that school year S. Mariella had been banished from the campus (so had S. Kristin Malloy and S. Thomas Carey). Someone else took over the pageant's direction. More and more of the sisters complained: too many hours of rehearsal, students needed more class time, trying to get 100 young women to march in formation seemed to be getting harder and harder, the language was dated. What had been so new and exciting in 1935 could still thrill the participants and certainly still imprinted itself on their memories. But its time was past.

The college put on the pageant several more times. In a community where dozens of people remember everything, no one can seem to recall exactly when it stopped.

When I see photographs of the fifties, everything is so clean.
The sidewalks are clean, the tar on the highways is clean,
the shirts of the men are starched, the women's skirts haven't
*a pleat out of place. I don't know if it was like that.**

FOUR

~

Everything Was So Clean

In 1953, the College of Saint Benedict celebrated its 40th birthday. S. Claire had made big changes in the 1930s, but Saint Ben's looked much as it had in 1913. Most classes still took place in Teresa Hall. S. Remberta Westkaemper had been teaching in the same classroom at least since 1920. Students ate in the same dining rooms. They no longer wore the original uniform, but they did abide by a dress code of skirts for all campus events (except room cleaning) and hose, hats, and gloves for all off-campus doings (even Saint John's football games). Sisters in traditional habit still filled the campus and ran the college.

The students still lived with posted hours and curfews and a clear set of rules. They signed out when they left campus and signed in when they returned. S. Mary Patrick Murray, the dean of the residence halls, welcomed students back on weekend nights (and reportedly took the opportunity to check on whether they'd been drinking). One student recalled that her parents seemed happy to leave her in the "prison" she felt CSB to be. The student yearbook wagered that many a first-year student would "hate the rules"—think them "old fashioned" and "exacting"—though, countered the *Facula* writer, the restrictions were a small price to pay

---

*Sebastian Barry, *On Caanan's Side* (New York: Penguin, 2012).

You can tell by the gloves that these Bennies are getting ready to go off campus.

for the "feeling of belonging and of togetherness in a lonely world" she would have the next year. Parents too must have been reassured by the presence of a sister who sniffed out the drinkers and dogged the daters. Many women's colleges actively cultivated the impression that they were conservative and would above all protect its young women.[1]

For all its history Saint Ben's had offered its students a rigorous classic liberal arts curriculum and training in traditionally female fields (home economics, teaching, English, and nursing at the sisters' nursing school in St. Cloud). There were other opportunities, too, for students to follow their own stars to uncharted universes. The college provided a path into religious life and paved the way to the married life that most students chose.

CSB had always tried to honor the three paths laid out (in the Church and in the larger society: religious life, single, married), but it did so in a context of deep social ambivalence about women's roles and women's education. The three paths did not have equal standing in society or in the Church, of course, and like virtually every other college in the United States, CSB struggled with the choices.

The ambivalence was especially chafing in the 1950s. The president of Mills—a women's college in Oakland, Calif.—expressed his concern that "the current liberal arts program does not adequately prepare women for the role of wife and mother." Should it, was the question.[2]

CSB students could follow a program leading to bachelor's degrees. For the bachelor of arts, the candidate was required to take 16 credits of philosophy, up to 14 in foreign languages, 13 of English, 12 of theology, 9 of social science, 8 of natural science/math, 1 of art, and 1 of physical education. For the bachelor of science degree, a student took slightly fewer credits of English, social science, and languages. In the 1950s the most popular choice for a major was elementary education, but students could also choose biology, business education, chemistry, English, French, German, history, home economics, Latin, mathematics, music, and sociology as well as minors in art, economics, philosophy, and physics. From 1956 to 1958, 34 of the 40 faculty members had a master's degree or a doctorate.

When Pope Pius XII wrote, "Every woman is meant to be a mother," he spoke what many Catholics and others believed and espoused in the 1950s. The hierarchy of priests and sisters, the keeping of women from the altar except to clean it, spoke loudly of women's "proper" role. When Saint Ben's displayed framed photos of alums with their husbands and 17 children, it honored the choice that many mid-century Catholic women made to have big families.[3]

But the sisters teaching the courses—from home economics to physics—modeled what it meant for women to be leaders and intellectuals. As one alum recalled, her time at CSB "gave me confidence in myself. I felt that if they could run a college, I would be able to do something equally significant with my life."[4]

Sisters enjoying a cookout

The college struggled with issues of who women should be and what they should do as a reflection of the larger society struggling with those issues. The Great Depression had thrown men out of work and destabilized family life. World War II further unsettled and undermined conventional gender roles. Men went away; women assumed family control. The government depended on women to do men's work. Childcare centers and middle-class working mothers became commonplace. At the war's conclusion, some women resisted the pressure to give up their jobs and go home. President Harry S. Truman appointed Minnesota's Eugenie Anderson ambassador to Denmark in 1949. President Dwight D. Eisenhower appointed Oveta Culp Hobby as his secretary of health, education, and welfare. In 1955, Minnesota elected Coya Knutson as its first woman representative to Congress.

At the same time, the "traditional" definition of women's roles and family life reasserted itself with a vengeance. The divorce rate fell and church membership rose, and home took on a new meaning and style. The GI Bill brought houses and higher education within reach for many more. Better jobs and easier money meant new furniture, cars, clothes, record players, and records. Televisions replaced radios. The promise of prosperity created a demand, too, for shopping malls, freeways, more and newer schools, and a college experience. Many new houses in the 1950s looked like each other and invited the people who lived in them to act like each other, too. Greater mobility put them in the suburbs, also fostering the at-work husband and the at-home wife.

Etiquette queen Amy Vanderbilt published through the 1950s the pamphlet series *Success Program for Women.* In "How to Help Your Husband Get Ahead," she advised women when out with their husbands to "be attentive to him when he speaks, and when you disagree with him say, 'Well you may be right, because you usually are, but—.'" The booklet offered other tips surely confusing for the educated woman. For example, "The wife of a big-corporation man needn't be a knock-out either physically or intellectually. In fact, it is better if she is not (or pretends she is not)."[5]

Family life took on new and greater importance. The depression of the 1930s may have undermined men in terms of their ability to bring home the bacon, and the war may have called on women to do much that had been called "men's work," but the end of the war and the new

S. Clarus Himsl and this "Home Ec baby" (of whom there were many) helped students learn how to care for children.

prosperity seemed to right the "disorder." Many women did leave those men's jobs and go back home; returning soldiers reclaimed their positions in work and as the heads of their families. The ideal of a particular kind of domestic tranquility—husband at work, wife at home, kids everywhere—held greater sway than it had for decades. The clearest indication of this new domesticity was the baby boom. Births in the United States jumped from 2.8 million in 1945 to 3.4 million in 1946 and climbed to a peak of 4.3 million births in 1957.

Catholic life in general and Catholic family life in particular flourished in the 1950s. Catholic churches overflowed with congregants, seminaries with priests, convents with sisters. Long discriminated against in a Protestant America, Catholics by the 1950s turned their separation into a vibrant common culture. Jobs outside the Catholic circle might be a necessary evil, but marriage outside was to be avoided at all cost. The Knights of Columbus, the Catholic Daughters, and other Catholic organizations provided social interaction. Every community of any size had at least one Catholic doctor, hospital, funeral home, cemetery, insurance man, and lawyer. Whenever possible, Catholics patronized their Catholic friends' paint or furniture stores and called on the plumbers and contractor of their parishes.[6]

The Catholic Church monitored the influences on its common culture: The Legion of Decency from the 1930s through the 1960s ranked the films shown in U.S. theaters, and Catholics faithfully selected movies based on those rankings. For 400 years the church published the *Index Librorum Prohibitorum* (or *List of Prohibited Books,* commonly "the Index"). Catholics were neither to own nor to read them. Catholic colleges did not place them in their libraries. One result was that they often offered courses on the Russian novel (those appeared infrequently on the Index) but rarely on the French (you can guess why).

Catholic schools were the heart and soul of the Catholic world. All good Catholics sent their children to Catholic elementary and secondary schools and to Catholic colleges, if possible. The schools supported and sustained the students' separateness and their distinct Catholic culture. Most but not all Catholic grade-school and high-school students wore uniforms, which reinforced Catholic commonality and de-emphasized class differences; they helped big families, and they set a standard for decorum and modesty. All grade-school students studied the *Baltimore Catechism.* They also used Catholic textbooks—even a Catholic speller. "Father" taught from time to time; laypersons, always Catholic, were hired to teach if necessary but with regret, and sisters ran the Catholic schools, often on a shoestring.

This vibrant Catholic culture shaped the College of Saint Benedict and flourished there. Catholicism was central to its purpose and identity. Former students report that no one talked much about what it meant to be Catholic or to be a Catholic college—there was no need. Catholicism was a way of being and seeing the world that, for most students and the college, was a given, presumed more than argued or articulated. Whether or not college rules required students to attend daily morning mass—few alumnae of the 1950s remember—they did attend. It was like brushing their teeth: if they were in the habit, they didn't need the requirement. The students gathered in the evenings to say compline and receive the blessing of one of the sisters before bed. Every January the students participated in a two- or three-day retreat. Whether or not each was a faithful Catholic—not all were—each knew Catholicism was part of the college's DNA.

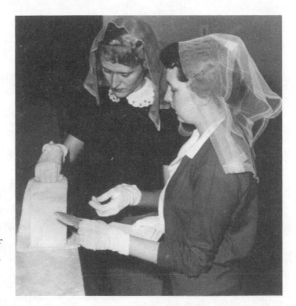

Mary Baker and Betty Bullock, members of the most popular on-campus club, the Sodality of Mary, help prepare for mass in 1956.

The sisters learned to conserve paper and pencils, to use nothing, to reuse everything. Their "mean" circumstances turned some of them mean—and into the butt of some 50 years of attacks and jokes, satire and memoir and fiction. So did the requirement that sisters teach what was needed no matter what they loved or whether they wanted to or *could* teach. Many sisters, of course, were beloved by their students and did their work with energy and vision and love.

One strong aspect of the Catholic culture was the separation of girls and boys, women and men. Catholic Daughters and Knights of Columbus for adults continued the single-sex approach for high school and college students. Separation supposedly meant sexual safety— really, safety from pregnancy—which served as a counter to the church's strong stance on birth control.

Did separation offer other kinds of safety, too? As one CSB student put it, the college offered "a place apart—a safe, secure, holding environment in which young women could grow."[7]

Catholicism permeated student life. Two of the largest campus organizations were the Sodality of Mary (its main function to encourage piety) and the National Federation of Catholic College Students (its main function to solidify Catholic cross-campus connections). Saint John's and Saint Ben's chapters met together from time to time, and both hosted and sent delegates to statewide meetings with students from St. Scholastica, St. Kate's, St. Teresa's, St. Thomas, and St. Mary's (the male counterpart of St. Teresa's, in Winona).

Sunday-night convocations brought to campus a variety of progressive (and conservative) Catholic speakers. Catholic artists, writers, philosophers, and historians were welcome at the College of Saint Benedict. The bishop, too, took a special interest in life at the college, making regular visits to campus and keeping his ear pricked for news (and gossip).

In 1953 all of this seemed likely to last forever. Enrollment at Saint Ben's steadied and then increased. Vocations to the Benedictine sisterhood in St. Joe also increased. Within a few years the buildings of the college and monastery—even the Ro, perhaps especially the Ro—were full to bursting.

Until the fall of 1956, all on-campus students at Saint Ben's lived and ate and took most of their classes in the Ro in Teresa Hall. The library that had served six students in 1913 had to accommodate 300 in 1956. From 1913 a phonograph, a radio, and then a telephone had

The college's many convocations usually took place in Assembly Hall, an original feature in Teresa Hall.

been installed in the Ro. A boy or two may have seen the inside of the Ro while helping his sister move in or during the panty raids that a few Johnnies claim they masterminded. This was a women's—or girls'—sanctuary, where residents could sit around in robes and slippers, curlers in their hair. Rocking chairs invited conversation and relaxation. Even candidates for the crown of Posture Queen could slouch among the pillows on the chaise lounges there. College students who lived in the nearby dormitory—a very large room with curtained partitions, lockers, and wardrobes—could use the Ro, too, as their living space.

The furniture in the Ro changed over the years, reflecting contemporary furniture and decorating styles, but soft, overstuffed sofas and chairs predominated. It was, after all, a living room. A piano eventually took pride of place. Carpets and coffee tables came and went. Stools and tables were moved in as needed.

In the 1950s, the college (and the academy and the religious community) could barely squeeze in one more person. Every spare space had long since been filled, and student enrollment would have to be capped just when those baby boomers would ready to attend college. The sisters' indebtedness had severely restricted their funds—and their physical building of the college. For purposes of "efficiency and economy of operation" the community decided that with nothing built at the college since 1913, it was high time. Yes, there was risk, but postwar prosperity and the rising tide of college applicants would make it manageable. So under the leadership of Mother Richarda Peters, the sisters hired the St. Paul architectural firm Hammel and Green to produce drawings for a new residence hall.

The new building would stand on its own, a bit apart from Teresa Hall, to create the centerpiece of a "fine interior campus" and open "new campus vistas." Nothing in the new dorm would remind one of Jefferson's Monticello or of the Pantheon. Instead it would be a "simple and serviceable unit" of three stories, with single, double, and triple rooms lining long corridors. For every 30 students, the building would include a common kitchen, living room, laundry, and bathroom. It offered several new amenities: a lounge where students could meet their dates, a snack bar, and a smoking room. The "family spirit" inherent in

The Rotunda changed with the times.

The Ro had cushier furniture in 1946.

*Students made good use
of the Rotunda common space.*

Benedictine life shaped the architects' plans especially for the "symbolically wide, protective roof sheltering the commons."

The architects estimated the cost of the new building at nearly $1 million. Not an unreasonable amount, it nevertheless generated an engine of fundraising effort by sisters, alumnae, students, and friends of Saint Ben's. Sisters Clarus and Magna, plus Clara Ann Donlin (Mrs. George) Condon '47 and undergraduates Mary Kay Heil and Margaret Johnson served on the first building committee, planning and setting up the Dollar-a-Year Club and the CSB Associates for those who could afford to give money, as well as a handiwork fair for those who could make items for sale (more than 100 sisters volunteered). Students, too, helped raise money for the building project, selling rings and holding fairs, going door to door. Each class had its project.

In return for these efforts, Mother Richarda promised the "earnest prayers of a thousand Sisters of St. Benedict" who would "ask for God's blessing upon all who assist us in bearing the great and necessary burden we are now assuming."[8]

The architects had planned a red-brick exterior for the new construction so to match the other buildings on campus. But John Alexander, president of Cold Spring Granite Company and a member of the CSB board of advisors, provided local granite, which read harder and more modern than the earlier façades. Molded plastic chairs, exposed-steel sofas, and leather benches—rather than soft furnishings like those of

These sisters were doing their part to raise money for the new Mary Hall by making needlework to sell. From left: Sisters Neomi, Mariella, Omer, Linnea, Remberta, and Agnesia

the Ro—were chosen to furnish the new commons area. This resulted in an interior of sharp lines and hard surfaces, in keeping with the design aesthetic of the 1950s. The new look dismayed some who preferred the style and metaphor of the Ro. The modern style and vibe of the new building thrilled others, including one prospective student who applied only on condition she could live there. Having grown up in a farmhouse, she loved every new thing about her new dorm, including her first experience of central heating. One alum of that generation saw the construction as an "amazing expansion for the college . . . in numbers and modernity."

The sisters might well have asked the architects for a traditional building, one more in keeping with the style of the main building and the Ro. But they didn't. They might also have moved all of the students from the main building into a new residence hall to relieve classroom, library, office, and monastery crowding. But they didn't. No doubt a variety of practical concerns explains their decision; regardless, the presence of such two different living spaces more than hints at the forces pushing and pulling on Saint Ben's in the 1950s. And it suggests the extent to which CSB was straddling—or perhaps bridging—the future with the past.

The old spaces and the new could not have been more different. Notice the soft and rounded furnishings of the original Rotunda and the hard, squared-off edges of the new Mary Lounge.

Clearly Saint Ben's was looking forward, not just to more students but to enough students to effect its transformation. A place of higher learning that could fit into one building was fundamentally different from one that sprawled, that allowed for subgroups, that required an effort to get to know everyone. The college was starting to turn outward.

Change was definitely on the horizon. Some people denied it was coming; some pretended it wasn't. There were, however, many indications. Sociologists wrote that men in their "grey flannel suits" were finding emptiness at the core of their new lives. More women worked outside the home in 1955 than at any time during the war, and their number was increasing, especially among those beyond childbearing age.[9] The postwar peace quickly turned cold as China "fell," nuclear weapons threatened the very existence of the world, and Sen. Joseph McCarthy of Wisconsin fueled an atmosphere of mutually assured suspicion in and out of Congress.

Many 1950s events portended change; some would not come into revolutionary fullness until "the Sixties" but were already making a difference The Soviet launch in 1957 of the first satellite—*Sputnik*—frightened Americans into an educational revolution. The U.S. Supreme Court struck down the constitutional protection of "separate but equal" in the *Brown* v. *Topeka Board of Education*. Rosa Parks refused to give her seat on the bus to a white person. And the African-American community in Montgomery flexed its muscles. Elvis Presley was already swinging his hips; John Lennon and Paul McCartney had already met. Rachel Carson wrote *The Sea Around Us* and was beginning work on *Silent Spring.* Michael Harrington was researching what would become *The Other America*. Birth-control pills were undergoing clinical trials in Puerto Rico. The students who crammed into grade schools in the 1950s would be part of a distinct and separate youth culture in the 1960s. The world Americans knew in the 1950s—however briefly—would soon implode.

However strong the Catholic world might have been in the 1950s, it was also eroding. The walls between Catholics and Protestants were crumbling. Catholic and non-Catholic soldiers had made common cause in the war. Catholics and non-Catholics at home did war work and suffered wartime rationing together. Afterwards, Catholics moved out

Sister Enid and her philosophy class tackle St. Thomas and the Problem of Evil.

of urban ethnic neighborhoods—parishes—and joined non-Catholics in the suburbs. They made friends at work and at home and not exclusively in their parishes. They attended—against church rules—the weddings and funerals of their Protestant and Jewish friends and co-workers. The Catholics' fear of godless communism meshed powerfully with the American fear of Soviet communism. That Senator McCarthy, who led the charge against internal enemies, was a Catholic, helped strengthen the Catholic-American bond, made Catholics seem less alien, and put them on the same team as their "non-Catholic" neighbors.

The Second Vatican Council, which shattered this Catholic world so dramatically, did not convene until 1962, but Pope John XXIII's plan for a council had grown out of changes already in the works in the 1950s. Pope Pius XII before him had loosened the strict rules for fasting before communion and called for more participation by the laity in the mass. Sisters received permission to modify their veils, so that they could see better when they drove, and more and more American religious communities were saying the Divine Office in English. The last edition of the Index was published in 1948 (and disappeared by the 1960s). The Legion of Decency added more categories and flexibility to

*Class officers,
1957–58, standing:
Elizabeth Dempster
and Irma Gentilini;
sitting: Mary Lee
Foley and Janet
McGuire*

its movie rankings. A few women dared to attend mass without a hat (or a piece of Kleenex bobby-pinned to the hair).

Catholics had long known how to bend the rules. Many CSB alums remember wearing academic gowns to mass—as required—but over their pajamas. They wore the required skirts to class but rebelled by wearing sweatshirts above them. Some admit ignoring Legion of Decency rankings (though no one ever saw a C movie) or tell of checking out forbidden books from the public library. There were formal avenues around some of the rules: The college library eventually owned many books on the Index—for scholarly use, of course. Saint John's kept its copies in what students called the "Hell Library"—a separate and locked room (for which the key could be obtained). Daring faculty members used condemned books in their classes. For example, S. Colman O'Connell, teaching theater at CSB, used the plays of John Paul Sartre, suggesting that the bishop surely would prefer that students read the plays under her tutelage than on their own. And at Saint John's, Fr. Eleutherius Winnance read Sartre's *Being and Nothingness* aloud to his modern-philosophy students.[10]

Much of such rule bending occurred in a kind of don't-ask-don't-tell way so as to avoid confrontation. In the absence of overt rebellion or challenge to authority, the powers that be could look away from infraction. In the 1957–58 school year, however, J. D. Salinger's coming-of-age novel *The Catcher in the Rye* provoked a crisis at Saint Ben's.

Published in 1951, the book was a searing critique of postwar American life, eliciting both praise and outrage. Its central character,

S. Mariella Gable

Holden Caulfield—a vaguely depressed, cynical, sex-starved teenager, prone to profanity, yearning for authenticity and finding too few adult examples to model it—was a new kind of protagonist. A Book of the Month selection, the novel became a huge bestseller and one of the most widely censored books in the United States.[11]

S. Kristin Malloy, fresh out of graduate school and up on contemporary literature, included it on a class reading list. Not to do so would be to announce that she was out of step in her field. S. Mariella Gable, chair of the English department, to whom being up in her field was a matter of honor, also paid it some due. *The Catcher in the Rye* never appeared on the Index, so there was no official, Catholic reason for excluding it and none for asking permission to read it. Every self-respecting English teacher in the middle 1950s was reading, assigning, and most certainly talking about it. Few English majors in America would have graduated without hearing some reference to the book.

*Sisters M. Thomas Carey
and Kristin Malloy*

Fr. Jerome Doherty, the college chaplain, got wind of Bennies reading this controversial and, in his judgment, morally dangerous novel. By one rumor, other faculty members took their worries to Fr. Jerome and asked him to do something. By another report, Fr. Jerome took action only after students in the confessional had talked to him about the turmoil that the book had caused in them. Fr. Jerome was a monk at Saint John's Abbey, a "lateral transfer"—that is, a person who as a fully professed monk moved from another monastery. As such he had missed the socialization that had allied the Collegeville-St. Joseph Benedictines, so rather than taking his worries to the abbot or the prioress he went to the bishop.

He condemned the novel as pornographic, referred to it as "Catcher in the Sty," and set out to remove it—and Sisters Kristin and Mariella, if necessary—from the college. He called the two sisters "occasions of sin" and ordered them to withdraw the book. When he tried to enlist the support of President Remberta and found her unsympathetic, he went over her head to Mother Richarda, more conflicted if also unsympathetic. Fr. Jerome found his most solid ally, however, in Peter Bartholome, Bishop of St. Cloud (or "Black Bart," as many irreverently called him).[12]

Bishop Bartholome claimed both a diocesan teaching prerogative

and an obligation to protect Catholicism from its enemies—including too much or the wrong kind of education and modernism in all its forms. Some in the Catholic intellectual tradition welcomed modernism as part of

Bishop Peter Bartholome often warned the sisters and students against intellectual pride.

the intellectual quest, but as he saw it, the purpose of Catholic education generally was to teach students to be good Catholics, the purpose of a Catholic women's college to produce good Catholic women. In service of that end, he agreed with Fr. Jerome that S. Kristin and S. Mariella were dangerous. He went even further, too, declaring "modernism" in all its forms a serious danger facing all American Catholics.[13]

The bishop took his position and his teaching prerogative seriously. He oversaw the appointment of confessors and chaplains for the sisters and kept a close eye on the doings of the college. He presided at formal CSB events and handed out diplomas at commencement. Every fall he addressed the students and faculty on some issue of Catholic teaching. Few remember much of what he said, but many recall his railing against "intellectual pride" and warning of the dangers of "too much education."

Bishop Bartholome and S. Mariella had been clashing for some time. Even before the "Catcher in the Sty," the bishop had written Fr. Jerome, instructing him to keep an eye on her "lest the spirit of the world should creep in" at CSB. By the mid-1950s, the bishop and the Benedictine had a 15-year history of tension around his authority and her scholarship, and *The Catcher in the Rye* presented as good a reason as any to suppress her.

For her part, S. Mariella had not been reluctant to show her feelings about the bishop. Many sisters and students remember that she walked out of mass while he was preaching and that, defying his authority, she bypassed him and turned to friendlier ecclesiastical authorities when she needed official approval for her writings.

Fr. Jerome, Mother Richarda, the bishop, and sometimes S. Remberta spent countless hours during the spring and summer of 1958 talking about what should be done about the "English Department trouble." Mother Richarda found the conversations painful. She was used to holding her own in her conversations with the bishop, but directly resisting the religious authority of her bishop was not her style or habit. And this case did not allow for indirect resistance. Fr. Jerome was correct that the book had many critics and censors. And CSB was not the only Catholic college where the book was an issue. Was she certain her students' souls were not in harm's way?

The threat of censorship must have had a bitter taste to S. Mariella, who took pride in her doctorate, in her accomplishments and reputation. She was a published author, better educated than either the bishop or the chaplain. As a priest, Fr. Jerome had authority that she did not, but he was not her intellectual superior. She believed that in this case her authority should prevail.

This conflict also seared President S. Remberta. Sisters in religious communities had long been cautioned against particular friendships (close relationships with another sister). Even so, Remberta and Mariella, like many other sisters before and since, had a particular friendship. In her 1979 autobiography Remberta wrote:

> Sister [Mariella] and I had been close friends for years. Nothing can be compared to a faithful friend (Eccles. 6–16), and such a friend I found in Sister Mariella. We have been friends ever since she joined the faculty, giving each other mutual support, sharing each other's joys and sorrows, and interests . . . In the beginning, our friendship was frowned upon as that bane of community life . . . We ourselves knew by experience that "a faithful friend is a sturdy shelter, a treasure" . . . I may safely say that Sister Mariella and I have helped each other to grow intellectually, morally, and spiritually. The community now sees our friendship in that light and fully approves of it and considers it an example for others.[14]

S. Remberta had been teaching since 1917, but she was not named (the first) full-time president of the college until 1957, the year of the dangerous book. Nearly 70 years old, with a voracious intellectual appetite for botany, she was completely trapped by the dynamics of the crisis. Supporting the bishop would endanger her friendship with S. Mariella; opposing him would draw his attention to their particular friendship and thus endanger it too.

President Remberta opposed the bishop, but she did not, could not, do so publicly. S. Richarda fought him too—on the matter of disciplining the "modernist" sisters—also not publicly. What happened in public is that Fr. Jerome called a formal gathering of students and posted an official notice: "On the first day of April 1958, Salinger's *Catcher in the Rye* was recalled from this campus. To date thirty copies of this book have been handed in to the chaplain, who wishes to thank all for their cooperation in this matter. If any student still has a copy in her possession, she is in duty and conscience bound to hand it in to the chaplain."

Nothing happened to the students who read or owned the book. At the end of the school year, S. Kristin was removed from the college and sent to teach high school in Cold Spring, Minn. S. Mariella was sent to a small Benedictine college in Oregon. S. Remberta remained president of Saint Ben's for three more years, and Fr. Jerome, after one more year as chaplain, was sent to North Dakota to do parish work.

The letters of Sisters Mariella and Remberta are full of anguish. Other records make clear that Mother Richarda was able to save S. Remberta from removal. She was not able to save S. Kristin, S. Mariella, or S. Thomas Carey. The chaplain and the bishop had wanted all of them gone. In the fall of 1958, their teachers' absence noted, the students picked up enough rumor to know that F. Jerome had had something to do with it. Otherwise, silence.

In 1957 Betty Friedan turned up for her 15th reunion at Smith College with a question: What were her classmates doing with their lives

A reunion of the class of '57

and were they happy? She had graduated—summa cum laude—taken a one-year fellowship at Berkeley, then married and raised three children. She worked as a magazine journalist until her child was born (and she was let go), then worked as a freelancer. Based on an exploration of her own and her classmates' experiences as educated women in American society in the 1950s, she defined and then named "the problem that has no name." She call it *The Feminine Mystique* "a strange stirring, a sense of dissatisfaction, a yearning . . . a stunting or evasion of growth."[15]

Colleges taught women to reach, and then their lives pulled them back. The live wire touched by Betty Friedan smoldered across the United States, even in the Catholic women's colleges, even at CSB. It wasn't long before it turned into an open fire—not the gentle flames of the Pageant, but the flaming radicals of the 1960s. Hold onto your hats!

The sisters of Saint Benedict in 1958 were responsible for

1 college, 342 students
4 high schools, 1,859 students
51 grade schools, 11,436
3 hospitals, 585 beds
1 school for medical records technicians
2 schools of medical technology
2 schools of nursing
1 school of anesthesia
3 foreign missions
3 homes for the aged
3 Indian missions
1 retreat house

As reported in [Mariella Gable], *1857–1957 Harvest*

Angeline Dufner Remembers

Every spring the seniors by popular vote determine which faculty member they will invite to speak to them at the Senior Dinner. In 1988 they tapped Angeline Dufner, professor of English, and class of '57. This is an edited version of that talk.

When I graduated in 1957, I had 36 classmates. I knew everyone in school: seniors through freshmen. I knew every faculty member, and I think every faculty member knew me.

When I arrived as a freshman, every class was held either on first floor Main or second floor, except gym classes. I had Moral Theology on the same floor space where Jane Haugen now gives out financial aid. In a Dante class I traversed Hell, Purgatory, and Heaven where public information now writes news columns. I learned philosophy in what is now the Business office.

At the ends of those two academic halls on the stair landings were great pieces of statuary, gargantuan and allegorical figures designed to remind us at each turn of the stairs of some noble thought or good deal. But it didn't take especially well—the thoughts and deeds, that is.

One figure, perhaps St. Anthony, served as a particular temptation, for he eternally held out his arms to us—empty. When we could no longer bear it, we could unstring the nearby fire hose and give him 20 feet of canvas tubing to hold.

On the next landing was a massive plaster statue of St. Joan. Whether it was the sheer ugliness of this figure or the pranks we pulled on Anthony and her other plaster kinfolk, we didn't know. But one moring, St. Joan and Anthony and all that other tribe which had so clearly failed to save us—all disappeared. Vanished. Not even a plaster flake.

Rumors afterward said that S. Colman and some of her friends, all of them faculty who hated those statues, had come with a truck in the dead of night, had loaded St. Joan and St. Anthony and the other heavenly bodies into it and driven in the moonless dark to the woods and the edge of Lake Sarah, where they drowned the whole saintly company of statuary.

Only main and second floor of the Main Building had classrooms. Third and fourth floors were dorms. We—or most of us in my class—lived on 4th floor in one dorm. The *We* was 25 or 26 sophomores in one large room. Each space, or "cell" as it was called then, had a bed, a curtain that could be drawn around the bed for privacy if you wanted, a stand beside the bed with a couple of drawers, a chair. Down the middle of the room and along one side was a row of lockers—the kind found today in swimming pool shower rooms. We each had one locker for our clothes, shoes, and coat. A wardrobe that didn't fit was not encouraged. If you had to, you could keep what didn't fit in your suitcase in the attic. Trying to shove it under your bed was judged bad form.

Where were the sinks and bathroom facilities? Down the hall.

S. Kristin Malloy was our prefect. Prefects were beings quite different from RAs. She was not required to sleep in the same dorm with us, as would have been true some years earlier. But she was obliged to see that we got our sleep. We might study until 9:30. Then we got ready for bed. By 10, we gathered to say Compline. S. Kristin then went round and blessed each of us goodnight. By 10:15 lights went out and we were expected to quietly fall asleep—or at least be quiet in bed so that others could.

By special permission we might stay up until 11 to study in the large study lounge at the end of the hall, but such an irregular behavior could not be frequent. Or you might write letters. Betty Stoltz wrote every night to Bob Spaeth, who was away in the army. They would be just one of many Johnny-Benny married couples a few years later.

On Friday nights you might go out, even to the bars, if you signed out at the desk and if you were back by 12 sharp. *Sharp* meant that. By the time the town clock finished striking, you had to be in. S. Kristin, who used to have to wait up for us to check us in, says she could hear two simultaneous sounds as the hour began: the town clock striking, and our feet running hard down the road to make that deadline through the door. If you weren't there, you were campused, a dire fate: you couldn't leave the campus; if you were lucky, that time was only a week.

On Saturday you might go shopping in St Cloud via the Greyhound—the possibility of student cars on campus was unthinkable—or, if several people pooled their money and called Linnemann's store, you could go via Linnemann's taxi service. You went with skirt, hose, hat, and gloves. Mandatory!

If going shopping Saturday afternoon was an event to look forward to, going to dinner Saturday night was not. Dinner Saturday night was regularly chow mein, a romantic oriental title for all the conglomerate left-overs of the week. If, as was rumored, the Convent ate our leftovers *during* the week, the sisters were fully avenged on Saturday night, when I think we ate theirs. Particularly obnoxious was the meat base in chow mein. Gristle. Archetypal gristle: tough, tasteless, unpalatable.

Bread you might have in plenty, but one pat of butter ONLY. A sister with a confirmed frown in her brow guarded those pats vigilantly. Simultaneously, she guarded the cookies, of which we might have one only.

On Saturday night, you went to bed. Going out Saturday night was not a good thing. Sunday mornings you were to be attentive for mass, not sleep-logged from the night before. There with you in the chapel were the sisters, dressed much as you were in dark gowns, some your teachers, some housecleaners, some cooks, some unfamiliar, but all a community of believers come to meet God, to beseech, to thank, to praise.

Like almost everything those days, even God's praise was prepared for and it was orderly. At 8 on Tuesday mornings all of us marched to chapel in rank to what was called Congregational Singing. Congregational Singing was a particularly unpopular day opener. A few truants tried to play hooky from this weekly rehearsal in chapel. Here S. Kristin went into action again. One of her roles was to go into the choir loft to take attendance at congregational singing. Since we were in rank and had assigned seating, delinquency was easily spotted from these heights. When she saw a hole in the seating, S. Kristin headed to our dormitory, where she might catch an unwary late riser still making her bed.

Even more cautious escapees rarely escaped our resourceful prefect. Delinquents who heard her coming sometimes dived under their beds. But they soon appeared in chapel, red-faced moles, routed by S. Kristin once again. More creative although no more successful were those who risked suffocation by squeezing into their lockers and pulling the doors shut after them. These too S. Kristin firmly found out and sent on to sing God's praises.

Unredeemed as we were, we usually preferred our own more irreverent songs, especially those we wrote ourselves. I remember one in particular that began, "Oh, clicker, clacker, clocker, I'm so happy in my locker, I refuse to go."

We began every weekday with breakfast—mandatory. 10-cent fine for skipping. Seating was assigned, and each table had a hostess. Classes followed shortly after. Like all our activities, these too had proprieties. Sweatshirts were forbidden, as was wearing coats during the class hour.

We had some curricular freedom—we might choose a major and a minor. But most other classes were prescribed by course. Since our numbers were small, there was little choice as to section or teacher. For instance, we had a requirement in ancient and medieval philosophy. The course had to be taken in the junior year. The college provided one teacher for that course. S. Enid. She was brilliant. From what we could tell, she knew all things. Besides teaching philosophy, we knew she could teach English. Tales had it the math teacher had sickened one day and S. Enid expounded co-signs and tangents with great effectiveness. She could teach Latin. She knew history and ethics. She could replace Fr. Cassian [Osendorf] in sacred scripture. Surely there was nothing she didn't know. Besides being brilliant, she was rigorous. According to upperclassmen, who knew almost as much as S. Enid, she was also unsmiling. A veritable Gorgon, we were sure.

She was, simultaneously, the dean. As far as we knew, she was the total administration, for there was no president, no vice-presidents, no faculty committees, none of the other multitudes of administrators, support staff, or secretaries you know now.

As far as we could tell, S. Enid, *did* all as well as *knew* all. She devised and oversaw the curriculum. We believe she recorded our sins along with our grades. At the end of each term, she called us to her office one by one to give us our semester grades and her comments upon them, our awards or delinquencies. Whatever mysteries made the financial operation work, we did not not know, but we were sure she marshaled the figures as she marshaled us. At the end of four years it was she who sent out the claim that we had arrived at a sufficient state of intellectual grace to warrant graduation.

To supplement our academic classes, we had physical education with Miss Allen, one of two laypeople then to be found among the faculty,

The Dufners, including Angeline's grandparents (grandmother inserted above), aunts (including two Benedictines) and uncles (including one Benedictine), and her father who's half hidden in the back row.

and we had convocation. In the middle of every week the college provided a common event: an off-campus speaker, a faculty lecture, or student panel presentations. Convocations were required. One might try to skip Congregational Singing, but one did not try to skip convocations. I don't know why. Perhaps we thought we might have to deal with S. Enid rather than S. Kristin.

Young men were not part of our education. We might see them on Friday night. We might meet them in the village. Or they might—and did—occasionally come to visit us in the College Parlor under the watchful eye of the portress, perhaps for an hour.

But we shared no classes or facilities. There were no buses. We were here to learn, and perhaps the sisters thought young men might interfere with our education. The monks were surely convinced we would interfere with the education of their young charges.

I did not know until I left for other places—the University of Minnesota, Notre Dame, Idaho, California—I did not know either the depth or breadth

Angeline Dufner as a student (second from left) with Mary Jo Matthews, Joan Marthaler, Mary Kay Braus, Rita Lukes, and Ann Marie Gaffrey

of what I had learned here. But I discovered I had gained a superb education and a value system that would serve me well in much of what lay ahead.

If one of you stands on this spot in 2018, seeing fresh, happy faces before you, yours will not be the same remembrance of things past. But yours is likely to hold the same respect and reverence for the quality of that which you gained here. And so, congratulations on arriving at this day, at this place, with this knowledge and these values.

Sister Formation Movement

Early in the 1950s Pope Pius XII called for more careful attention to the spiritual and intellectual needs of professed women. In 1952 the National Catholic Educational Association, the professional organization for Catholic school teachers, founded the Sister Formation Conference, launched in 1954. The conference supported religious women's aspirations, indeed ambitions, and their professional education and helped religious women stand up to their bishops.

The Sister Formation Movement gave mothers superior of religious communities, including Mother Richarda, authority to change what had been 60 years of undereducating religious women and the premature assigning of them to work for which they were only barely educated. Rather than sending sisters out to teach after only a year or two in the motherhouse, the prioress could give the new sisters time to develop their vocations, to deepen their spirituality, to get an education that matched their vocations.

This shift came just as the post-war baby boom put pressure on virtually all Catholic schools in the United States to expand. Local parishes wanted sisters to staff their Catholic schools, for their students' religious education and edification and because the salaries they paid the sisters were so small.

This insistence by the mothers superior and by many women's religious communities on spiritual formation strengthened women's sense of themselves and their abilities as well as their spirituality. Their ability to make a demand and have it met proved a boon, too.[1]

Mother Richarda took the pope's encouragement to heart and carried on running battles with pastors and bishops about school staffing. S. Remberta—herself a Ph.D.—as part of her presidency urged her faculty members to get more education and helped make that possible with the wind of the pope's authority to speed her along.

S. Mary Anthony Wagner—a Ph.D. in theology and a vibrantly intelligent and quietly determined woman—with Fr. Pascal Botz, established a Benedictine Institute for Sacred Theology (BIST) that in the summers offered advanced theology courses leading to the MA.

S. Mary Anthony Wagner, one of the leading forces behind the Benedictine Institute for Sacred Theology

The BIST was a specific response at CSB to a specific need for more formation. Its education in theology fed the sisters' hunger for more education, more religious education. Yes, it was, like the sisters' college, in the summer, but it was a graduate school. It spoke to the sisters' needs and their passions, indeed to their ambitions, too. It also appealed to women of other religious orders—Franciscans from Little Falls and Rochester, Benedictines from Crookston and Duluth. Others, too.

The small library at CSB in the 1950s proved to be a problem for BIST and resulted in its moving it to the campus of SJU. It developed into the School of Theology, the *SJU School of Theology*.

FIVE

~

Merger from the Bottom Up

From its founding, the College of Saint Benedict was connected to Saint John's University through families, religious tradition, location, employees, parish work, and parochial schools. Saint Ben's had long hired Saint John's monks to serve as chaplains and to teach undergrad theology (ordination required for each), as well as specialized courses in the sisters' summer colleges. The CSB students had long paid notice to those at SJU (and vice versa).

In the 1950s, the two colleges inched toward each other. Their theater departments cast women in women's parts and men in men's, regardless of which produced a play. Their communication and theater departments moved toward merger. Nine Johnnies traveled to CSB to take S. Inez Hilger's sociology course, and S. Johanna Becker and S. Mariella Gable taught classes at Saint John's. All three of these women were stars in the CSB firmament, and the SJU students were lucky to have such remarkably accomplished and talented scholars and teachers. They worked the CSB and the SJU students pretty hard. Johnnies and Bennies both still credit S. Johanna with a lifelong appreciation of art, and a few even straighten up a bit when they recall their days with S. Mariella.

A complex historical context has shaped every step in the cooperation between the two colleges. Societal inequalities of opportunity and

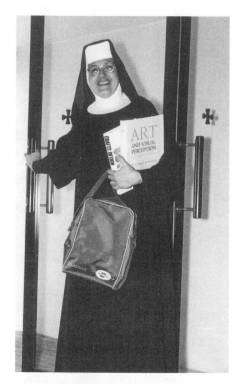

*Like most of the Benedictines,
S. Johanna taught for years and then
went off to finish her graduate work.
Here she is on her way out the door.*

S. Inez Hilger's seventh book, Together with the Ainu *(1971), examined the lives of the
Ainu people in Japan.*

income have meant that on average Johnnies got better jobs for more pay and had more "disposable" income. These economic facts as well as the legacy of the sisters' debt on the hospital—and the sisters' frugality generally—deeply permeated college life. They also created another inequality between the two colleges: a significantly larger endowment at SJU than at CSB. All of this is shifting and the current financial footings of both CSB and SJU are complex, but until the 2000s it was safe to say that SJU felt, and was, wealthier than CSB. The outcome of these various factors was that while going into closer cooperation SJU has worried about having to carry or support CSB and CSB has worried about being absorbed into SJU.

The inequalities in the Catholic Church structured some inequalities in the relationship, too. Priests have always had more power in the Church than have the women in religious orders. Saint John's Abbey and University at one time relied on sisters to cook and do the laundry.

Inspired by her friend and mentor the anthropologist Margaret Mead, S. Inez Hilger pursued fieldwork among the Objiwe (or Chippewa, the corporate tribal name) of Minnesota, the Great Plains Arapaho, the Araucanians of Chile, and the Ainu in Japan. Her fieldwork required travel, which S. Inez loved, and a lot of money, which she secured with remarkable success through grants. By the mid-1950s she was a research associate of the Bureau of American Ethnology of the Smithsonian Institution. She published eight books and more than 70 articles.

S. Johanna's and S. Mariella's stars were bright, too. Johanna was becoming the world's expert on Asian ceramics, and having published four edited collections of Catholic short stories between 1942 and 1950, Mariella was a widely regarded authority on Catholic literature. S. Mariella Gable's books include *Great Modern Catholic Short Stories* (1942), *Our Father's House* (1945), *They Are People: Modern Short Stories of Nuns, Monks, and Priests* (1947), *This Is Catholic Fiction* (1948), and *Many-Colored Fleece* (1950). S. Johanna Becker earned her bachelor of fine arts degree at the University of Colorado, her master's at Ohio State University, her doctorate at the University of Michigan. S. Mariella earned her bachelor's degree at CSB, did graduate work at Columbia, and earned her doctorate at Cornell.

The college and monastery at Saint Benedict's still must rely on Saint John's Abbey to provide chaplains to say mass and administer the sacraments.[1]

The combination of social, religious, and economic inequality and its resultant fears complicated the moves toward more cooperation and made the two colleges competitive with each other. They have often compared themselves to each other (some version of sibling rivalry, perhaps, too?) where they might have supported each other instead.

Regardless of their legacies, CSB and SJU, aided by the winds of change, took giant steps toward each other in the 1960s. Those winds included the trend in higher education toward greater cooperation generally, a growing student preference for coeducation, and steeply rising costs. Even stronger were the tornadoes of Pope John XXIII's Vatican II, the Cuban missile crisis, the integration of the University of Mississippi with use of the military, and a race riot in Oxford, Miss. Also Doris Lessing published her *Golden Notebook,* which some called "a feminist bible," and Rachel Carson's *Silent Spring* topped the *New York Times* bestseller list. John F. Kennedy was the youngest president to date. The wedge end of the baby-boom generation was pushing its way into college. In the midst of these events and the social change they portended, many colleges locked hands for safety, for partnership, for cooperation. CSB and SJU did, too.

In February 1963, the presidents of the two colleges—S. Mary Grell and Fr. Arno Gustin—appointed a joint Committee on Cooperative Academic Policy. The deans—S. Firmin Escher and Fr. Dunstan Tucker—and the committee pointed to several reasons for cooperation: "To provide a better education, to avoid duplication of courses and faculty, to increase enrollment in upper division courses, to increase the breadth and variety of courses offered in the major." Cooperation would make both colleges better, and the two administrations hoped it would save money, too.

The completion of the Benedicta Arts Center in 1964 was to be a game changer for CSB. It represented the audacity with which the sisters saw their future. It has "given back" for decades, and will for decades more. It has received several American Institute of Architects awards and featured countless national and international performances.

In 1964 the sisters formally opened the Benedicta Arts Center. The Escher Auditorium honors S. Firmin Escher, violinist, dean from 1961 to 1972 and founder of the college orchestra and Campus Singers.

Most importantly, it put onto the CSB campus a building that was better than any arts facility at SJU. Music and art students, especially, could feel enormous excitement about taking classes there.

Most of the 1963–65 efforts toward academic cooperation focused on getting people used to the idea of working together. The changes were small: In the fall of 1963, 48 CSB and 4 SJU students took cross-campus classes; in the spring there were 36 from CSB and 42 from SJU. The *St. John's Record* noted that a few students feared mixing would inhibit class discussion, but most—at least in the abstract—thought cooperation a good idea.

One student who in 1963 was the only female in a class of 35 found it at first "a little disconcerting." And she was annoyed to find assigned readings available only in the SJU library. Otherwise, she didn't mind. Some students on each campus thought the mix could improve everyone's performance, and one SJU faculty member agreed: "It might work that way." One Bennie, who believed she spoke for many, said sharing classes could "shatter a rather prevalent belief among Bennies that all Johnnies are intellectuals."[2]

Students voted with their feet, too. By 1965 nearly 300 students were taking classes cross-campus. And there were other changes, for example as noted in the *Record*: "After progressing from the dance floor to the classroom, the exchange program between CSB and SJU has moved to the cafeteria."

Certain they needed change but not so clear on what that change should be, the schools tried whatever they thought might work. The 30-day trial of a meal-exchange program was launched, for example, with the hope that the two food services would find no need for the exchange of money. The trial made clear the impossibility of an even exchange—the girls ate more often at Saint John's, and the boys ate way too much more than the girls.

Practical problems limiting cooperation cried for attention: calendars, transportation, and the numbering of courses, for example. By 1965, the two colleges agreed to a common calendar (4–1–4), to a bus running on a regular and published schedule, to classes running on the same schedule, to a joint course catalog, and perhaps most importantly, to the appointment of committees charged to work toward a common curriculum.

The CSB and SJU catalogs were combined in 1967–68 with an introduction announcing "A New Beginning" with a "complete revision of the curriculum and the adoption of a new academic calendar." The goals of this "fresh stance" were "to strengthen the quality of education, to permit a fuller exchange of ideas among faculty and students, and to increase the offerings."

In 1967, the two colleges applied for and received a grant from the Hill Family Foundation to hire a panel of consultants to advise them about how much more cooperation was desirable and feasible. Chaired by Stanford professor of education Lewis Mayhew, the consultants visited the campuses, talked to faculty members and administrators, surveyed each department, and looked at other schools in similar situations. The panel brought to its work wide familiarity with the higher-education landscape—it included Rosemary Park, past president of Connecticut and Barnard Colleges, and Alan Simpson, the president of Vassar.[3]

After months of study, Lewis Mayhew met in March 1968 with the boards of both schools. He reminded them that "these are perilous times" for private colleges. Real solutions to real and imminent problems had to be found if CSB and SJU were to survive in the increasingly competitive, increasingly secular, market. As the study panel read the tea leaves of higher education, more and more students were attending public colleges and the cost of higher education was increasing. Almost every college was looking for ways to cooperate. CSB and SJU, the panel recommended, should go beyond cooperation: "Our panel has thought most seriously about the problems of the two institutions and has reached the unanimous conviction that merger of the two into a new corporate entity is the only plausible solution. Thus, we recommend that the two institutions merge and merge quickly. We believe to delay more than two years would so irreparably damage either or both institution that ultimate merger or cooperation would no longer be possible."[4]

The panelists acknowledged that a merger would not be simple, that many significant differences would have to be bridged. The structure of governance was one problem. Until 1961 both colleges remained legally joined to their religious sponsors, but in that year Mother Henrita Osendorf, prioress from 1961 to 1973, had spun off Saint Ben's as a separate corporation. Even so, the sisters maintained nearly full control over the college for another decade: All the members of its 1967–69 board of trustees were sisters; laypersons comprised an associate board of trustees (the descendant of the board of advisors of the 1930s). In the meantime, SJU remained part of the Saint John's Abbey corporation. SJU could not form a single corporate entity with Saint Ben's until after it was separately incorporated too.[5]

The committee pointed out that despite several years of cooperation, "plans for future building have been made at each institution as though the other did not exist." Moreover, the two institutions were looking in opposite directions for funding: "Saint John's is planning a capital development program of perhaps three to five million dollars, and Saint Benedict is actively searching for federal loans to aid it in building a new residence hall." Each of these might be a good thing, but survival required financial cooperation.

Differences in the student bodies—real and perceived—posed another significant issue. One real difference was size: in 1968, Saint Ben's enrolled just over one-third (420) the number of students that Saint John's did (1,202).

Other differences were even more troublesome. As Mayhew reported, "There appears to be a strong feeling both among the faculty and the student body of Saint John's that the students there are a more capable group who, for the most part, are heading for graduate or professional schools, while Saint Benedict students, according to stereotype, are heading for marriage, teaching, or religious orders."

Test scores for the entering class of 1967 offered some basis for this feeling. The Johnnies' math-score bell curve peaked at 550–599, the Bennies' at 500–549. Johnnies' verbal scores peaked at 500–549, Bennies' at 450–499. That might reflect native intelligence, but more likely it mirrored the high schools from which the students were graduated. There were also important demographic differences: 34 percent of Bennies and only 11 percent of Johnnies came from farms; 55 percent of Johnnies came from urban places and only 31 percent of Bennies.

The "strong feeling" noted by Mayhew reflected the societal truths about men and women that were propelling the national women's movement of the 1960s. More men than women did go to law school, medical school, and professional schools; for too long that had meant to many that men were smarter, more ambitious, and more able than women. Reading social norms as markers of intelligence had led generations to misread women and generations of women to underestimate themselves. In the 1960s, women were beginning to challenge the facts and stereotypes that had led to those differences. Of course, this was also a part of the dynamic between CSB and SJU.

A related, third obstacle to merger was CSB's fear of being swallowed up and SJU's of being weakened. Fears rarely make it to official records, but Mayhew ferreted out and reported several of them, recommending that the merged entity be "Benedictine University." The joke at SJU was that the new college should take the first word of its name from Saint Ben's and the second from Saint John's—resulting, of course, in "Saint John's." SJU business officers reportedly felt that since Saint John's was subsidizing Saint Ben's, it should "simply absorb" the smaller school. These jokes only confirmed S. Linda Kulzer's fear that to merge meant to be submerged.[6]

Some at SJU reportedly felt a merger would be fine if SJU "were granted the balance of power," as it held the balance of resources (and, many believed, talent). Because they were the better educated and stronger, many on the Saint John's faculty believed "they ought to be leaders in any cooperative venture." The report itself gave grounds for fear. It noted, for example, the absence of a unified library catalog and stated, "It would be easier for Saint John's to absorb Saint Benedict's catalog." Would it be easier for Saint John's to absorb Saint Ben's, too?

SJU's sense of superiority—and no doubt the differing treatment of women and men in the Catholic Church—kept CSB from trusting its intentions or actions (and perhaps rightly so). "Do they really want cooperation, or are they trying to phase us out?" was one fear Mayhew reported hearing at CSB. Many at Saint Ben's believed those at SJU were "deluded about their own greatness and their contribution to the cooperative effort." What kind of partnership could come of that? Especially, as Saint Ben's admitted, with its own people "too timid in listing their strengths."

In their statement appointing the committee in 1963, presidents Mary Grell and Gustin had asked for ways to work together that would protect the identities and traditions of both colleges. That seems straightforward, but determining the essential components of identity and tradition was not. In 1963, the semester calendars were similar except for Christmas vacation. Bennies stayed a week longer before Christmas and returned a week later than the Johnnies. Was this habit, tradition, or did it even matter?

Yes. CSB went a week later because the Pageant took up so much time in September. Saint John's students wanted to be home early enough to work pre-Christmas jobs. It took four years—and retirement of the Pageant—to settle on a common calendar. Given the fears of both schools—spoken and not—how much more would it take to decide the larger issues of a merger?

The cooperation of the two schools took on an edge among students in the form of Bennie jokes. An exchange between *The Torch*—CSB's student newspaper—and SJU's *Record* reveals the dynamics of that edge. *Torch* staff writer Debby Merickel reported in her November 6, 1967, column "Yup, the Johnnies Really Love Us" that a war between the two campuses was in progress. In the Johnnie tradition, on-air radio announcers at Saint John's were making jokes about Bennies, some of whom called the station and "counterattacked." Merickel wrote: "Johnnies have attacked the Bennies in this manner for years" and lamented that the complainers had lost their sense of humor. "If the Johnnies truly hated the Bennies, they wouldn't bother with wise-cracks," she said. So, instead of defending her "sisters," she urged them not to resort to "all out war" but simply to change radio stations if they weren't satisfied with KSJU.

A *Record* editorial a few days later agreed: "The campuses of St. John's and St. Benedict's seem to be battlefields upon which great wars are waged with an outcome not too clear . . . Tradition calls for the Benny jokes." He called them the "'Johnny slam Benny' game . . . They show up in St. John's variety shows and in daily conversation—most recently on air on the KSJU station." Bennies, the editorialist allowed, "seem concerned," but the students—females—who were in college for the "right purpose" wouldn't bother themselves about the slams. Only the "husband hunters" would. Ouch.[7]

The women's movement was not new in 1967, but it was still small, especially among students. The exchanges above were characteristic of the late-1960s movement: men made statements, women considered them demeaning, men replied that the statements were only jokes (though even the editorialist called them "slams") and that the women had no sense of humor; some women replied that some women don't have a sense of humor, and the complaining women went silent.

In 1968, the student development offices of the two colleges also saw trouble. Saint John's encouraged a less protective atmosphere, and Saint Ben's challenged it. Saint Ben's wanted a more protective atmosphere, and Saint John's challenged it. Which would prevail in the event of a merger? More issues of identity.

Other deeply held differences also surfaced. For example, the art departments, looking for ways to cooperate found "fundamental philosophical differences" not just between the two schools but also between male and female schools in general: Men "intending to work as lifetime professionals" had needs different from those of the women, for whom art is "more . . . an avocation than a vocation." How then would a combined department accommodate its courses to meet the perceived different needs? Would one group suffer?

Propelled by the urgency of the Mayhew recommendations, the boards of CSB and SJU voted to merge, despite the obstacles:

> The joint meeting of the two Boards was held on 12 July 1968. After a thorough discussion, the following Motion was made and seconded: "Be it resolved that the joint Boards of Saint John's University and of the College of Saint Benedict today declare the desirability of a merger, to take place within the next thirty months, and that the Boards engage immediately in the hiring of a coordinator for this task; the final decision on the merger is to be made not later than thirty months from this date."
> The vote on this Motion was 19 affirmative, 1 negative.[8]

Merger made all sorts of sense at the time. The alternative, it seemed, was for Saint Ben's or Saint John's or both to go coed, each of which would have harmed one or both and carried no guarantee of success. In 1968 no one wanted that—those choices portended catastrophe, for sure. Within weeks, some say days, of the vote, the merger fever cooled. Within a few months, both boards "clarified" the meaning of their votes (in a not entirely clear way), declaring they would be "separate colleges with a single corporate identity."[9]

Apparatus and momentum rolled toward merger nonetheless. The boards had agreed to hire a coordinator to manage the transition, and they moved forward, though it turned out easier said than done. In the first year of searching, the colleges found no one willing or able to take on the job. Finally in 1969, after having turned down the position at least once, Sylvester Theisen accepted the job offered by the boards' Committee on Cooperation. The job placed him as equal to the two presidents, reporting to a committee of members representing the two college boards.

Sy Theisen, a graduate of Saint John's, class of '47, held a doctorate in sociology from Notre Dame University, and he was part of the SJU faculty. His sister, S. Dianne Theisen, was part of the community of CSB. He had long, strong ties to both institutions. More than that, he was known to be fair, cool, and smart. He was patient and dogged. Talk about "the merger" turned to talk about "merger from the bottom up," so he focused on students and faculty, leaving be for the time being the proposal for a joint academic vice president and a "single corporate identity." No one even hinted at a joint president.

One contextual problem with cooperation and merger had to do with the changing composition of administrations and the changing ambitions and temperaments of their leaders. S. Remberta Westkaemper served as CSB president from 1957 to 1961, S. Linnea Welter from 1961 to 1963. S. Mary Grell served from 1963, when she ushered in with Fr. Arno Gustin the first phase of cooperation, until 1968. S. Johanna Becker was dean from 1957 to 1961, S. Firmin Escher from 1961 to 1972. Mother Richarda Peters served as prioress from 1949 to 1961, Mother Henrita Osendorf from 1961 to 1973. Under their leadership, the college and the community—funding evenly split—built the Benedicta Arts Center, opening in 1964. The center, representing a new vision and public position for CSB, enhanced its identity and reputation. Its only connection to Saint John's lay in Fr. Gunther Rolfson's blessing of the groundbreaking in 1962.[10]

S. Mary Grell in 1963 brought to the presidency the same energy characterizing her work as a biologist. A graduate of Saint Ben's, she had earned a doctorate in cytogenetics at Fordham University and done advanced work as a Fulbright Scholar at the Max Planck Institute in Germany. She had received grants from the National Atomic Commission and the National Science Foundation, and she had taught 30 years in the CSB biology department. Like earlier college leaders, she had deep Minnesota roots, starting with her birth in Pierz in 1912. She played an active role in moving the college toward greater cooperation with Saint John's.

S. Mary stepped down in 1968. Without advertising for the job or appointing much of a search committee, Mother Henrita Osendorf called Dr. Stanley Idzerda and offered him the job. He had visited central Minnesota at least twice, so he was not entirely new to the college. He had consulted at 11 Benedictine colleges in the 1950s and '60s.

Mother Henrita and her family

After earning his undergraduate degree at Notre Dame, he earned a master's and doctoral degrees in European history at Western Reserve University. He had served on the faculty at Western Michigan, as director of the Honors College at Michigan State, and simultaneously was dean at Wesleyan in Connecticut and adjunct professor of history at Yale. At the end of his on-campus "interview" during which time he'd decided not to take the job, he and his wife Gerry attended the Saint Benedict's feast day mass. The sisters' (in full habit) and students' (in caps and gowns) "glorious singing" changed his mind. Six weeks later, he and Gerry and their seven children landed in St. Joseph—just after the merger vote took place.

Continuing Education and the Bahamas

Minnesota and Bahamian Benedictines—women and men—have long and many ties with each other. Bahamians pursued religious vocations at the Saint Benedict's and Saint John's monasteries and welcomed North Americans to St. Augustine's Priory. Sisters of Nassau attended CSB. The Benedictines welcomed S. Remberta Westkaemper when she went there to do botany research. CSB and SJU faculty members have spent time with students and faculty in the Bahamas. Bahamian faculty members have visited Minnesota.

Since the 1920s, CSB and SJU have welcomed Bahamian students— more than 1,000 women and men—to their campuses. Many of those students are "college-aged" and throw themselves into multiyear degree programs; they join campus organizations (often the International Student Clubs) and serve in student government.

Today Bahamian students make up one of CSB's largest international student groups, but historically there were never very large numbers of Bahamians who attended CSB at one time. In 1949, Helen and Virginia Baker from Nassau were the only ones enrolled at CSB. In 1950, Helen was the only Bahamian student at CSB. She was not, however, the only student of color—from the 1930s several African-American students also attended CSB, and a few Chinese students were registered as well. The international student population was small, and it is likely that these students never thought of themselves as an organized group on campus.

By 1982–83, CSB had 40 international students, the majority from the Bahamas. The college appointed a foreign student advisor, and each student had a host family. Bahamian Marie Roach especially appreciated being linked with a family "within walking distance." But imagine the Bahamians' initial journey—stopping en route in the still largely segregated South and continuing to a very white central Minnesota uncomfortable with outsiders (even Catholic ones)!

Despite the differences in geography, race, and culture between the Bahamian students and the white Minnesota students, CSB and the Bahamian students from 1975 to 1994 developed a special relationship that grew out of CSB's continuing education program.

The CSB Center for Continuing Education (CCE), which no longer exists, was organized to offer three kinds of programs: 1) short, life-enrichment classes such as Music through History or Chemistry for Enjoyment; 2) refresher courses for women (almost exclusively) who wanted to step back in the job market or meet specific certification requirements; and 3) a path to an associate's or bachelor's degree in liberal studies. All three offered opportunities for education then in demand by central Minnesota women; the third catered to nurses, especially.

Some of these developments were initiated by changes in state laws that increased degree requirements in various fields. Minnesota required associate of arts degrees for nursing home directors, for example, beginning in 1975; by 1980 they needed bachelor's degrees. After World War II, the expectations for nurses' and teachers' training also rose. Where RNs had been sufficient, bachelor's degrees became the norm. St. Raphael's—the nursing school connected with St. Cloud Hospital and run by the Benedictines—had been training registered nurses for decades, but it was not equipped to offer a bachelor's degree. Yet hundreds of Benedictine sisters and their students needed such degrees if they wanted to retain (or get new) jobs.

CSB was quick to adopt continuing education programs, as some other institutions were doing as an answer to increasing standards. These programs devised ways to give students credit for life experience. For traditional undergraduates this developed into a comprehensive curricular focus on "competency-based" education, meaning that students would demonstrate the mastery of pertinent material rather than simply accumulate credit hours. In a college using that approach, returning students—nurses and teachers especially—could advance more rapidly toward bachelor's degrees.

Under the direction of S. Kathleen Kalinowski, the Center for Continuing Education welcomed these nontraditional students and offered them individual testing and counseling to help determine their most appropriate course for each. Recognizing that they might find a college campus intimidating, the CCE intentionally presented itself as a welcoming place where students could obtain information, advice, or just a cup of coffee and a comfortable chair.

Critics worried that the degrees earned in continuing education programs tailored especially for women might not be up to par, but S. Firmin Escher, the academic dean, insisted that the college be both rigorous *and* flexible. CSB President Idzerda wholeheartedly supported the program and reassured critics that the degrees met CSB's high standards.

CE programs—both those for enrichment and for degree advancement— are now ubiquitous nationally (though CSB no longer offers them). But when Saint Ben's started its program, the opportunities for adult education were considerably more limited. Elderhostel (now Road Scholars) and the Fromm Institute for Lifelong Learning (parent of the Osher Lifelong Learning Institute) did not exist, and junior colleges had not yet been reinvented as community colleges. In short, adult learning was only beginning to flourish, and the first wave of participation was overwhelmingly female.

CSB never identified its program as feminist, but the key to its success was a central feminist idea: valuing women's lives. CCE programs awarded academic credit for life experience. Nineteen-year-old students received college credit for courses on child rearing, nutrition, and family life.

S. Enid Smith, professor of philosophy and member of the Continuing Education Council, explained, "We are devising ways of evaluating experiences so that credit can be given for knowledge obtained outside the classroom." Among those ways was the development of a standardized college-level examination program to determine student mastery and award credit based on the result. In addition, rather than asking participants to conform to a schedule designed for full-time students, the CCE offered independent study courses and a flexible schedule.

The degree work proved popular and beneficial to teachers needing more formal education, to nurses—Benedictine and lay—working toward higher professional standards, to stay-at-home moms who wanted to improve their resumes, and to working women wishing to expand their horizons.

But the program had less to do with degrees than with meeting the interests and needs of the wider community. The CCE deployed faculty members to teach short courses—The Christian Woman, Women and the Law, Career Development for Women, and Assertiveness Training, for example. S. Enid herself taught a course on death and dying as well as one on Dietrich Bonhoeffer. The center also tapped into its wider community for teachers. One St. Cloud businessman offered a popular class on auto mechanics for women.

S. Kathleen and her board found just the right mix of serious and fun, flexible and demanding, accommodating and rigorous courses to make the program work at Saint Ben's. The program also provided a ready new basis for CSB's engagement with adult students from the Bahamas.

In 1974, S. Kathleen went to the Bahamas to meet with Telzena Coakley in the Bahamian Ministry of Education and with S. Maedene Russell, superintendent of Catholic schools in the Bahamas. (All three women were CSB alumnae.) Together they devised a plan to assist in the education of Bahamian elementary school teachers, using the structure of the CE program being perfected in Minnesota. The Bahamas had a long tradition of sending students to England (or elsewhere in the Commonwealth) for college and thus had already developed a domestic system of two-year programs leading to associate degrees.[1]

In 1973, when the Bahamas gained its independence from Great Britain, its government turned attention toward improving the country's educational infrastructure. Its only homegrown college was a two-year teacher-training institution. The Bahamas needed more teachers with degrees—and its own bachelor's-degree-granting colleges—and they asked CSB for assistance.

CSB's board of trustees approved a program in Nassau, where local teachers offered evening and weekend courses and CSB faculty members offered classes in summer. Students in the program followed the practices of CSB and met CSB graduation requirements. The first of the Bahamian women to register was Valderine Turquist, in 1975–76. More than 400 students participated during the program's first 20 years.

The program succeeded because of the work of many, but a few key individuals carried much of the load. S. Kathleen, S. Emmanuel Renner, and S. Delores Super ran the program in St. Joseph from 1978 to 1994. In the Bahamas, S. Clare Rolle ran the program for a few years, as did S. Mary Patricia Russell in her wake. Telzena Coakley directed it from 1977 to 1990. In 1997, longtime CSB faculty member, dean, and vice president Chuck Villette was named director and dean of Benedictine University College, CSB's operation in the Commonwealth of the Bahamas.

Still today, Coakley is considered a trailblazer, both at CSB and in the

Bahamas. Aside from directing Benedictine University College, she has had a powerful role in enriching, molding, and strengthening the relationship between CSB and the women of the Bahamas. Coakley, in 1962, was one of the first Bahamian graduates from CSB. She has a bachelor of arts in math and history, and with minors in philosophy and secondary education. She also pioneered the first four-year degree program entirely in the Bahamas, which began in 1974. The creation of the program coincided with the newly found independence of the Bahamas in 1973, and its inspiration came from the belief that if the Bahamas were to succeed in their newfound independence, education was of the utmost importance.

In addition to strong leadership, the program at CSB thrived during its heyday because it met the educational needs of Bahamian women, who were willing to make sacrifices to get their degrees. In 1983, Pamrica Ferguson graduated from CSB. She was 45 years old, a hospital infection control officer in Nassau who, upon graduation, planned to become an elementary school teacher. Her son was a SJU junior, and her daughter

Pamrica (second from left) is joined at her graduation by her siblings Pandora ('78), Telzena ('62—director of the CSB extension program in the Bahamas), and Dorothy ('77). The gold rope around her neck denotes her membership in Delta Epsilon Sigma (the Catholic Honor Society).

completed two years at CSB. She was the fourth female in her family to attend CSB. Her three sisters all came from the Bahamas for their graduation.

Until 1994 the program was almost entirely a CSB program offering women CSB degrees (the few participating men earned SJU degrees). The Bahamian students generally spent their last semester on the CSB campus. Most of them—well into adulthood and settled in their lives—left husbands and children behind, arriving in central Minnesota in late January to live in the International House Apartments in St. Joe. In a show of Benedictine hospitality, coats, boots, mittens, and scarves awaited the Bahamians arriving for the "spring" semester each year. Many reported finding welcome and support, especially among their teachers and especially in the education department.

Despite the welcome, some Bahamian students reported a certain chilliness beyond the weather at CSB. As one student said, "I came to Minnesota well prepared for the winter cold, but no one could have prepared us for the cold, racial undertones existing in the college environment." Not every Bahamian student reported experiences of implicit or explicit racism on campus (though few were eager to spend time in St. Cloud), but the homogeneity of central Minnesota did show a hardness to outsiders that could be painful to these women.

Several students spoke more of cultural than racial differences—Americans being more reserved and Bahamians more expressive by one account, Bahamians more formal and Americans more playful, Bahamians more mature and Americans less so. That's the thing about cultural differences—different people may read them differently.

For Bahamian students trained in the British educational system, the American way of testing was difficult. The library could be intimidating too (though it may have been intimidating for central Minnesota students as well). Senior Bennie Keva Cartwright wrote in 1975: "I avoided the library for a whole semester. It scared me." She also said, "If more people were consciously aware that there were cultural differences . . . everything would be a little easier to adjust to."[2]

Cultural differences and racism explained some of the challenges. Some might have been academic: most of the Bahamian students, especially the older married women, brought a seriousness of purpose to their studies, instead of the conventional "senioritis," or lack of energy that traditional students sometimes show. They demonstrated a fierce desire to pack the semester full of schoolwork.[3] In some instances, the Bahamian students were 20 or 30 years older than the rest of the Bennies.

Still, accomplishments, and especially Commencement, were cause for celebration, and the graduating Bahamian seniors cheered by their husbands and children, and friends looked just as pleased and proud as the sisters and faculty members watching them receive their diplomas. Even those who hadn't taught them beamed in admiration of the Bahamians' determination.

The CCE program admitted many fewer students to SJU, though its longer history of enrolling traditional-aged Bahamian men continued. Over the years, CSB developed a stronger base in the Bahamas, consisting of non-traditional students and an increasing number of college-aged Bahamian women. From 1975 to 1999 the Bahamian program was a CSB extension program. In 1995, the CSB and SJU boards agreed to jointly sponsor the Benedictine University College program.

Officials in the Bahamas, as well as those in Minnesota, agreed that students in the Bahamas must hold to the same requirements as the students in Minnesota. The Education Department of the Bahamas extension program received accreditation by the National Council for Accreditation of Teacher Education (NCATE). In multiple ways the Benedictine University College demonstrated its high quality.

The College of Saint Benedict was and continues to be enriched by its Bahamian alumnae and has always had a strong and intimate bond with the Bahamas through the monastic link of the sisters of the Order of Saint Benedict. That initial bond has grown into a lifelong partnership grounded in liberal arts education, women's leadership and sustaining opportunities for future generations of women. This exceptional partnership has kept lit a beacon of hope for many to follow. The lives of so many have been enriched by the work and endeavors that have evolved for nearly 100 years. Today, the Bahamian alumnae sisters continue to foster their proud connections to CSB and offer their support through philanthropy, volunteer opportunities, student mentoring and more. They are vibrant, accomplished and ambitious women whom the college is proud to call alumnae.

SIX

~

Cooperation from the Bottom Up

Stan Idzerda was Saint Ben's first lay *and* first male president. He was also the first who had not been a student or graduate of the college. He was neither from Minnesota nor German. His history specialty was France, and his father was an immigrant from Holland. As an eight-year-old, Stan had worked with his father on the fishing boat that was the family business. He entered the Navy ROTC at Notre Dame and in December 1941 was aboard one of the ships bombed at Pearl Harbor. He was an adult convert to Catholicism. He had a habit of speaking his mind, and he liked other people to speak theirs, too. He came from a remarkably different culture than the one he entered in St. Joseph.

On the occasion of Stan's inauguration in that late fall of 1968, SJU's President Colman Barry remarked:

> For one hundred and eleven years Benedictines from Saint
> John's and Saint Benedict's have worked together in upper
> Midwest schools as Minnesota's oldest educators in continu-
> ous existence . . . We have grown together and developed in
> our service of adults and youths. Since 1926, the C of SB and
> SJU have enjoyed close and friendly relations both among
> faculty and students. During the last five years, much progress
> has been made in developing inter-institutional cooperation

between our two undergraduate colleges. We look forward to future integral and organic growth in the development of our Benedictine academic consortium.[1]

In his essay, "Saint Ben's and Saint John's: 'Why Should We Travel Together?'" Stan championed the "values and activities typical of a single-sex campus" and the advantages for women "to be able to exercise leadership and creativity in many areas which are not typically prerogatives on a completely coeducational campus." He also recognized the value of coeducation—members of the faculty "testify that men and women have improved as a result of our collaboration."

Cooperation resulted in direct savings to Saint Ben's and Saint John's, in more opportunities, less duplication, better planning, stronger departments, more resources, indeed in a "brighter future." Did Stan pour water on the merger fire? He did express the belief that "our destiny is to grow together in mutual reliance." He also went to great lengths to set Saint Ben's on a course that would materially change the game.[2]

Particularly given his experience at Wesleyan and Yale—and the experience of both of those places with single-sex and joint programs—Stan had given much thought to mergers and cooperation. While he was at Wesleyan, he saw conversations about a Vassar/Yale merger progress, then break down, and by 1970 both had gone coed. In the 1960s, many women's colleges wrestled with financial uncertainty and whether or not to merge or go coed. Virtually every men's college moved toward admitting women. Two members of Mayhew's committee were deeply involved in merger/coeducation discussions at other places. Alan Simpson, the sitting president of Vassar, was a strong proponent of its merger with Yale.

The sisters of Saint Ben's loved the new president, and they love him still.[3] Sisters Colman O'Connell and Emmanuel Renner—the presidents succeeding him—reported what nearly all the sisters and lay members of the time believed, namely that Stan profoundly affected the college. He was the champion it needed, a mirror reflecting to CSB its possibilities. Did he share the "strong feeling" Mayhew had identified—that SJU was superior? Not for a second. Bigger, yes, better, no!

About "bigger" Stan could and did do something. He set out immediately to increase the size of Saint Ben's. Whatever happened with Saint John's, he believed, Saint Ben's had to get bigger. It could not afford to be small. By 1972, his third year as president, enrollment at CSB had nearly doubled, and students were housed in every nook on campus. Such a dramatic increase demanded an aggressive building program—Corona Hall first, then temporary trailers, then West Apartments. The college couldn't build fast enough to keep up. From its founding to 1950, a total of 394 women graduated from CSB. In the next decade, nearly 700 women graduated. That number doubled in the 1960s.[4]

With so many more students on campus, the faculty of every department had to expand as well. Both CSB and SJU had long depended on alums, but with increased competition for jobs, being an alum with a master's degree wasn't enough. Stan urged current CSB faculty members to complete their doctoral work, supporting them with sabbaticals and other kinds of funding. The proportion of CSB faculty with doctorates was about 25 percent when he took the reins—quite respectable for a college like Saint Ben's—and by MaryAnn's time it had more than tripled. Most importantly, the bachelor's-only faculty had shrunk to four by the end of Stan's term.

During Stan's tenure, the decision was made to close the Benedictine Academy at the end of the 1972–73 school year. The high school's enrollment had taken a dive, but its cost had not. The sisters' devotion to their students could not outweigh the demands of the school on the Benedictine community, and the decision to close both strengthened the college and expanded its physical plant. The HAB—or Henrita Academic Building, as the high school was renamed—provided desperately needed classroom and office space, though its high-school origins remained evident.

CSB continued its struggle with finances. It carried only the tiniest of endowments—less than $200,000 at the start of Stan's presidency. The sisters had a long history of making do. Most of them had lived through lean community times. Many of those in the Catholic hierarchy—and laity too—thought the prospect of women raising money was "unseemly." Accepting what was offered rather than asking for what they needed was the "appropriate" stance for women in the

United States, in the Catholic Church, in the Midwest. Furthermore, most colleges received most of their donations from their graduates. On that basis alone, CSB would have a small endowment because it was small, because so many of its students and graduates entered religious life, and because of its history of alumnae entering traditional "women's fields." The fact that women received less pay on average—even in those occupations—than men did added to the problem. Stan thus faced an uphill battle. But CSB needed money, so he went friend- and fund-raising.[5]

The smaller, more timid Saint Ben's that embarked on cooperation at the start of the 1960s had grown wings and buildings and students by the time the two colleges were working out the details of greater cooperation in the 1970s. What CSB needed, what it aspired to, and the circumstances in which it acted, were enormously different. There was physical change, yes, but CSB also had more energy, more confidence, wider horizons. Stan had a lot to do with that; so did changes in the larger society; so did changes in the Church.

In the 1960s all the CSB students lived with strict dorm hours, with clear and enforced dress codes. By 1970, students on both campuses had raised the issue of coed dorms (they were springing up on campuses across the country), and a dozen or so students lived together in Avon, another dozen on "The Farm," in experimental coed communities. The dress code has disintegrated—though both Bennies and Johnnies admitted to dressing up a bit more for coed classes—and dorm rules were crumbling. Anything but "natural" birth control was forbidden for Catholic women, but "the Pill" was widely available off campus. The student movement had forged new behaviors and demanded new practices in American colleges. The assassinations of Martin Luther King Jr. and Robert F. Kennedy in 1968, the Vietnam War, the civil rights movement, the women's liberation movement, environmental movement—and dozens of other activist causes—engaged students on college campuses and culminated in the killing of students at Jackson State College in Mississippi and Kent State University in Ohio. CSB–SJU cooperation played in company with the many issues occupying students and college life in that decade.

The sisters (and priests) grappled with huge issues, too. In 1960, the sisters wore full habits. They traveled in pairs and rarely drove cars. They lived a significantly cloistered life. They cultivated attitudes of obedience and conformity. By 1970 their habits—clothing and practice— had profoundly changed. More and more Catholics were talking about the ordination of women.[6]

The convents were bleeding women. Between 1965 and 1970 more than 25,000 women—most of them among the best educated—left their religious communities.[7]

Saint John's Abbey and University administration also changed during the years from 1961 to 1973. Abbot Baldwin Dworschak served from 1950 to 1971, then Abbot John Eidenschink until 1979. Fr. Dunstan Tucker was dean from 1958 to 1967, then Fr. Hilary Thimmesh for two years, mathematician Jack Lange from 1969 to 1972, then O. William Perlmutter. Fr. Colman Barry, who replaced Fr. Arno Gustin as president in 1964, had big dreams for Saint John's. He was the "father" of both the Ecumenical Institute and Minnesota Public Radio, both of which enhanced the identity and reputation of Saint John's. Neither included Saint Ben's in any way.

In 1971, Fr. Michael Blecker replaced Fr. Colman. He was no less ambitious but more direct, even confrontational. He was late in coming to the cooperation table, but his Chicago upbringing and Harvard doctorate equipped him to fight when he thought it necessary. He often thought it necessary to fight for SJU.

As coordinator of cooperation, Sy Theisen, worked with this changing cast of strong characters who held powerful positions. He could hardly take a step without landing on someone's toes. He worked with the dozens of department chairs, hundreds of faculty members, thousands of students, and hundreds of sisters and monks, all of whom had a stake in cooperation and an even higher stake in merger.

As the chair of and with the backing of a committee including prioress, abbot, and trustees of both colleges, Sy marched forward. He might have thought that Solomon had an easy job in comparison with his! He coordinated the unification of the registrar's office, the appointment of a single library director, the opening of all departmental courses to all students, and the organization of regular cross-campus bus service, just for starters.

With mixed success, he spent enormous time and energy on uniting academic departments. Mass Communication and Theater was already an "inter-institutional" major, housed at CSB. It was a joint department, except that the mechanics of jointness—budgeting, hiring, course numbering, for example—remained sluggish. Its faculty was small, and all its members had long recognized the advantages of having women and men together, especially for theater performances, so they made it work. The Benedicta Arts Center, with its two performing spaces and sophisticated lighting and backstage facilities—and the absence of such at SJU—proved a strong incentive to cooperation and placed the department at CSB.

Based on its research, the Mayhew panel had reported that most departments, "with [a] few marked exceptions," were willing to merge; several had done so or were well on their way. The economics departments and psychology departments operated jointly by 1968, with both housed at Saint John's. Education operated as one department at Saint Ben's. Sociology functioned as one department, with classes and faculty located on both campuses. History, too, moved with apparent ease, at least, toward unification.

Indeed, the academic departments of the two schools moved toward unification with varying speed. Both colleges offered majors in chemistry and physics; neither had many students. Unifying the departments was possible without much difficulty. Saint John's had better laboratory facilities—everyone agreed—in its new science building, and its faculty respected the ability and competence of CSB colleagues.[8]

The Mayhew report had predicted that the biology departments would be the last of the departments to unify. It wasn't. And in some ways biology offered a way to sidestep the perceived differences in quality of Saint Ben's and Saint John's. Both had crackerjack departments including lay and Benedictine faculty. The CSB department had more members than its counterpart. Though, as Mayhew reported, none of them "have shown a great willingness to cooperate," they made it work. Moreover, the decision in 1970–71 to move the Saint Ben's faculty to Saint John's—also based on its greater lab space—resulted in no loss of status or self-respect for the women, whose qualifications were readily apparent. S. Remberta's talent and reputation, in particular, were widely recognized. She was a charter member of the Minnesota Academy of Science, which had cited her for Distinguished Service to Science. She was named Outstanding Educator of America in 1972. Students at CSB and SJU still benefit from her work in local botany, and her collection forms the basis and bulk of the CSB/SJU Herbarium.

In the fall of 1971—having worked on cooperation for two years—Sy Theisen reported "excellent progress" in unification on many fronts, but there were some "laggards." Philosophy would take some work. The SJU department had eight faculty members (mostly priests, most of whom had provided education for seminarians), for example, while the CSB department comprised only two.

The English departments also proved difficult. As Sy reported in November 1971, "I have not been successful in bringing the English Department members from both schools together." He called on the two deans for help. The CSB chair did not speak for all her department members when she said they "would be delighted to meet with and cooperate with the staff of the Saint John's English Department." The SJU chair probably did speak for his when he reported that SJU wanted "to go it alone." Both departments were strong; neither wanted to give ground to the other. Both wanted to keep their own courses and approach. Would cooperation mean that only one college had a Shakespeare teacher? Would the outcome of that decision diminish one college? Would it mean the loss of status, position, identity, perhaps even of faculty members? The future wasn't clear.[9]

At one joint meeting, many of these issues surfaced: "Can some rearrangement of teaching assignments occur without personal pain over the next few years? Are our institutional images of each other outdated; are they residues of the past?" Sy hoped that the election of a joint chair would occur soon, but he feared "the process of coming to feel and think as one department will take a year or two." In both he was too optimistic. The plan to elect a joint chair did not come to fruition for nearly a decade. Thinking as one department took longer still.[10]

The talk of merger had long since morphed into talk about merger from the bottom up, then into the unification of departments, then into talk of cooperation. In 1970, the boards' Committee on Cooperation advised waiting to make unification plans beyond the department level and recommended that the boards refrain from merging at that time (with the implication that they not do it ever).[11] In a 1972 letter to his SJU counterpart, Stan reported that he had publicly taken "the damnable heresy of merger" off the table so had "stilled many fluttering hearts in the CSB faculty."[12]

One of the knottiest issues in the cooperation enterprise concerned finances. It's not clear what the exchanges "cost" either college, but that they spent huge amounts of time and energy figuring out who owes what to whom is evident.

Already in 1967 Fr. Gervase Soukup, treasurer for Saint John's Abbey and University, worried that the original purpose of cooperation (at least as far he was concerned) was being forgotten. As the presidents promoted the improvement of students' education and opportunity as the purpose of cooperation, Fr. Gervase listed "financial savings" as of "paramount importance," in hope of lowering per capita instructional costs at both schools. As he saw it, "Because the importance of financial considerations have not been adequately evaluated . . . there is bickering and strife regarding costs and charges." Further, "the present level of cooperation is not sustainable." The two schools had to become one university or abandon the effort.[13]

Financial considerations took up many hours, and the two colleges calculated annually what each owed the other for cross enrollment, for the salaries of faculty members teaching cross-campus, for its share of bus rides and meals. The strong scent of one side taking advantage of the other permeated the air. Complicated formulas and calculations kept the business managers of both colleges deeply involved and invested in the matters of cooperation. The interests of academic officers versus those of the financial officers sometimes pulled the colleges in opposite directions. Financial considerations certainly affected the speed and nature of cooperation.

In 1970–71, CSB paid SJU $43,740 for credit hours that Bennies took at SJU (more than Johnnies took at CSB). Saint John's paid Saint Ben's a net amount of just over $20,000 for the exchange of faculty. (Three CSB faculty members taught full time at SJU; two SJU members taught full time at CSB; 24 others taught on the opposite campus part time.) The two schools also figured out that somewhere in the neighborhood of 20,000 meals were eaten on the other campus; this cost Saint Ben's $16,000. For transportation CSB paid $14,000 and Saint John's $6,500 because fewer Johnnies used the bus.

The precise amounts are not in themselves important now, but they indicate the effort going into financial arrangements between the two schools. The reporting of them indicates the tension engendered by the negotiations:

"It is easy for erroneous notions to arise when not enough facts are communicated," Theisen's report begins. "[We must] see these items in the context of our common values and goals . . . One must see the cash element in the student exchange in realistic perspective . . . Some SJU professors say there are many Bennies in classes at SJU, and CSB pays little money . . . The food service exchange system is equitable and fair, despite persistent unsubstantiated rumors to the contrary . . . A few SJU persons complained . . . that CSB did not provide its share of recreational facilities."

In 1971 Fr. Michael Blecker took over as president of SJU. Stan and Sy and Fr. Colman had spent two years getting to know each other. Fr. Michael had a different style, and when he and Stan and Sy worked together, they sent out a lot of sparks. They clashed about words, about memos sent, about speeches given and rumors reported.

"I was deeply distressed to read your memo to Sister Firmin," Sy wrote Michael, and "I deeply regret the existence of your memo to Sister Firmin." More starkly he wrote, "Before you became president, there was a spirit of mutual trust and respect which had developed among the presidents, coordinator, and deans. There were weaknesses, but we did speak with mutual respect." The memo of note, according to Sy, offended both S. Firmin and President Idzerda.[14]

All hell broke loose when Sy received reports that Michael had been "ridiculing CSB" and that he'd "made fun of" the CSB vice president for finance. In response, Stan had threatened to pull CSB science students from Saint John's. Fr. Michael abolished the group that represented Saint John's on a joint academic committee. Finally, Sy wrote, "I am told that you were quoted [as saying] "SJU would build a dormitory for women soon.""

Michael's copy of that memo is deeply creased with penciled responses.[15]

Relations continued to deteriorate. In December Sy was at wit's end: the minutes of an SJU student government meeting quoted Michael as saying "Father Blecker said his main concern was how much money he could get out of Saint Ben's." Clearly, Sy felt stuck in the middle: "I try to defend Saint John's when I am at CSB, and I try to defend Saint Ben's when I am at SJU." In response to the student minutes, he said, "I am blamed at CSB for trying to give an interpretation to SJU [that] is better than the facts." Worse still, such comments "undermine my attempts to make CSB believe that Saint John's wants to have a just and fair financial arrangement."[16]

In response, Fr. Michael was "amused and dismayed" that the CSB officials put so much faith in student minutes. Despite his having a serious cold and laryngitis but "in order to assist the cooperative effort," he said, he had attended the meeting, telling students only that he believed the exchange with CSB was not fair to SJU "considering our costs." He charged the CSB people with a "lack of elementary etiquette" for not checking with Michael first and indicated that though "it would be too much to expect an apology, it seems to me courtesy might recommend that course of action."[17]

Fr. Michael had his own complaints. In April of 1972, he wrote Sy that he had "patiently borne with actions which CSB has taken in its own best interests" without enough regard for SJU. More pointedly: "I am tired of being painted a villain at CSB for my concern for SJU, and of hearing that all ladies are heroines."[18]

Both colleges tended to mistrust the other, to worry that the other was out for its own ends, and that their ends were in competition. Stan wrote to the presidents of both St. Kate's and St. Thomas to see how they managed the finances of cooperation. No money changed hands, they reported, agreeing that both were the better for it. CSC's president, S. Alberta Huber, wrote, "We find the exchange beneficial in so many ways that we have not considered limiting it or trying to balance it."[19] This attitude did not characterize CSB/SJU financial dealings at the time (CSC and UST did not end up cooperating while CSB and SJU did).

Another issue affecting cooperation was that SJU looked rich from the outside, certainly richer than Fr. Michael found it to be when he entered the presidency. The Breuer buildings—Abbey Church, Alcuin Library, Science Hall, and new dorms—gave an air of modernity and prosperity to the campus. Fr. Colman's expensive initiatives had done much to raise Saint John's visibility. By all reports, however, he had jumped first and worried about financial consequences later (or never), so Fr. Michael faced both an operating deficit (about $250,000 for the year preceding his tenure) and long-term indebtedness of $5.5 million. In his report to the SJU faculty shortly after taking charge, Fr. Michael talked about this indebtedness and, looking for solutions—or perhaps scapegoats—he intimated that CSB was paying SJU "less than we should rightly have."[20]

Financial considerations derailed discussion after discussion, such as the one about the location of classes. "I am distressed," Sy wrote in 1971, that too many decisions, in this case where a class should be held, seem to hinge on "whether one school can get more money out of one location or another." Such consideration, when put at the heart of the relationship, "turns cooperation into selfish manipulation."[21]

Through that year, conversations about finance filled the papers of the administrators of the two colleges. So did talk—indeed threats—of dropping cooperation entirely and going coed. CSB felt SJU might invoke that threat without notice. The Committee on Cooperation recommended in April that each board promise it would not go coed without a two-year warning.[22]

By early 1972, the coordinator expressed a deep "sense of futility." The two presidents, Sy wrote them, had "wrested the initiatives for co-operation from the coordinator and made him into their employee." The two schools, he reflected, "have lost our sense of direction." He took some of the blame—for letting the initiatives be wrestled away when he might have resisted more strongly. He wrote this at a low in his tenure; on reflection, he might have couched his message in more gentle language. Still, it makes clear the deep conflict of the colleges regarding their cooperative venture.[23]

In early June 1972, Sy Theisen stepped down. His final letter to the Committee on Cooperation and the two college presidents conveyed the depth of his discouragement and disaffection for the process of "cooperation": "Since I wish to be freed from involvement with cooperative questions, I ask that I not be asked next fall to undertake any task relative to cooperation."[24]

By the time he left the office of coordinator, a Joint Study Committee on Cooperation had determined five assumptions that guided cooperation for decades:

1. No legal merger is seen in the immediate future.
2. There are unique and separate qualities in each institution; these qualities may cause conflicts [that] will need to be resolved.
3. Each school will maintain authority and control over its own internal affairs.
4. To the extent that institutional autonomy is not threatened, areas of cooperation between the two schools are to be explored and implemented.
5. The intent of cooperation is to provide a more effective educational experience and in some areas to make possible more efficient management.[25]

Remarkably, cooperation has survived and thrived. Hard work over decades—and perhaps a miracle or two—has made it happen. We're both better for it.

Key actors in this merger story included Stan Idzerda (CSB president), Sy Theisen (coordinator), Fr. Colman Barry (SJU president) and Jack Lange (SJU dean), Fr. Michael Blecker (SJU president).

The Library

The library was one of the showpieces of the new Teresa Hall in 1913. The wood paneling made the area welcoming. The built-in bookcases gave it permanence and substance. Big windows let in good reading light and stained glass hinted that this was sacred space. Small sofas invited readers to sit down and stay. Fireplaces with surrounds of hand-painted tiles warmed the space.[1]

From 1913 to 1961 this space held the college's collection of books and magazines and study space. In 1930, the college catalog boasted the library's almost 17,000 volumes and subscription to at least 50 periodicals. By 1962, the library was bursting and the 38,500 volumes and 350 magazine subscriptions filled every inch. Students had long given up actually studying in the library.

The college solved the crisis of crowding by building a new gymnasium—not the normal response to a library problem, perhaps, but the gym took up the space immediately below the library. By relocating the gym, the college could nearly double the size of the library. The students still wouldn't have enough study space, but the books would be accessible, and there was room to expand the collections.

The college enlisted the help of the sisters to move the books. Like a line of firefighters, they passed the books from shelf to sister to sister, out the window, down the ladder, through the window, down the ladder, from sister to sister to shelf. The work took dozens of sisters only a few days.

About the same time, Saint John's also outgrew its library and looked to Marcel Breuer to design one in the same style as the Abbey Church. SJU broke ground in 1964 and formally opened the Alcuin Library in 1966. The new library gave CSB students an expanded place to study as well as an excuse to visit the other campus, just at the time when the two colleges were beginning to move seriously toward greater cooperation and students were taking classes on both campuses.

While some aspects of college cooperation met roadblocks, the two libraries walked to merger along a comparatively clear path. In 1979, presidents Fr. Michael Blecker and S. Emmanuel Renner called on the two

Moving the library books

academic vice presidents—S. Linda Kulzer and Fr. Gunther Rolfson—and the directors of the two libraries to come up with a plan. They were not seeking counsel on *whether* to cooperate but *how.* They made clear that saving money and improving services to students would be the goals of the cooperation. If the two colleges had one library, many kinds of duplication could be eliminated—did both libraries need copies of the same books? Could the libraries develop specialties?

Two proposals emerged—one calling for a slow evolution of cooperation, the other for rapid merger of everything but the library buildings. The second carried the day. Each campus was to continue having a library. Librarians would still be hired and paid by one college, but would have responsibilities on both campuses. The move toward merger uncovered strong institutional loyalties.

"None of us realized," wrote Michael Kathman, director of the new joint libraries, "how strong the sense of institutional identity was bound up in . . . policies and procedures." Whether to keep book jackets, for example, needed discussion, the format for the library letterhead as well. Most of the library differences were accommodated. But some administrative ones pockmarked the path forward. The libraries might act as one, but the business offices and budgeting practices remained separate. Paying for library materials remained subject to different paperwork requirements and procedures.[2]

The two libraries and their staffs exhibited many of the fears central to cooperation on all fronts: Would Saint John's be weakened by cooperation? Would Saint Ben's lose its identity? Some people may have felt so at first, but that was only temporary.

CSB wanted a larger library even so, and in 1983 Saint Ben's announced it would build a new one. Clemens Library opened in 1986—a moving

company as well as teams of students and staff members carried 137,000 volumes to the new space—and the junior partner became an equal. Graduating senior Patty Cousins '89 felt a tie to the library she called her "old friend," but she welcomed the new and modern library.[3]

A few people are still fond of the warmth and intimacy of the old library space in Teresa Reception Center, but Clemens Library, full and busy, is no one's little sister. At its most recent count, the library housed nearly a million volumes plus subscriptions to 700 paper and 27,000 electronic journals. Clemens today is one of the most used academic-social spaces on the two campuses, the group work location of choice, and a welcoming place to work after a meal at the adjacent Gorecki Dining Hall.

The libraries—or do we say the library—have come a very long way!

Bella Abzug

In the fall of 1979, the CSB Student Administrative Board and the Women for Equality Association organized the third annual Women's Week. They chose "Challenge of Choice" as the theme and included talks by Paula Treckel, from the History Department, on the single life ("She made us feel that being single was definitely a choice," one woman reported), by alumna Anne Ford "on surviving in the man's world of banking," by Del Marie Drake, "Former Prostitute Tells Her Story," and a program on women and athletics. The week started with an exploration of female and male images of God and ended with a talk by President Emmanuel Renner. One organizer noted that the "overall awareness of women increases every year," so attendance was much higher than in previous years.

Nothing in that week generated the controversy that the appearance of former Congresswoman (D-NY) Bella Abzug did three weeks later. The CSB/SJU Joint Events Council invited the fiery, outspoken feminist to talk on campus on "Women and Politics." The students—and the college—worried about public opposition to Abzug's appearance.[1]

Abzug, a three-term congresswoman and a 30-year lawyer, had a long history of political activism, particularly in support of women. She was an active proponent of the Equal Rights Amendment. She did not speak about abortion or abortion rights, but her well-known support of the Supreme Court's 1973 *Roe* v. *Wade* decision meant that her speech—intentionally *not* on abortion—ignited both fiery opposition and spirited defense.

The disagreement did not center on abortion—but on whether a Catholic college should host a speaker who held a pro-choice position. Students supported and opposed Abzug's appearance. One side asked: isn't this supposed to be a Catholic college? The other side countered: isn't this supposed to be a liberal arts college? Fr. Paul Marx the director of the Human Life Center at Saint John's, objected. Pro-life/anti-abortion organizations from Chicago and Washington, D.C., who kept a close eye on Catholic colleges, objected and mounted a campaign to encourage donors to withdraw their support of CSB and SJU. One D.C. official argued that inviting Congresswoman Abzug to campus was like "The Pope sitting down to chit-chat with the devil."

S. Colman O'Connell—the "pope" in this analogy, perhaps—would have been able to hold her own in such a conversation! She strongly defended the right, indeed obligation of the college, to provide a forum for controversial ideas and speakers. So did SJU President Fr. Michael Blecker. So did many students. SJU alum and local attorney Roger Nierengarten (and twin brother of S. Ruth Nierengarten) published a strong (and controversial) defense in the local diocesan newspaper, the *St. Cloud Visitor,* and reprinted in the SJU alumni magazine. The Forum, the student debating society directed by Joan Steck, chair of the Media and Communication Department, made the issue the topic of the spring debate.

The same controversy blew up again in both 1984 and 1997 when students invited first Judy Goldsmith, then Patricia Ireland, sitting presidents of the National Organization for Women (NOW), to campus. One of NOW's central issues has been pro-choice; one of the Catholic Church's central issues has been pro-life. Students knew this and the colleges, too. In both cases the student organizers asked the speakers to talk about issues other than abortion. In neither case did that matter to the campus controversy about their appearances.

CSB weathered these and other controversies. It may have lost some financial support (the records are ambiguous on this matter); it tested the loyalty of some friends; it defended the right of the students to invite controversial speakers to campus; it worried about the right balance between Catholic and liberal arts. It has worked hard—sometimes quite bravely—to uphold the idea of the Catholic college—this Catholic college—as a place where even the most difficult issues can be discussed.

The 1970s at CSB

~

Artist Joe O'Connell taught and worked at CSB from 1962 to 1995. Among his sculptures is this one, titled Work, *one of a series of three commissioned by the sisters. All three live in the Gathering Place of the Sacred Heart Chapel.*

From College of Saint Benedict and Saint John's University *Combined Catalog 1975–76:*

The College of Saint Benedict is an academic community for undergraduate women. It maintains close cooperation with Saint John's University, a college for men. We are committed to providing an educational content and process in an environment that fosters liberal, Christian, Catholic education in a Benedictine setting.

From: *1994–1996 Course Catalog:*

The College of Saint Benedict and Saint John's University are two liberal arts colleges located four miles apart in Central Minnesota. Saint Benedict's is a college for women and Saint John's a college for men. The students of these two colleges share in one common education, as well as coeducational social, cultural and spiritual programs. The colleges encourage students to come to terms with their own personal development in relation to their peers and to bring that enriched understanding into the lively coeducational life which characterizes the two campuses. . . .

The liberal arts education provided by the College of Saint Benedict and Saint John's University is rooted in the Catholic university tradition and guided by the Benedictine principles of the colleges' founders and sponsoring religious communities. These principles stress cultivation of the love of God, neighbor—and self—through the art of listening, worship, and balanced, humane living. The liberal arts, valuable in themselves, are the center of disciplined inquiry and a rich preparation for the profession, public life and service to others in many forms of work. . . . [CSB and SJU] seek to exemplify an authentically Christian concern for human rights and to make education broadly available to students on the sole criterion of ability to benefit from enrollment in the colleges.

From *Catalog 2012–2013:*

The mission of the College of Saint Benedict is to provide for women the best residential liberal arts education in the Catholic university tradition. The college fosters integrated learning, exceptional leadership for change and wisdom for a lifetime.

Our history is characterized by a fierce belief in the power of liberal education, an engagement with the world around us, responsiveness to the needs of society, an enduring commitment to our Catholic and Benedictine Heritage, and an unwavering focus on women's development as leaders, professionals, and scholars. We envision our future as grounded in these same commitments, and we embrace the changes and challenges impacting the world with the same courage, strength, and boldness of our foremothers.

A student in the mid-1970s reading in her dorm room.

2 Colleges to Start Inter-School Plan

ST. JOSEPH, Minn. — While | During the past school year | the interim month, to Europe, | Sr. Patrick Joseph said there | eral years. This will be the
Yale and Vassar, Columbia and | an inter-campus bus had trans- | to Mexico and New Mexico on | will be many more combined | first year, however, that an

TO AND FROM CLASSES—Students from St. John's University and the College of St. Benedict are more and more often walking in pairs. The two colleges will cooperate in a single, inter-campus bulletin this fall.

From the St. Cloud Times, *July 31, 1967*

St. Ben's-St. John's in Academic Transformation

ED. NOTE: This is part 2 of a series written by Times | and then four courses again dur- ing spring term. | emphasis is placed on depth within fewer subjects." | of the students, their back- grounds and wants," Fr. Hilary said | ban area of our times. This will provide a background of other topics." Fr. Hilary said. | prefects, types of managers, in charge of discipline and other dorm living problems.

CSB-SJU changes made the news on November 7, 1967 in the St. Cloud Times.

S. Ingrid Anderson before Second Vatican Council

S. Delores Super, S. Shaun O'Meara, S. Mary David Olheiser after the Second Vatican Council

St. Cloud Times *ads 1971, 1976*

The Weber family, including sisters and monks, in the mid-1970s.

Shirley Chisholm, first African-American Congresswoman, visited CSB in 1973.

The 26th Amendment lowered the voting age to 18.

CSB has had choirs since 1913 (good choirs, too).

18   Daily Times, St. Cloud, Minn.   Sat., May 13, 1978

Local/Area news

Program gives opportunities to women on welfare

By SALLY THOMPSON
Times Staff Writer

Sandra, a 23-year-old St. Cloud woman, felt herself caught in a frustrating rut about a year ago.

The mother of a 3-year-old son, she had been forced to seek public assistance because of her child's high medical bills.

While receiving Aid to Families with Dependent Children (AFDC) payments, she worked at a local manufacturing plant, earning the minimum wage.

"It was just impossible," she recalled. "I was working full time, but with AFDC, by the time they took deductions out for my wages and after I paid the babysitter and transportation, I just couldn't make it.

"You get stuck in a rut and there's no way you can get off AFDC. It's tough to get a good job with a high school education," she said.

Sandra and two other local women receiving AFDC are getting an opportunity to break out of the welfare cycle by studying for a college degree at the College of St. Benedict.

The women are enrolled in a two-year program that will train them for jobs in the growing mental health field. Their tuition, books, child care expenses and transportation are paid by a grant from the Bremer Foundation.

"Welfare is a situation that perpetuates itself," said Bob Gephart, coordinator of CSB's mental health associate program who is supervising the women's program.

"These women have felt the helplessness of it all — having kids, and knowing they have the ability, but no money or job and no skills or training," he said. "We want to get them off welfare, to where they're paying into taxes."

Since February, the women, in their 20s and 30s, have attended classes part time at CSB while their children stay at Children's Rainbow House, a nursery school run by the college.

After they graduate, their two-year associate of arts degrees will qualify them to work as "general practitioners" in human service agencies, Gephart said.

Job opportunities in the mental health field are expanding rapidly, and the associate degree qualifies graduates for many jobs in dealing with people that do not require more extensive education, he said.

The two-year degree will give the women a good basis should they want to work toward a four-year degree, he said. He added that 89 to 90 percent of the program's graduates have gone on for more advanced degrees.

Gephart said he is not aware of any other college with a program for women on welfare.

He expressed confidence that the experiences of the women on AFDC in dealing with social service agencies as clients should help them in their work after graduation.

A $5,000 grant from the Bremer Foundation is funding the program for women on AFDC for two years. Yearly expenses for a participant total about $1,000, Gephart said.

After the grant was awarded, letters were sent to inform agencies dealing with AFDC recipients that the program was available.

Nine women applied and four were accepted. One has since become inactive in the program, Gephart said.

Women who would be mature students with a sense of direction were selected, he said.

"We didn't want to set people up for failure," he said. Women considered most able to finish the two-year course and get jobs afterward were chosen because if the program succeeds, its chance of receiving more funding is greater, he explained.

Mary (not her real name), another woman in the program, hopes to use her training by counseling alcoholics or the mentally retarded. She is also interested in a nutrition-related job, but that would require more study.

The mother of a 4-year-old son, she has received AFDC for three years. She spoke firmly about the program's value to her.

"No, I wouldn't have the opportunity to do this otherwise. The expense is just too great," she said. "This will give me a chance to get a good job, and it won't be necessary to be on AFDC."

Continuing education at CSB went in many directions, as reported in St. Cloud Times, *May 13, 1978.*

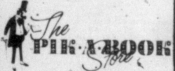
The local bookstore offered this list of most popular books in 1973.

A local St. Joe lounge adapted to the lowered drinking age.

Senior photos in the 1973 yearbook show the new informality.

The interior of the Sacred Heart Chapel (post-Vatican II, pre-renovation)

Peggy Landwehr (who graduated in the last Academy class) and Mike Roske are among the married Bennie-Johnnie couples.

CSB student Rita Knuesel—like others before and after—went away to graduate school, then returned to teach at CSB, then to become provost at CSB/SJU.

St. Benedict's explores upturn
Enrollment's up, but why?

By LIZ SCHEVTCHUK
Times Staff Writer

Maybe it is because of the sense of "community." Or. maybe it is the quality of academic programs or the women's liberation-era trend towards women's careers.

Whatever the reason. the College of St. Benedict (CSB) has an increased enrollment that makes CSB administrators, students and national women's college representatives happy.

The college has the largest enrollment increase this year in a survey of member institutions with increased enrollments by the Women's College Coalition. (Of the 70 institutions in the coalition. 64 were included in the enrollment survey.) CSB has grown from 1,163 students in 1975-76 to 1,870 students this year.

According to the coalition, CSB's increase reflects national upward trends for women's college enrollments. Private college enrollment is up 1.2 per cent nationally, and women's colleges' enrollments have increased 3.4 per cent. the coalition reports.

In full-time students. CSB had an increase of about 212 students, compared to a 170-student increase at Marywood College in Pennsylvania, the institution with the second-highest increase.

St. Benedict's has been growing over the past several years, from about 500 in 1968 to its record year, this year. CSB administrators explain.

They attribute the increase to a variety of factors. especially the college's emphasis on a community atmosphere and friendliness.

The spirit of community and togetherness is part of the college's four-point mission as a Christian. Catholic. liberal arts and Benedictine, CSB officials say. The college is affiliated with. but not the same as St. Benedict's Convent.

According to CSB Presdent Beverly Miller, the college's students and faculty "live the sense of community in a participatory way" by maintaining the small size, friendly atmosphere and ethical and spiritual values.

Despite the students' serious academic interests, "they are seeking a value orientation and a perspective." a philosophy for living, Miller said last week.

"Even though we've grown in size, we're residential." said Sister Mary Mark Donovan, vice president for student development. "We try to keep the personal contact with people." Among

students, she added, there seems to be an attitude of "wanting to have a larger identity with a group."

"Going to college is really a means to increase one's ability to live life to the fullest in a personal way" and in terms of a career, explained Sister Katherine Howard, vice president for academic affairs.

Attention to both a student's personal and professional growth is part of the general appeal of women's colleges, Nancy Lasersohn of the Women's College Coalition staff explained. "They want women to be aware of the options available" and to find "success in whatever they do," she said.

This means the colleges have improved and adopted innovative programs designed to help the modern woman handle careers and changing roles in the world. The institutions have lost their image as finishing schools for rich girls and are intensely involved in offering quality education for women in both traditional and non-traditional fields, she said.

At the College of St. Benedict, "some of their programs are really innovative." she said. She cited a program for women in management, receiving national attention, as an example.

Miller mentioned the school's horsemanship program, which grants students a minor degree, a new minor degree program in coaching, and various community services and childhood development programs as other new advantages of the institution.

Even such "traditional" women's fields as raising or teaching chilren are receiving professional emphasis, she said.

She, her colleagues and students also listed the college's high job placement rate of its graduate's as another reason for St. Benedict's popularity.

About 99 per cent of last spring's graduates seeking work have found jobs, she said.

Freshmen entering the college and seniors leaving it echo the administrators when they discussed reasons for their school's increasing popularity and their presence at the institution.

Several said they wanted to attend a small college not far from their homes (85 per cent of CSB students are from Minnesota) and one with a good academic reputation and spirit of friendliness.

"It's smaller, it's unique." said Carrie Schliesman, a freshman from Glenwood.

"I like it here. It's a small college, for one thing. The atmosphere was really friendly" during visits before she enrolled, she said.

"It was close to St. Cloud, and three of my sisters went here," said Patti Grundman, a freshman from St. Cloud. "That's why I'm here but I made the final decision."

"I really like the Christian environment." added Ann Preiss, a freshman from Wayzata. "It's an overall attitude, and a different type of people. People here are a lot more open to you."

The seniors gave nearly identical reasons for being at the college.

"There's a great relationship between the faculty and students," said Carla Stevermer, a senior from Granite Falls.

"I think the atmosphere probably decided me," said Marcia Enney, a senior from St. Paul.

One senior, Maria McDonald, from Minneapolis, said the college's generous financial aid drew her. Others agreed the assistance offered them had been a decisive factor.

The college and its counterpart for men, St. John's University, awarded 750 freshman scholarships this year. The scholarships range from $200 to $2,000. In the 1975-76 academic year, the two institutions awarded about $1 million in various forms of aid, with the average amount being $2,300.

Aside from the financial benefits, "I was really impressed by the friendliness." McDonald added. "The college admissions officers have a very winning way. I was very impressed by their correspondence. It didn't look like a form letter."

However, life at St. Benedict's is not without its potential problems. The college administrators mentioned the increasing costs of education and forthcoming years of declining enrollments at all colleges as obstacles to be overcome

Currently, one year at CSB costs students from $3,500 to $4,000. With enrollments likely to drop again by 1980, more attention is warranted to draw older, non-traditional women students to the college, administrators said.

Already, the school has a large continuing program expected to expand in the future.

The seniors also suggested the college's isolation and sheltered atmosphere are drawbacks. Students can easily be lulled into forgetting about the rest of the world, they said.

From the St. Cloud Times, *Sept. 21, 1976*

Basketball fans turned up at "Rat Hall" for CSB games.

The Rotunda transformed into offices and meeting spaces

SEVEN

~

The Embodied Bennie

On Saturday night, March 13, 1993, the CSB Blazers scored a triumph in their final regular-season basketball game. The Blazers—as all Saint Ben's varsity teams have been called since 1976—beat the Concordia Cobbers 84–57 and claimed an undefeated season (28–0).[1]

This victory sent the Blazers to the NCAA Final Four, the team's players and fans to euphoria. For the last several minutes of the game, the crowd chanted, "Final Four, Final Four." Even Concordia's coach praised the Blazers: "They have all the ingredients—post play, perimeter play, coaching, depth." The team had a lot of stars. Senior center and team captain Kelly Mahlum scored 14 points; another senior, Janine Mettling, scored 22; Tina Kampa, a first-year student, put in 15; and Colleen Carey scored another 13 points.[2]

Among the team's biggest fans and loudest cheerleaders that night were some of the people who had made it all possible: S. Grace Donovan, Stanley Idzerda, S. Lois Wedl, Margy Hughes, Elaine Henke, Carol Howe-Veenstra, Mike Ryan, and John Gagliardi. Sitting on the bench, or more likely standing on the sidelines as proud as he could be, was coach Mike Durbin. He had coached CSB teams for many years. This team's success must have tasted very sweet to him. Before the year was done, he was named Division III Coach of the Year. The spirits of generations of CSBers must have been cheering, too,

The winning Blazer team of 1992–1993

about how far Saint Ben's athletics had come since the days of the Women's Athletic Association (WAA) and the Women's Recreation Association (WRA).

Women's colleges since their founding have navigated a landscape zoned by gender, nowhere stricter than around women's bodies. The "content" of that zoning has certainly changed over the history of Saint Ben's, but the cultural norms about women's bodies are the landscape upon which women's colleges—and women—have invented and known themselves.

The notion of women as "the weaker sex" has long contributed to the idea that women need protection. This basic premise led colleges to set hours for women. In late 1967, the Saint Ben's Students' Hours Committee approved a loosening of the hours requirements to allow seniors to be out until 11:00, juniors until 10:30, sophomores until 10:00, second-semester Bennies to 9:30 (first-semester Bennies had to be in by 7:30). In 1969, the college experimented with no weekend hours for juniors and seniors. The rules gradually eroded.

The same notion has long shaped how "respectable" women are to perceive themselves. By 19th-century standards a "true woman" was dainty, fragile (or pretended fragility); she was likely to faint at the least provocation. She was so refined that she could be overcome by strong language or truth too directly told. The solution to her physical ailments was bed rest.

In the 1918 novel, *My Antonia,* Willa Cather offers a searing portrait of the respectable young women of the fictional Midwestern town of Black Hawk: "When one danced with [the town girls] their bodies never moved inside their clothes; their muscles seemed to ask but one thing—not to be disturbed. I remember those girls merely as faces in the schoolroom, gay and rosy, or listless and dull, cut off below the shoulders, like cherubs, by the ink-smeared tops of the high desks that were surely put there to make us round-shouldered and hollow-chested."

Cather contrasts the town girls with the less respectable country girls, immigrants most of them, who "were almost a race apart, and out-of-door work had given them a vigor which . . . developed into a positive carriage and freedom of movement, and made them conspicuous among Black Hawk women" and a "menace to the social order." But, Cather continues, "Anxious mothers need have felt no alarm. They mistook the mettle of their sons. The respect for respectability was stronger than any desire in Black Hawk youth." The Black Hawk boys might dance with the country girls, but they married the townies.

That lesson was not lost on generations of America's young women. Women before and since have shaped—and misshaped—themselves to prescribed body types, whatever their actual body types might be. Corsets and girdles and their contemporary cousins—Spanx—have been designed to make sure that women's "bodies never move inside their clothes." Diets, too, aim to make women's bodies "taut." Overweight as well as anorexic women and girls, according to the research, are equally disconnected from their bodies, and neither has a healthy relationship with her appetites. Neither has the ability to see what her body really looks like.

Few issues have strained that gender zoning more than athletics. Physically active girls get called tomboys. To "throw like a girl" is a negative description of a boy or a girl, a man or a woman, who throws

A star player

without engaging the body. Girls and women who fully occupy their bodies are likely to be thought of or accused of being not feminine enough (or lesbian). Like the town girls of Black Hawk, "ladies" don't have bodies. It's hard to be athletic without a body!

Some women have been willing to flout the social conventions. Something about basketball has appealed to many of them since its invention in the 1880s, and Smith College took up the game as early as 1893. By 1895 five other of the women's colleges had fielded basketball teams, and women's colleges came to be known as "hotbeds" of women's basketball. Many coed colleges and high schools took up women's basketball as well. Berkeley and Stanford women played the first intercollegiate women's basketball game in 1896. Saint Benedict's Academy fielded teams—by class—and CSB students formed a team as soon as they had enough players.

From the beginning, women's teams played by women's rules. Senda Berenson, Smith's "director of physical culture" and the strongest proponent of basketball for women, worried about the game's "rough element" and how it could be eliminated. "It is a well-known fact that women abandon themselves more readily to an impulse than men." As a result, she said, "Unless a game as exciting as basket ball is carefully guided by such rules as will eliminate roughness, the great desire to win and the excitement of the game will make our women do sadly unwomanly things."

Berenson therefore proposed rules for women's basketball that stayed virtually intact until 1971: six players to a side—two guards, two forwards, two centers, each assigned to only one-third of the court. She preferred no dribbling, but the rules allowed three dribbles and prohibited stealing the ball.

She was, no doubt, gauging the tolerance of her audience in making her arguments, recognizing the social and, indeed, the medical resistance to women's physical activity. Almost from the time of basketball's invention, the Athletic Conference of American Women worked to make women's basketball more "feminine." For good reason. Since opposition to women's participation grew with the game's popularity. One critic asserted: "Women who were able to excel in the rougher and more masculine sports [that is, basketball], have either inherited or acquired masculine characteristics." Berenson worked hard to make basketball palatable to outsiders and to the players themselves, by couching their playing in ladylike terms and working toward ladylike ends.[3]

From 1913 CSB students participated in physical activity. Not all of the students joined in with equal vigor, of course, but they did meet the college's not-for-credit requirements. The original college buildings—in addition to classrooms, a library, a science lab, and the Ro—included a gym. Not a great gym, mind you—it was located in the basement of Teresa Hall, where a set of load-bearing columns broke up the playing space. The gym's low ceiling limited volleyball, and size cramped. But there it was. Just the fact of the gym's existence indicates that CSB was paying attention both to women's higher education elsewhere and to the value of physical activity for its women. Students could and did use it for floor gymnastics and modern dance, volleyball, badminton, and basketball.

Basketball took flight, too. In 1923, one Bennie noted that being captain of the basketball team was the thing that made her most happy about college. The campus was alive that spring, the *College Days* reported, with "as much excitement here as at a World Series game." It was all about the basketball round-robin tournament in which the one college team and four high school teams played for the title of champion of the school. The high school seniors finished with a 3–1 record; the sophomores 1–3; the college team and the freshmen finished 2–2.

Students took part in these (and many other) physical activities.

*Six captivated fans at
a St. Patrick's Day
basketball game*

Several players, including Irene Simonet, Mary Tibbetts, and Jeanette Wimmer for the college, emerged as stars. One of the most important basketball games in later years was the annual Germans vs. Irish match held around St. Patrick's Day.

Constance Zierden (from 1933), S. Grace (Mary Mark) Donovan (from 1945), and other physical education teachers long dedicated themselves to the students' physical well-being. S. Grace taught in habit. Those black wool gowns looked elegant, but they were so heavy and slow to dry that they were washed only once or twice a year. That wasn't enough for the very physically active S. Mary Mark. She requested permission to make a habit of polyester that could be laundered weekly at least. The new habit was indeed lighter and easier to wash, but, oh, was it hot!

From the 1930s, if not earlier, Saint Ben's prescribed two years of physical education, and students belonged to the WAA/WRA that organized everything from volleyball to bowling and badminton tournaments, from play days scheduled for area high school girls to skate and ski, from archery and tennis and ping pong (now called table tennis) to soccer and swimming and softball and slimnastics (the 1960s

Archery, too

equivalent of aerobics). The programs were as varied as the women in the association and the CSB facilities allowed.[4]

In the college's physical education program, students took their two years of required activity and then had the opportunity for two more years—one in team sports and one in individual and dual sports—during which they could also study coaching and officiating.

In this, as in so many other areas of Saint Ben's (and American society), big change occurred in the 1960s and 1970s. In 1961, the new gym—now called Murray Hall—opened. It had a ceiling high enough for even the most enthusiastic volleyball players and a regulation-size basketball court without pillars—heaven by comparison to what they'd had before! What the new gym didn't have was room for spectators. Clearly, it was a gym for the players. Regardless, the new gym brought with it the hire of Elaine Henke for the physical education department—and she coached the basketball team. The changes brought new life and energy to CSB athletics.

So did the hiring in 1966 of Margy Hughes in physical education and Mike Ryan in education. Margy taught and then chaired the department for nearly 40 years. Mike was quickly tapped to help out,

*Cross-country
team runners
in 1983*

*A pitch in the
Saint Ben's vs. Carleton
game in April 2011*

then to direct student services, then to head up the recruitment of students. He campaigned hard for better athletic facilities. Without them, he argued, the college was losing recruits. The flame of athletic passion was sweeping through grade and high schools, and girls wanted to play too. Increasingly, prospective students visiting the campus asked to see the gym and the locker rooms. Many cared more about those than about the dorms. Mike and Elaine and Margy campaigned for funds to hire coaches and staff, to buy uniforms, and to pay for travel—all keys to a successful athletic program. They oversaw revolutionary changes in the college's athletic life and physical plant, including the construction of a sanctioned-competition swimming pool. Their effort culminated in the opening in 1985 of Claire Lynch Hall—a state-of-the-art gymnasium. That really was heaven! To this day it is a wonderful venue in which to play or be a fan.

Title IX of the Education Amendments of 1972 reads: "No person in the United States shall, on the basis of sex, be excluded from participation in, be denied the benefits of, or be subject to discrimination under any education program or activities receiving federal financial assistance."

Blazer basketball team in 1977–1978 season

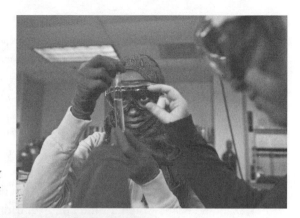

*Bennies exercising
their strong brains*

As separate women's and men's colleges, CSB and SJU were exempt from the enormous changes that Title IX wrought in athletic programs at virtually every coed institution in the United States. Nonetheless, the legislation created a significantly changed environment for women's sports. Opening Little League and grade- and high-school sports to girls created greater demand for college-level sports. Girls who had been active—stars, even—in high school wanted to be just as active in college. Terri Lammers, a #1 seed tennis player, transferred out of CSB for example, to be able to play on a tennis team. Before long CSB had its own tennis team as well as dozens more teams in multiple sports. CSB and its women certainly benefited from the spirit of Title IX.

The last slat in the bridge from the WAA to the Final Four was admission to the Minnesota Intercollegiate Athletic Conference (MIAC).

In this, John Gagliardi—longtime SJU football coach and father of two Bennies, won the undying loyalty of CSB athletes and staff. In the early 1980s the MIAC had only one women's college member—St. Kate's. To ease scheduling conflicts, the MIAC paired women's and men's teams for "home" and "away" games. Because SJU wasn't paired and neither was St. Kate's, the MIAC planned to put them together. CSB had applied for admission, but the MIAC hadn't yet acted. When it did—and it certainly would—as CSB had long since been ready for a full program of inter-collegiate athletics—Saint Ben's would be isolated, and scheduling games would be impossible. John Gagliardi saw the damage that the pairing of SJU and St. Kate's would do and put up a roadblock. He even threatened to withdraw SJU should the MIAC not admit CSB immediately and pair it with SJU. His intervention speeded the process and cheered the college on. His two CSB daughters and the college thanked him.

With such people, buildings, memberships, and spirit in place, the CSB volleyball team—under coach Carol Howe Veenstra—took its

Saint Ben's volleyball team huddled up during a 1976–77 game.

CSB softball team, 1991–1992

Volleyball team 1989–1990

first MIAC title in 1987 after a 34–0 season. The members of that team were all stars and, as a team, they were inducted into the CSB Blazer Hall of Fame.

The only other team in the Blazer Hall of Fame is the 1993 basketball team, whose captain, Kelly Mahlum, was named All American in 1993 and went on to a successful college coaching career. She was added individually to the Hall of Fame as well. Her team did not take the Division III NCAA title in 1993. Its players were deeply disappointed, and their fans were, too, of course, but as the *Independent* reported, "Blazers win hearts." Two loyal faculty fans, Steve Stelzner and Richard Wielkiewicz of the psychology department, traveled to the Final Four games, writing later that they were "proud to be associated with the College of Saint Benedict team, not only because of [its] performance on the basketball floor but for the class and maturity [its] members] demonstrated all season long both on and off the court."[5]

The sisters have been some of the teams' most loyal fans—S. Lois Wedl, a thwarted athlete herself, is most faithful of all. As a high school student she watched the boys' teams and felt deeply the unfairness of having no girls' teams. She marched herself to see the principal, who was also the boys' basketball coach, to complain. His answer: "Girls don't play sports." For the past 50 years, she has had the pleasure of cheering on

Some sister sports fans

A *"ladylike" jump ball in 1981*

the students who, day after day, prove him wrong. In recognition of her support, the athletic department has established the S. Lois Wedl Endowment for Blazer Athletics and the alumnae association holds an annual "S. Lois Scramble" golf tournament.

Many members of the Saint Ben's faculty and staff as well as its sisters and friends have fueled the change and cheered the results. But its students provide the focus, the force, the engine, and the motivation for this growth. Bennies wanted to play and they did. And do.

Oh, by the way—that winning team played five women on the full court, with unlimited dribbling. One of the key plays was a scoring drive capped by a three-point shot. Dainty indeed!

Athletics demonstrates one way that women upon the college's 100th anniversary relate differently to their bodies than they did in 1913. Sex is another. It's as if women in the last 100 years have discovered their bodies, taken more control of them (or have tried to, in the case of eating disorders), and lived more fully in them.[6]

Behaviors have also changed—many more young women in America are sexually active in 2013 than in 1913—and the topic is more fully

A 2013 campus program

talked about. What's considered taboo has shrunk, and the amount of skin most women are willing to expose has expanded! Where once a young woman might have presumed she would be a virgin when she married, now young women who make this decision feel themselves in the minority, out of step with their peers. Where once an "unwed" mother was sent into hiding or "to visit an aunt," single mothers now proudly tend their children.

CSB women have always, of course, known about sex. No doubt some were sexually active. Older alums report that if their classmates were having sex, however, they didn't talk about it. It was so severely taboo as to be undiscussable, almost unthinkable. School rules made an active sex life (even a furtive one) difficult. Catholic training made it more difficult on principle.*

As late as the 1960s, a widely circulated Catholic pamphlet taught that "French kissing" was a mortal sin. Sex with another woman? Virtually unthinkable. One alum recently reported being so innocent and chaste herself that it occurred to her only years after she graduated that some of her classmates might have been having sexual relations

---

*In her short story "Matinmas," published in the *New Yorker,* Nov. 15, 1947, Betty Wahl (Powers), class of '43, depicts a schoolgirl asking the priest in religion class, "Is it sinful to French kiss?" He considers it a silly question, "so theoretical that chances are a million to one [you'll] ever meet the problem." Furthermore, he advises, "If you want to know how to French kiss, ask your French teacher. I am a theologian."

and that a few friends might even have been lesbians. (Some alumnae discover this about each other only much later, at reunions.) A Bennie newspaper columnist in 1984 reported on a "stifling atmosphere" at Saint Ben's that kept sexual issues secret and shameful and kept the "closet door . . . jammed, if not locked."[7]

From the perspective of some CSB students then and now, these strictures are as they should be. Catholic teaching on premarital sex and homosexuality has not wavered over the college's history. Many Catholics may ignore these teachings, but a significant minority of CSB students uphold them. Some don't know *what* to think.

Many former students report that in their generations at Saint Ben's, the students were naïve, the atmosphere at the college religious or repressive (depending on the student's point of view), the relationships mostly chaste, and the consequences of sexual misbehavior severe (and shameful). The most sexually titillating stories center on flirtations from a distance, meeting up with a roommate's brother, and panty raids—many of them! In one story, the Johnnie raiders were so unfamiliar with the women's living situation at Saint Ben's that they miscalculated and went into the convent rather than the Rotunda. Yikes! Fortunately, one of the young men was the nephew of a Saint John's monk, who got them off the hook. Later, in the 1950s, a panty raid got a couple of the Johnnies tossed out of school, a punishment still grating on their classmates. A third panty raid, during the time Stan Idzerda was president, cost the raiding Johnnies only the price of replacing the underwear.

The sexual revolution of the 1960s and '70s took a while to storm through CSB, but storm through it did. In 1971 the Boston Women's Health Collective published the first edition of its pathbreaking book *Our Bodies, Our Selves.* Nothing signaled the new age for women more decisively. Gone was the delicate woman, and in her place was a woman of appetites, passions. The book encouraged women to hold mirrors up to their own bodies (literally, to their genitals)—and the book to their eyes (metaphorically) so as to see themselves for the physical creatures they are.

The sexual and student revolutions of the 1960s churned up all sorts of controversy on college campuses generally and at CSB in particular. How much supervision did women need? How many inches did the door need to be open during "visiting hours"? How many feet on the floor? (Three at any one time was one rule). Graduates from the mid-1970s remembered the time a Johnnie was in their room after closing hours. S. Brian Spain, supervisor of the dorm, happened to stop by, and the Johnnie hid in the closet. S. Brian was especially talkative that night, or she knew something was amiss. She stayed, talking to those roommates for a long time. The Johnnie did nothing to betray his position and so outlasted her. The young women swooned with relief that they weren't found out.

Other alums (and current students, too) tell of boyfriends climbing in and out of windows, of "accidentally" missing the last bus, and of various other ruses. Others report that through the most revolutionary days of the sexual revolution and its aftermath, they continued to feel safe, protected, even removed from the sexual activity. The dorms housed women standing at many points on this spectrum. They all reported feeling equally at home there, too.

Some of the most vigorous controversy about sex-related topics centered on contraception, which, like abortion, contravenes official Catholic teaching but which, unlike abortion, is widely practiced even among devout Catholics. The campus sentiment about contraception, then, was mixed. The AIDS epidemic and the American campaign for safe sex intensified the ambivalence. Getting pregnant was one thing, but dying was quite another consequence of unprotected sex.

In the 1980s and 1990s, much of the student activism about sexual issues took place at Saint John's (and most of the sexual activity, according to the lore).[8] In the mid-1980s the CSB Wellness Program director put condoms out at its annual health fair. And the mid-1990s Bennies and Johnnies handed out condoms and campaigned to have them sold in the college bookstores or bathrooms (without success). Loso's—the only store in St. Joe that sold condoms—closed at 8:00 p.m. The Midi (one of the St. Joe bars) stocked them in vending machines in its men's room, accessible only to those of drinking age (or those with a fake ID). One *Record* editor decried the students' inability to procure condoms: "We must protect ourselves and each other, even if our schools refuse to." The Saint John's on-campus pharmacy did not carry condoms, and in 2002 the monastery had all birth control pills removed from the pharmacy, too. The medical staff could continue to make medical decisions to prescribe the pills, but students had to fill their prescriptions elsewhere. Saint Ben's did not have an on-campus health center until 2010. Avoiding the on-campus contraception debate was one of the few positive by-products of this.

Sex also was a topic of public debate. Three Bennies in 1994 wrote several "Wildways" columns for the *Independent*. After columns on menstruation and midwifery, the authors took up the matter of women's orgasms. In addition to commenting on women's right to orgasms, they excerpted a long description about women's physiological response to sexual stimulation from *The New Our Bodies, Our Selves* (1992). Some students applauded the frank writing; others found it too intimate and not right for a Catholic college newspaper.[9]

That same year, two CSB editors squared off over whether condoms should be sold on a Catholic college campus. The "con" editor argued from the perspective that birth control runs counter to Catholic teaching. "Condoms suggest that sex is easy, sex is fun, and that premarital sex is fine as long as you're protected," she wrote. "These are all false assumptions." The "pro" editor approached the issue from a more feminist perspective: "For a women's college, isn't it funny how sexual issues . . . are limited exclusively to date rape and abuse?" She continued, "As much as we'd all like to deny it, women at this college have sex, and many of them do not know how to protect themselves against serious diseases [and pregnancy]." 1994 was quite the activist year!

In Saint Ben's first 60 years, should a student became pregnant—and some did—she usually disappeared without comment. Alums report that a roommate might know about such a thing, but rarely did anyone else. Loyal to the "disgraced" one, the friend on campus kept the secret, too.[10]

Jeanette Moriarty '45 was one Bennie who attended CSB after having a child. She was a student who had dropped out to marry. After the death of her soldier husband in 1944 and the birth of their child, she applied for readmission. Her application met some resistance and consternation, but she was admitted as a dayhop (not living on campus). But she made an active campus life for herself: she was an attendant to the posture queen in 1945. Her classmates elected her to the position of senior class president. She lived as "normal" a college life as she could manage.[11]

Former Bennies will know of other mothers who attended CSB, but there aren't good records of the number. In the late 1990s at least four mother-child pairs lived on campus. While the students went to class, their children went to daycare. Other students in their dorms did occasional babysitting; many took an active interest in the children. The mothers' lives seemed to go well enough, but from 1998 the college students with children lived off campus. The college currently has no policy about this. In the few cases where students have had children (and did not choose to have them live with guardians, like grandparents), Student Development staff members have worked with them to find the best alternative and to provide a support system, case by case. In recent memory, none have lived on campus with children.[12]

Students at Saint Ben's now know that others are sexually active (though lots of false information circulates about its extent). A *Record* writer in 1997 declared: "In a community of nearly 4,000 consenting adults, sex happens"—not just after midnight, on weekdays, and after 2:00 a.m. on the weekends (the female-free hours at SJU). Three years later the *Record* covered Sexual Responsibility Week on both campuses, and one reporter again declared, "It is not a secret that students at CSB and SJU are having sex." A 1999 survey of incoming first-year students on both campuses asked, "Have you had sexual intercourse in the last year?" To which 31 percent answered yes.[13]

An equally informal and unreliable poll of students of other years puts the figure much higher—more than 50 percent is the estimate of graduates of the 1990s, closer to 80 percent for those of the 2000s. Whatever the talk of hooking up, the number seems to be down: In 2012, 49.9 percent of CSB students reported that they had had consensual sex.

For many women, easier access to birth control pills, to morning-after pills, and yes, to abortion, have changed the dynamics of sexual activity. At CSB none of those was considered a good Catholic option. The term *pregnancy* shows up most often in the CSB newspaper in ads for Birthrite and Birthline, both strongly anti-abortion, offering help for women with unwanted pregnancies. One couple put an ad in the *Independent* seeking to adopt a baby boy. Planned Parenthood did not advertise in the student newspaper. Some students have supported public readings of Eve Ensler's *Vagina Monologues*. Others, like one group in 2004, formed a Students for Life Club. Many on both sides identify themselves as Catholic; some are feminists. There's almost as little middle ground as between the sex lives of students of the 1910s and those of the 2010s.

By the 2010s, a kind of post-sexual-revolution revolution had taken place. The pendulum seems to have swung from one extreme of naiveté and shame to the other of "hooking up." Likely neither characterizes the typical CSB woman. Contemporary commentators on the college female/male "scene" argue that the pressure on women (from themselves, their parents, the culture) to succeed and excel, to set themselves firmly on a path to a fulfilling career, has profoundly altered young women's relational habits and practices. It must be confusing to navigate between the drive to put studies and career first and the desire to have a partner. If she puts her career first, what does she do with that need for intimacy? Do these factors cause women (and men) to choose transient sexual relationships over real long-term relationships? We don't know the answer, but we do know that the choices aren't easy for women, including CSB women, in the early 21st century. The CSB culture does permit, indeed actively supports a more open environment in which women can explore and express their sexuality.

The lives of lesbian students also shifted dramatically between the "stifling atmosphere" of 1984 and "Coming Out Week" in 2009. FLAG—Friends of Lesbians and Gays—had organized on campus in the interim. So had PRISM—People Respecting Individuals and Sexual Minorities. Many GLBT faculty members came out themselves, giving courage to GLBT students by example, then offering them support and a safe space. In 2004, four students attended the Midwest GLBT College Conference, there presenting their video *Creating Safe Space for GLBT Students on a Rural, Midwestern, Catholic Campus*.[14]

The CSB Student Development Office long ago initiated a variety of programs to assist Bennies in dealing with their bodies. For a time CSB had a college nurse. In 1980 the vice president for student development—and former PE teacher and coach—S. Grace Donovan spearheaded a grant application to the Fund for the Improvement of Postsecondary Education (FIPSE) for a program on women's heath. When it was funded, Miriam Hof, the new vice president, appointed Kathy (Paden) Thornbury as the campus wellness coordinator. The grant application recognized the trend in higher education toward keeping students healthy, and to taking seriously the host of significant body issues facing women. Thornbury's wellness program and her team of student health advocates focused on physical fitness, nutrition, and "awareness of risk-taking activities." This language only slightly disguised the issues that CSB students grappled with then—and grapple with now. Some of the greatest risks for women have to do with unprotected or forced sex and with alcohol, which often contributes to the first two. The health advocates put on workshops, met with other students in small and large groups, and conducted various support groups. They engaged in student conversations, trying to break through campus taboos.

The campus today is replete with programming about health, wellness, physical activity, nutrition, and sex. The Student Development Office has shifted some of its attention to related and pressing issues: date rape and sexual assault in particular. The recent opening of a full-service health center, run by a nurse practitioner with several full-time professional staff members is part of the overall health and wellness structure on campus, which also includes ready access to professional psychological services.

Finally, there is a new kind of openness among contemporary students (on and off the campus). Students in 1913 might have kept their sexual lives a deep secret. Many current CSB students do not. They will casually mention that they stayed overnight with a boyfriend at SJU or that they're taking birth control pills, for example. Some also dress in body-hugging and revealing ways. It's the style, of course; it's also very different from the women of 1913 or 1953. As the larger American culture has changed from pre-Oprah to post-Oprah, so has the campus culture. Americans generally have learned how to talk differently and how to talk about subjects that once seemed too intimate, too personal. In 1957—when the college was just 50 years old—Americans

Every woman over the age of 25 can understand the complexity of sexual issues and body image. It's easy to identify and sympathize with those who struggle with these issues. But tattoos? Talk about a generation gap!

Once the body markings of sailors and circus women, tattoos are now "gentrified" and "feminized" and meaningful, the work of body artists. CSB students describe their "tatts" as a special way of telling their stories, marking transitions, registering special relationships.

"Scars with a story," one 2012 student calls them. Her stories include a phoenix on her ankle to signify her rebirth after a particularly difficult period in her life. Two roses and a hummingbird represent her maternal ancestors. "To Thine Own Self Be True" reminds her of her study in London and her commitment to being herself. Another student of the class of 2013 is inscribed with a rhetorical "Why Not?" to commemorate her survival of something she otherwise keeps to herself. Another Bennie and her sister have matching tattoos. A sociology major, class of 2012, reflects, "My body used to be just like everyone else's, but now it is covered with art." She has seven tattoos and plans to get more. Each student interviewed for this project described her tattoos as a way of expressing herself, of being different from the rest, of standing out, of saying her piece. Earlier in Saint Ben's history, women spoke of their lives with their words. Now these and dozens of other women on campus have taken to speaking with their bodies.

were titillated, scandalized, by *Peyton Place*. S. Mariella Gable and S. Kristin Malloy were banished over *Catcher in the Rye*. In 2013, the year of the Saint Ben's 100th anniversary, *Fifty Shades of Grey* has been on the *New York Times* bestseller list for more than a year. Memoir constitutes an especially popular genre of contemporary literature. We want to know about the insides of other people's lives, and we want to show our own.

For much of the 19th and 20th centuries, the ideal American woman was "disembodied." Like Cather's town girls, they tried to make their bodies small and frail. To be weak was a mark of femininity. To be sexually passionate was to be unladylike (or worse). To be

Baseball player, 1977

hearty—like Cather's country girls—was to be less feminine. Aspects of these values and ideas still paralyze and limit many women. Body-image problems plague them. Many of us still "throw like a girl," a phenomenon that one scholar suggests is the result of inability to be fully in one's body (divided between throwing and watching oneself throw).

CSB has for all its history focused on a student's intellect, moral compass, and spiritual life. That's what college is/was supposed to do. CSB has done it well—just look at its alumnae. It has from its start required that women be physically active as well. Like most American Catholics and American women, the members of the CSB community have held ambivalent ideas about the right balance, the right relationship between mind and body. Though Catholics have had enormous regard for the Body of Christ, that body and that flesh have been symbolic and metaphorical, not corporeal. CSB women of the most recent generation have discovered their bodies in a new way and are living more "embodied" lives. Sometimes those bodies cause them pain (eating disorders), sometimes they cause confusion or confusing pleasure (sex), sometimes they tell stories (with tattoos), and sometimes those bodies take them to the NCAA finals.

The College of Saint Benedict that walks confidently, with vigor and purpose, into its second century is led by strong, challenging women. It is as it should be!

Bonnies and Jennies

When I joined the SJU faculty in 1980, I didn't know much about Saint Ben's and nothing about the relationship of the two institutions. I'd grown up Catholic and attended a Catholic grade and high school so I did know about Fr. Godfrey Diekmann, who had played a role at the Second Vatican Council, and about *Worship,* a magazine edited at SJU, that championed liturgical changes that my guitar-strumming friends and I appreciated.

Most significantly, I did not know how good CSB was and had been for a long time.

I knew about Saint Ben's only through her alumnae, especially "Mrs. Hough," my mother's best friend, and her daughter Mary Ellen, one of my high school friends, both of whom loved CSB with a devotion that I do not feel for my own undergraduate college. Don't get me wrong, I had had a terrific experience at Southwest Minnesota State College—amazing teachers, life-changing classes, formational relationships. I donate to the college and happily keep up on college news in the alumni newsletter. What I don't share but what so many CSB grads do, is an intense sense of community, a strong bond to other alums, lifelong friendships, that deep emotional tie to the college. I envy it slightly, I admit.

Jean, as Mrs. Hough invited me to call her when I turned 21 (I never did, she was always Mrs. Hough), attended CSB only briefly in the late 1930s and did not graduate, as was the case with many students of her generation, but she attended every reunion she could manage for the next 50 years. She was thrilled when I joined the SJU faculty, even if it was second best! In 2011 I was thrilled to meet up with Mary Ellen at her 40th class reunion, faithful like her mother and still close to so many of her classmates.

If, in 1980, I had been hired at the College of Saint Benedict, I'd have entered the same department that I entered as an SJU employee and had the same colleagues, but my experience of CSB/SJU would have been different. At CSB I'd have been part of a predominantly female faculty. The president and most of the administration and trustees were female. I would have taught female students primarily, meeting curriculum

Me in the early 1980s

requirements designed specifically for them. My office would have been in St. Joe in one of the converted student rooms in the Rotunda. I'd have attended college meetings that included only CSB faculty and professional staff. I'd have been paid less with significantly fewer benefits and had access to fewer faculty development funds. I'd have spent a good part of my off-campus time explaining where Saint Ben's was and having to identify it in relation to Saint John's.

As it was, my morning routine included a cup of coffee in the faculty lounge on the second floor of the Quadrangle in Collegeville, where a coterie of male colleagues met up before class. The regulars included many Saint John's alums, who generally called each other by last name. They didn't know what to call me. They amused each other (and me) with lore of the old days, tales of colorful teachers or prefects, of Fr. Martin Schirber (economics), Fr. Ernest Kilzer (philosophy), and Steve Humphrey (English). The faculty (on both campuses) tended to stay forever, so alums had the happy experience of knowing many of the same people.

As a newcomer in my first full-time teaching job out of graduate school, I was plenty busy, so I didn't pay much attention to questions of identity or location (or pay or benefits, for that matter). I did feel the powerful maleness of Saint John's. I was one of about a dozen women on a faculty of about 120 men. I taught classes full of men (in my second year I had a total of 10 female students all year). I quickly took up with two of those dozen female colleagues: Janet McNew (English) and Linda Hansen (philosophy). I also made friends with the army of women secretaries, support staff, and cleaners at SJU. Oh, how I came to depend on them: Lynda Fish Bennetts and Pam Reding in the Academic Affairs office; Maxine Richmond and Chris Poff in the Christian Humanism office; Jane Opitz who ran the Writing Center; Nita Jo Rush and Barb Peterson who worked in Counseling and Career Services; Connie Miller in the library; and Delphine Stotz, who cleaned the Quad offices.

I don't mean that my male colleagues weren't extraordinarily valuable and helpful because they were—Bob Spaeth, Dave Bennetts, Joe Friedrich, Ken Jones, Ernie Diedrich, Lee Hanley, Fr. Ray Pedrizetti, and Fr. Rene McGraw especially—but that being female made the Saint John's waters a little chilly and choppy and left me feeling like I often rocked the boat. There was so much I didn't "get." It took me an embarrassingly long time, for example, to learn how Saint John's humor worked and to feel teasing as affection.

I was struck by what seemed like class differences between SJU and CSB. The Benedicta Arts Center was (and is) a fine venue for the arts, from the Theater Department productions to the Minnesota Orchestra. Otherwise, facilities at Saint John's dwarfed in size and expense everything else at Saint Ben's. The Marcel Breuer church, library, and science and monastic buildings, then residence halls had in the 1960s transformed the small, red-brick Saint John's campus into a showplace for modern architecture and an important Minnesota tourist site.

SJU also spent two years renovating the oldest building on campus—the Quadrangle—which reopened in the fall of 1980. In line with the Breuer aesthetic, the walls had been taken back to the original brick. Big oak doors and desks, made in the Saint John's woodworking shop from locally harvested wood, contributed both to the beauty and the rich feel of the place. The Henrita Academic Building at CSB, by contrast, one of the newest buildings on campus looked like the high school it once had been. The desks were leftovers too, and had never been good desks to begin with (much too small for athletic women and men). When Saint John's faculty members attended events at Saint Ben's—less often than Saint Ben's people went to Saint John's—they expressed their disdain for CSB's weak coffee and bad wine. To my feminist soul, all of this felt awkward, at best, or downright painful.

Was I teaming up with the oppressors by being at SJU and, especially, by loving my office? I didn't join in the "even the wine is better at SJU" chorus, but I did love Saint John's. Would I be a better feminist if I were unhappy at SJU? But I *was* unhappy in some ways. Very confusing.

Janet, Linda, and our fourth musketeer, Joan Steck, in Media and

Communication, secured faculty development funds to organize a series of discussions called *Listening to Women's Voices—Women on a Men's
College Campus*. CSB faculty and staff members were invited, and some
significant issues about women and men surfaced, but many of them
were campus specific. My problem with the three locker rooms at the
Saint John's Palestra—Men, Women, and Faculty—and with the men-only
sauna didn't resonate much at CSB. Neither did my irritation that so
few people could seem to tell Janet and me apart (despite differences
in our hair color and weight and accents). We took to calling ourselves
"Janette" as a slightly bitter joke. These and more serious forms of invisibility troubled us (no wonder we became trouble-makers and loud
talkers!). Raising these issues irritated nearly as many people, it seemed,
as it sensitized, but discussing them made it possible for the women at
Saint John's to find each other, to make common cause, and to survive.

That I was a woman complicated my life at SJU. That I was at SJU
complicated my relationship with CSB. S. Linda Kulzer, the CSB academic vice president, responded cooly when I objected to her formula-
tion that CSB cared about the education of women and SJU about the
education of men. I cared about the education of women and I was SJU
(this felt like another version of that invisibility that had already troubled
me). As I hadn't understood some of the Saint John's culture, I also mis-
stepped a few times at CSB, especially in speaking my mind, as CSB culture favored indirection.

The CSB version of feminism wasn't mine. The strong focus on wom-
en's spirituality at CSB made enormous sense, but it was unfamiliar to
me. And so I learned quickly about Boston College theologian and "radical feminist" Mary Daly, whose books *God the Father: Toward a Philosophy of
Women's Liberation* (1973) and *Gyn/Ecology: The Metaethics of Radical Feminism*
(1978) rattled many religious cages and excited many at CSB. As one re-
viewer wrote, *God the Father* offered not only "a critique of the sexism of
the Christian faith. It was also an attempt to articulate an alternative
faith, the faith of feminism."[1] Many CSB women—including some OSBs—
found this deeply compelling. I felt it less so.

For a long time, it seemed, I felt odd and a bit out of place on both
campuses. Things changed for me and my relationship with CSB when
Carol Gilligan's *In a Different Voice* was published in 1993, and members of

both faculties talked about "women's ways of knowing." Increasingly, we explored the huge educational and academic ramifications of a feminist perspective.

I especially found common cause and made friends with Ozzie Mayers (English) who was a member of the CSB faculty, a man on a women's college campus. (We could identify with each other.) He and I and a small group of CSB and SJU faculty applied successfully for a Fund for the Improvement of Postsecondary Education (FIPSE) grant to "Engender the Curriculum." This grant allowed feminists on both campuses to focus on getting women authors and issues and perspectives into the curriculum. This grant fed eventually into the formation of a gender requirement in the curriculum, the formation of a Gender and Women's Studies program, then a minor and eventually a major. Ozzie and others also focused specifically on Men's Studies and, with Gar Kellom, the vice-president for student affairs, instituted an annual Men's Studies Conference, and created a conversation about men as men.

Upon Saint Ben's 100th anniversary, I am 33 years away from my original impressions. A few things have stayed the same: In 2013 I'm still in the Quadrangle at Saint John's—just three doors away from the office I moved into in 1980. Ken Jones and Dave Bennetts and I are the only members of the CSB/SJU History Department still at Saint John's. The rest have moved to Richarda Hall at CSB. Our new officemates—Jean Keller and Chuck Wright—are philosophers. After officing 15-plus years at CSB, they've moved to SJU. We are all part of a reshuffling of departmental locations. We've found over the years that dividing departments has negative effects—difficulty of communicating, absence of community, division of departmental resources. The natural sciences have long since learned this lesson. The faculties of the humanities and social sciences are in the process. The long-range plan for CSB/SJU projects the physical joining of most departments, timing depending mostly on the construction and renovation of buildings. The new History Department offices are in what once was a CSB dormitory.

Where once I identified myself as from Saint John's, I now say I'm from CSB/SJU. People unfamiliar with the workings of the two schools often presume that, as a woman, I'm on the CSB faculty. I don't correct them.

After meeting separately for many years, the two faculties began to meet together but vote separately. Eventually we met and voted together, making sure we alternated campuses for meetings. Now there's a single faculty senate, and the chair position rotates from campus to campus.

As long as each college remains legally separate and faculty members are hired by one or the other—which is still the case—the process for review and tenure (and approval by the trustees) continues to be separate. The two rank-and-tenure committees, however, report to a single chief academic officer—the provost—who recommends tenure and promotion to two boards of trustees.

There are other pockets of separation—parking permits, bill-paying practices, Christmas parties, teaching prizes (one named after a CSB person, one after an SJU person). Some of these are annoying, but all are manageable.

Students, too, live with campus differences. Locked/unlocked doors, women's/men's spirituality groups, faculty residents/residence directors, CSB Senate/ SJU Senate, who gets first reservations at the Thanksgiving dinner, who is more willing to take the bus, which has the better coffee.

One odd consequence of the continued legal separation of the two colleges is that at the beginning and end of the students' time in college, we separate them. On the first day of class each campus offers an opening convocation. A CSB faculty member addresses the incoming students at CSB. A SJU faculty member addresses the incoming students at SJU.

The students also graduate separately—on Saturday at CSB and on Sunday at SJU. The students march in, clad in caps and gowns, without each other. There's not enough room for the CSB seniors to attend the SJU ceremonies. Students belong to separate alum associations, and the two colleges hold their reunions separately, too—CSB in the summer and SJU in the fall. As more and more students identify as CSB/SJU students and graduates, these artificial separations might fade, too.

Once we go into the classroom, from a curricular point of view, the separateness falls away. Yes, there are differences between the CSB and the SJU students—or are they differences between women and men? There are also differences between "gamers" and "study-ers," drinkers and teetotalers, Californians and Minnesotans and Bahamians, between Chinese Americans and Hmong Americans? Once in class, though, we're all together.

In the early 1980s, Prof. Bob Fulton (chemistry) took on coordinating the move from separate college requirements to a common core curriculum. He led the two faculties through that process for nearly five years. Students came and went and kingdoms rose and fell in the time we took to agree to a common and joint curriculum. Fulton took us from being two distinct faculty groups to as close as we could be to one faculty. The genius of the exercise is that it asked all of the faculty members to focus not on the two colleges or on one college or the other but on the students, on our common enterprise. No meeting schedule favored one campus over the other. Everything was repeated, then said again, so no one was left out or behind. No faculty group is ever quick to change, especially in regard to curriculum, but even many of us were crying "uncle!" toward the end of the process. But getting to a joint curriculum that we all "owned" required that.

We're the better for it. Students navigate their campus/college differences as they do other variations among them. They make friends (and enemies) and study groups out of each other, and they know how to work together. They think of themselves as Bennies and Johnnies, for sure, but increasingly as Jennies and Bonnies!

We somehow make the whole complicated, complex enterprise work. CSB and SJU have not merged. Neither is coed. Neither has collapsed. Neither has partnered with another school. Both have survived. For people who believe in the Holy Trinity, the idea of two in one isn't all that hard to comprehend.

Afterword

by MaryAnn Baenninger

I write this afterword on April 8, 2013. Margaret Thatcher, Britain's first (and only) female prime minister, died today. The news is filled with stories of Thatcher and with speculation that former U.S. Senator and Secretary of State Hillary Rodham Clinton will make a second run for president in 2016. Christine Lagarde, the managing director of the International Monetary Fund, figures highly in the attempted resolution of the continuing economic crises in Europe in the aftermath of the Great Recession. Yesterday, the news included the sad announcement that a young U.S. diplomat, Anne Smedinghoff, was killed by terrorists as she took time from her daily work in Afghanistan to deliver donated books to children. We also saw news footage of former Secretary of State Condoleezza Rice playing golf for the first time at Augusta National, a formerly all-male bastion, where she is one of the first two women—and the first African American woman—to have been admitted. Very recently, Julia Pierson was sworn in as the first female director of the U.S. Secret Service. Closer to home, Minneapolis was named one of the best cities in America for women entrepreneurs.

It is now a matter of course that women appear in the news in roles—powerful, happy, and sad—that were previously reserved for men. But if you are reading this book at the time of the College of Saint Benedict's centennial, you also know that questions of true equality for women, here and around the world, are still the source of much debate. A few weeks after its publication, Sheryl Sandberg's book, *Lean In: Women,*

Work, and the Will to Lead, mentioned here in the *Foreword,* has become a cult piece and/or a lighting rod for those on various sides of the debate about whether women have full equality today, and if they do not, about whose responsibility it is.

Sandberg's thesis, essentially, is that women must take more responsibility for their own equality, their representation in positions of leadership, and their acquisition of power. She does not blame women, nor does she believe that women should opt out of traditional roles. She also understands implicitly, and explains explicitly, how society continues to pressure women into making certain conscious and unconscious choices. Nevertheless, whatever the cause, she believes it will take the actions of women themselves to actively break through this cycle.

The historical record, rightly, focuses on the successes and the struggles that the college had on the way to being fully responsible for its own destiny. In this afterword I focus on what the College of Saint Benedict looks like today and its recent accomplishments.

To me, this notion of responsibility for one's own destiny is an essential purpose of a college for women. I had the honor of speaking at the inauguration of Elizabeth (Beth) A. Dinndorf, Bennie, class of '73, and the 18th president of Columbia College, a women's college in South Carolina.

I spoke in part about the role of women's colleges:

> At Columbia College and my own institution, College of Saint
> Benedict, we are also faced with the misperception that unique
> opportunities for women's education are no longer necessary . . . .
> I say simply, "access does not equal success." What I mean by
> this is that roughly 50 years of nearly universal coeducation has
> not produced a woman president of the United States. It has not
> produced equal pay for equal work. It has not produced work
> environments and expectations that are conducive to raising
> a family—for women or for men. And it has not unshackled
> women or men from the bonds of society's expectations.
>
> Perhaps if there were as many colleges for women today as

there were 50 years ago we would have broken those barriers and many others by now.

Clearly the work of colleges for women is not done; that is one of the things that compelled me to come to Saint Ben's in 2004.

This afterword gives me a chance to describe further the College of Saint Benedict today, which differs markedly in many ways (though never at the heart of the mission) from the College of Saint Benedict of the past. I hope that this accounting of where we are today is evidence that pushing Saint Ben's to be its best has been the right way.

Presidents Love Buildings

Despite my acquired love of buildings and construction, deep in my heart I know that it is not the buildings themselves, but what happens in them that is at the core of an educational enterprise. Buildings have always figured highly at Saint Ben's, more often for what they represent, than as entities unto themselves. There are particular buildings that punctuate the history of the college and that serve as markers of important college events and changes.

In the Main Building and its constituent buildings one sees the rich history of the sisters, their glorious successes, their triumphs over adversity, and the evolution of the college, like the age rings on an ancient tree. Alumnae can tell many a story about living and studying here. This building is alive, well, and cherished, and it is the place where most of the administrative team and I make our professional homes. But it is no longer the place where our students eat and socialize over meals.

Facilities for hospitality and stewardship. In 2007, the Gorecki Dining and Conference Center became the social hub of the campus. This venue, named for Ben and Dorothy Gorecki, longtime friends and benefactors of the college, serves more than one thousand meals per day to Bennies and Johnnies, and has made its mark on our campuses as "the" place to eat, and as a leader in sustainability and healthy eating. The upstairs at the Gorecki is where we congregate for celebrations, milestone events, and stimulating talks and presentations, and where we welcome the community at large to our campus to host wedding receptions, corporate events, and civic meetings. We miss the old Café in the Main Building, but the spirit of community and togetherness that exemplified the Café is alive and well in the Gorecki.

A building with the arts at its heart. When the Benedicta Arts Center (BAC) was finished in 1964, it was an audacious undertaking for the sisters and it deservedly became renowned as one of the finest performing arts centers in the Midwest. When we substantially expanded the BAC in 2006, we knew we had to live up to this reputation. The building now directly serves dozens of faculty members and hundreds of Bennies and Johnnies majoring or performing in the arts, and within its five performance venues the BAC provides exceptional entertainment to the rest of our campus community and all of central Minnesota. It has received awards from the American Institute of Architects, the International Interior Design Association, and the Society for College and University Planning. Our students pack the more than 1,000 seats in Escher Auditorium (named after S. Firmin Escher) for Saint Ben's annual opening convocation.

Living in community. The College of Saint Benedict campus has expanded east over the past decade. The empty fields on College Avenue that many alumnae may remember are now home to Renner House and Centennial Commons. Renner, the president's residence, named after S. Emmanuel Renner, was completed in 2005, and was financed entirely through the generosity of anonymous donors. My husband Ron Baenninger and I are fortunate to be the first residents of this wonderful home that serves as an intimate gathering space for college conversations and celebrations of faculty, staff, students, alumnae, and friends. Ron is also the first president's husband to reside on campus!

Centennial Commons, completed in 2012, is home to 124 senior women. The townhouse residence complex, with buildings named after S. Lois Wedl, S. Cecilia Kapsner, S. Mary David Olheiser and S. Mary Anthony Wagner, was awarded LEED Platinum Certification for its sustainable features. Its front porches, individual bedrooms, and open plan kitchen and living spaces provide a true homelike atmosphere for our students. The only complaint about this facility is that all of our senior women cannot live there.

The Promise of a More Diverse Community

All college presidents have particular passions or, some would say, fixations. Mine is creating and nurturing a more diverse community. I am a white woman who was born and raised in Philadelphia, a thriving city where whites make up only 39 percent of the population. Coming to central Minnesota for me was culture shock in many ways, and the lack of racial diversity was one of them. But I found Saint Ben's to be a welcoming environment that truly recognized the value of diversity. It was eager to make that welcoming spirit a reality. I found that my personal experiences could help make our aspirations come true in part because I was not afraid to really talk about diversity.

Numbers never tell the story of a diverse community. They are merely a representation of a start, of a commitment. It is the actions and the behaviors of a community that tell the tale. We do know, however, that 52 percent of babies born today in the United States are not white. Fifty-two percent is, by definition, not a minority. We must look to the future and ensure that when these children enter college, we are welcoming, and we are equally likely to enroll all of them and serve them well, regardless of race or ethnicity.

In 2004 when I arrived, College of Saint Benedict's entering first-year class included 4.6 percent American students of color. In 2012–2013, 16 percent of our first-year students are American students of color. Our nascent success in recruiting students of color began with a program called Intercultural LEAD (Leadership, Education, and Development). This program, for high-achieving first-generation students who have demonstrated leadership potential in high school, is not explicitly for students of color, but the overwhelming majority of students in the program are of color. Because these students excel in leadership and are deeply engaged in campus activities, their presence has had a transformational impact. It has been one of my great joys to form what I hope will be lifelong friendships with the early graduates of this program.

We have much work to do toward achieving the goal of a fully diverse community, particularly in the area of recruiting and nurturing a diverse faculty and staff, but we are committed and moving forward. History will show that the last decade of the first century of the College was a pivotal time for Saint Ben's in this regard, and I will consider this to be one of my greatest leadership successes.

Academics and Accolades

It is impossible to cite all of the accomplishments of our faculty, staff, and students in the last decade of the first century. Here I list only a few, and for the most part I focus on those that most exemplify the College of Saint Benedict and its people at this point in our history. While a few of these cite one individual, each is a team effort in some way: a student has faculty mentors who supported her, faculty and staff join together to help us reach an institutional goal, and the administrative staff always works as a team. Lastly, the institutional accomplishments of CSB and SJU are always intertwined, but this is CSB's history, so here I focus on those accomplishments for which the College of Saint Benedict, my team, or our students can claim a particularly important leadership role. I also resort to a bulleted list to highlight each individually.

- A *Phi Beta Kappa* chapter was awarded to College of Saint Benedict/Saint John's University in 2009.
- College of Saint Benedict/Saint John's University was recognized for its leadership in comprehensive internationalization with the Senator Paul Simon Award in 2012.
- The Intercultural LEAD Fellows Program for first generation students, instituted in 2005, attracts historic numbers of underrepresented students.
- The MapCores (Mathematics, Physics, Computer Science Research Scholars) program, begun in 2009, and funded by the National Science Foundation and the Hearst Foundation, attracts academically gifted, primarily first-generation women to mathematics, physics, computer science, and pre-engineering programs
- The FoCuS (Future Chemists Scholarships and Support) program, begun in 2012, and funded by the National Science Foundation, attracts academically gifted women and students of color to the chemistry program.

- College of Saint Benedict was named to the President of the United States' Community Service Honor Roll with distinction, 2011, 2012, 2013.
- College of Saint Benedict was named a *U.S. News and World Report* "Up and Coming" institution, one that others look to for strong and innovative programming, 2010, 2011, 2013.
- Student Stephanie Wegmann '10 was awarded a Pickering Fellowship.
- Student Rachel Mullin '14 was awarded a Truman Fellowship.

Catholic and Benedictine Identity

The College of Saint Benedict rejoices in its Benedictine heritage and all the sisters have done for the college, all they have taught us, and all of the support they have provided. We live the Benedictine values, or, at least, aspire to live them to the fullest extent possible. The Benedictine values provide a compass for decision-making, a roadmap for sustaining the college, and a spirit of community that I have never experienced before and will never experience again in my life. All who are touched by Benedictine life are forever changed for the better. That is most certainly true of our students and alumnae. Our surveys show that regardless of their own faith traditions, the Benedictine ethos of Saint Ben's and the values themselves have a profound impact on the lives of Bennies.

At our centennial, we are blessed with a wonderful prioress, S. Michaela Hedican. Michaela is strong, wise, resilient, warm and generous with her time and talent. She and I have become fast friends and confidants and I am pleased and grateful to have her by my side as we begin our second century. I was also privileged to serve alongside Prioress Ephrem Hollermann, who was a great mentor and friend to me when as a novice president I desperately needed both, and Prioress Nancy Bauer, whose wit, wisdom, and expertise in canon law were always welcome.

We are equally strong in our Catholic identity, our Catholic ethos, and our commitment to the Catholic intellectual and social justice traditions. Saint Ben's is infused with our Catholic heritage and myriad opportunities abound for our students to grow in their faith. There are fewer Catholics among our student body than in the past. At our centennial about 60 percent of our students are Catholic. We take care to welcome all students in the Benedictine—and Catholic—tradition, and to ensure they feel at home in Catholic worship, in campus ministry programs, and in our theology courses.

It would be disingenuous to say that leading a Catholic institution at this time in history is easy. The Church struggles with so many issues, issues on which the faithful of good conscience are divided. These issues play out openly at Saint Ben's and Saint John's, frankly, as they should. We hold our heads high and endeavor to remain true to both our Catholic identity and the intellectual and academic freedom that a liberal arts college demands. We are very lucky to have the Benedictine perspective to guide us in this important task.

College of Saint Benedict/Saint John's University, Bennies and Johnnies, Equal Partners

Many of the stories within this book speak directly or indirectly to the relationship and partnership between Saint Ben's and Saint John's, and the sisters and the monks. Neither of our communities' stories exists without the other. And that is as it should be. The coordinate relationship today, as it has been for 50 years, is the key sustaining force of our two institutions. As I said in my inaugural address in 2005, "Without each other, we would be nothing." I was referring both to interpersonal relationships and to the relationship between Saint Ben's and Saint John's. We cannot move together in strength if one institution is perceived to be, or is, weaker than the other.

When I came to Saint Ben's, we needed to live our own motto, *Sic Luceat Lux Vestra, "Let Your Light Shine."* It was a time for Saint Ben's to get stronger and to assert where it was already strong, to the benefit of Saint Ben's and the Saint Ben's and Saint John's partnership.

Over the years I have seen dozens of peoples' faces express incredulity when they learn that CSB enrolls more students than SJU. This becomes humorous at times when they tell me, "No, you must be wrong about that!"

Recently, someone asked me if Saint Ben's has a basketball team!

For the record, Blazer Basketball, under the coaching expertise of Mike Durbin, two-time NCAA Coach of the Year, has won the Minnesota Intercollegiate Athletic Conference 13 times, and has gone to the NCAA playoffs 16 times. Our volleyball team has made several NCAA appearances as well.

College of Saint Benedict student-athletes have been recognized for their success both on the playing field and in the classroom. In fall 2012, the National Collegiate Scouting Association honored CSB among the 10th annual collegiate power rankings. The Blazers were one of just three women's colleges to make the list, and one of just two in the Division III rankings.

I bring up these examples because they so strikingly show how misconceptions live a very long life. Women's colleges today still labor under many of the patriarchal ideas that they have throughout their history. This is not about patriarchy from SJU; this is about patriarchy from society at large. One result is that Bennies sometimes feel that they need to describe Saint Ben's by first describing Saint John's. My hope is as we enter the next century that our students and alumnae are confident in describing Saint Ben's by describing its own strengths, one of which is our great partnership with SJU.

Data show that women must work harder and accomplish more to be given the same credit as men, that women are less confident in their talents than are men, and that women are less willing to tout their own accomplishments than men.

These disparities must change. It doesn't matter what career (inside or outside the home) that women choose, it doesn't matter whether they choose to be mothers and leaders, mothers or leaders, or to be engaged citizens who chose to contribute by following. We must offer equal opportunity and encouragement to women (and men) to make these choices.

It is my firm belief—and under my leadership we have expressed this in our actions—that Saint Ben's must practice what it preaches for women, and it must exemplify true self-determination *and* true partnership.

This, indeed, is where we are in the coordinate relationship at College of Saint Benedict's centennial. I have been fortunate to work with four SJU presidents during my presidency. I wish Michael Hemesath '81, SJU's first permanent lay president, a very long and fruitful tenure. We

see eye-to-eye on most important things, and we are of a similar generation (though I am a bit older, I admit ruefully). We both have experience
in a world where women often lead. That is a characteristic that was not
always part of the colleges' history.

I am grateful, too, to Dan Whalen, who graciously stepped up to lead
at a time when SJU really needed him, and to Fr. Bob Koopmann, who
played the pivotal role of leading SJU through its corporate restructur-
ing in 2012. I miss deeply Br. Dietrich Reinhart who was an excellent
partner, mentor, and dear friend. Peace to you, Dietrich, it was grand!

Model Leadership

Saint Ben's is nearing completion of its second strategic plan since I
arrived on campus. Strategic Directions 2015 has eight components.
Most of them focus on the core mission of the college, teaching and
learning. One component, *Model Leadership,* speaks to how those of us
in leadership positions fulfill our roles as servant leaders. I believe that
Saint Ben's is the strongest that it has ever been.

Leadership by its essence means to move forward, to reach, dream,
and to grow. At its centennial, Saint Ben's benefits from the strength of
all the leaders who went before.

History owes a debt of thanks to the "modern" presidents, the
ones who provided the foundation on which I and my team have been
able to lead: Drs. Stanley Idzerda, S. Emmanuel Renner, S. Colman
O'Connell, Mary Lyons, and Carol Guardo. To President Guardo,
I owe personal gratitude. She served as my "guardian angel" during
her interim presidency. Every action she took was to pave the way for
the new, as yet unknown president, and my leadership benefited enormously from her preparation.

The history should also acknowledge the strength and commitment of the College of Saint Benedict Board of Trustees and its current
chair, Lynn Newman '79. There are more alumnae board members
than ever before and a strong collection of men, too, some Johnnies
and some Bennie dads, all equally committed and professionally and
personally engaged in ensuring that Saint Ben's will soar.

Last, but certainly not least, history will show that the "Centennial

Cabinet," the members of the CSB leadership team, were essential to both creating the Saint Ben's of today and paving the way for the Saint Ben's of the future in 2113. I know that their names will go down in history, but I leave nothing to chance. I offer love and deepest gratitude to the "Centennial Cabinet": Rita Knuesel '75, Sue Palmer, Mary Geller, Kim Ferlaak Motes '89, Jon McGee '84, Cal Mosley, Joe DesJardins, Anne Oberman, '82, Brad Sinn, Jody Terhaar, Kathryn Enke '05, and Diane Hageman.

Let Our Light Shine into the Second Century

The College of Saint Benedict's history is characterized by a fierce belief in the power of liberal arts education, an engagement with the world around us, responsiveness to the needs of society, an enduring commitment to our Catholic and Benedictine heritage, and an unwavering focus on women's development as leaders, professionals, and scholars. During this, our centennial year, we celebrate our first century, a century of connection, and we eagerly commence into our next 100 years in women's education with vision, imagination and joy. We have come far—from a quiet college on the open prairie to a nationally recognized, top-ranked institution, home to 2,100 students and 20,000 alumnae who are prepared to see the world, identify its great needs and conquer them. We envision our future as grounded in the same commitments as our founding community, and like our foremothers, we embrace the changes and challenges impacting the world with the same courage, strength and boldness. *Sic Luceat Lux Vestra.*

MaryAnn Baenninger
President
College of Saint Benedict
Saint Joseph, Minnesota
April 8, 2013

Notes

Preface and Acknowledgments

1. The sisters worked to convert and educate Native Americans to Euro-American "civilization" and religion at Minnesota's White Earth (Saint Benedict's Mission) and Red Lake (St. Mary's Mission) Ojibwe reservations and at Onamia (Little Flower Mission). Only later in the 20th century did they realize that no matter how well-intentioned their effort, the imposition of Euro-American culture was damaging to Native American children. After much soul-searching, the sisters apologized, and they are working to repair their relations with native communities.

2. Barbara Miller Solomon, *In the Company of Educated Women: A History of Women and Higher Education in America* (New Haven, CT: Yale University Press, 1985), xix.

1. We Are Bennies: CSB at 100

1. Irene Harwarth, Mindi Maline, Elizabeth DeBra, *Women's Colleges in the United States: History, Issues, and Challenges* (Washington: U.S. Department of Education, 1997). See: http://womenscolleges.org/about/history. Accessed March 6, 2013. Between June and October 1968, 64 women's colleges closed or went coed.

2. M. Grace McDonald, O.S.B., *With Lamps Burning* (St. Joseph, Minn.: Saint Benedict's Priory Press, 1957).

3. See *US News and World Report,* "Up-and-Coming Schools," at http://colleges.usnews.rankingsandreviews.com/best-colleges/rankings/national-liberal-arts-colleges/up-and-coming. Accessed March 6, 2013.

4. MaryAnn Baenninger and Dietrich Reinhart, "Presidents in Action," *Presidency* 9 (Fall 2006); MaryAnn Baenninger, "Institutional Strength: From CAO/CFO Partnerships," *University Business* 12 (October 1, 2009); MaryAnn Baenninger, "For Women on Campuses, Access Doesn't Equal Success," *Chronicle of Higher Education* 58 (October 7, 2011).

5. New Advent, "Pope Pius X," *Catholic Encyclopedia,* at http://www .newadvent.org/cathen/12137a.htm. Accessed March 6, 2013.

6. Thank you to Annette Hendrick for her e-mail of March 6, 2013, about her and her classmates' experiences in that first year of study abroad programs.

7. http://www.csbsju.edu/IPR/Strategic-Directions.htm. Accessed March 12, 2013.

Mother Benedicta Riepp and Abbot Boniface Wimmer

1. M. Incarnata Girgen, OSB, *Behind the Beginnings: Benedictine Women in America* (St. Joseph: Saint Benedict's Convent, 1981) uses the letters exchanged among the many actors in this drama to show the fullness of the dispute between Benedicta and Boniface. She makes clear that the money, though significant, was only a small consequence of a disagreement also "touched on matters dealing with the whole of religious life." The resolution of the dispute between these two enormously powerful—and equally headstrong—people of faith changed the relationship between the American sisters and their Bavarian motherhouse and ultimately put the sisters under the control of the local bishops. See pp. xii, 86–87.

2. Benedicta Riepp, "Mother Benedicta Riepp Defends Nuns' Autonomy," in Mark Stephen Massa and Catherine Osborne, eds., *American Catholic History: A Documentary Reader* (New York: New York University Press, 2008), 39. Girgen, *Behind the Beginnings,* 118.

3. In his history of Saint John's, *Worship and Work,* Fr. Colman Barry tells the story of the "stolen" florins and a bit of the story of the challenge of authority. Calling it a "faux pas," even the "most auspicious faux pas of his life," however, could not have salved any lingering wounds over the affair. (p. 82) At the 150th anniversary of Saint John's Abbey the sisters of the Saint Benedict's Monastery agreed that they would no longer tell the story. They would bury it as their gift. For many years, however, the sisters had been only one set of storytellers. Some of the lay faculty members have helped keep the story alive. Many job applicants tell of hearing a version of the Saint-John's-stole-Saint-Ben's-money story during interviews. Interestingly, students don't

tell or even seem to know the story. If, as historians all know, every story has a meaning and a purpose, it's worth meditating on why this one continues to be meaningful.

2. Here We Come, Ready or Not!

1. S. Claudette Scoblic, majoring in math, entered late but was the first graduate. The students varied in their postcollege paths, too. Josephine Misho remained in St. Joseph as S. Olivette, teaching math and secondary education. Margaret Grant clerked in the Hennepin County Treasurer's Office. Josephine Skluzacek became a nurse and worked in St. Paul before marrying Bartlett Corser. Helen McDonald taught public school in Eau Claire. Esther Mueller married Martin Linnemann and stayed in St. Joe. Margaret McKeon moved back home. See *College Days,* 1923, p. 94.

2. American bishops "saw a fundamental split," historian Philip Gleason reports, "between the Catholic view and the secular view" in America generally, and in the public schools especially, Protestantism had to be resisted. Gleason, "Baltimore III and Education," *U.S. Catholic Historian,* 4:3/4 (1985), 276.

3. "God made me. God made me to know, love and serve Him in this world, and to be happy with him in the next"—that last phrase about being happy with him was an addition by the time my generation came along.

4. Here and below, Carol K. Coburn and Martha Smith, *Spirited Lives: How Nuns Shaped Catholic Culture and American Life, 1836–1920* (Durham: University of North Caroling Press, 1999), 131–34.

5. Merrill E. Jarchow, *Private Liberal Arts Colleges in Minnesota: Their History and Contributions* (St. Paul: MHS Press, 1973), 16.

6. S. Kathleen Kalinowski has been my main teacher on all things financial about the college. As the longtime community treasurer, she knows where every dollar was buried! I thank her for her generous gifts of time and information.

7. In *Minneapolis Morning Tribune,* O. Terence, "Miss Jane Addams, Greatest American Woman 53 Today," Sept. 6, 1913; "Careers for College Girls Treated in a 'U' Bulletin," Jan. 8, 1913; "Should a Girl Continue to Work after Marriage," March 17, 1913.

8. A few historians of women have begun to integrate the stories of Catholic sisters into the larger account of women in the Progressive Era, but that they have paid little attention to the separate category of "women" and

"women religious." Mary Dillon Foster's remarkable compilation, *Who's Who Among Minnesota Women* (St. Paul, 1924) includes biographies of hundreds of laywomen, including none of women religious.

9. For much information about these early sisters, see McDonald, *With Lamps Burning.*

10. Saint Benedict's College differed from the Seven Sisters in that while the latter recruited male faculty members and in 1910 three of the seven had male presidents, Saint Ben's for its first half-century had almost exclusively female teachers and administrators.

3. A Force of Nature

1. For a fuller story of the mission, see Grace McDonald, *With Lamps Burning,* and the Saint Benedict's Monastery website that includes three videos from the Haehn Museum's 2010 exhibit on the sisters' work in China. See, http://sbm.osb.org/history_haehn_museum. Accessed March 13, 2013.

2. S. Adelgundis Bergman to Aloysius Malloy, OSF, March 1, 1932, Saint Benedict Monastery Archives, 22.4a.2.

3. Jane Lamm Carroll, Joanne Cavallaro, and Sharon Doherty, *Liberating Sanctuary: 100 Years of Women's Education at the College of Saint Catherine* (New York: Lexington, 2011).

4. S. Adelgundis Bergman to S. Aloysius Malloy, OSF, March 1, 1932, SBM Archives (22.4a.2).

5. S. Claire wrote the secretary of North Central about this: Could the college and would North Central consider S. Luann a virtual "doctor," given her vast amount of post-master's coursework? (It would). What about S. Grace McDonald? (Yes)

6. [S. Claire Lynch], "Administrative Reports, 1933–1934," SBM Archives.

7. The most frequently earned major in Saint Ben's first 60 years was English, followed by home economics and sociology. The number of elementary education majors surged from its invention in 1953, in response to state requirements. From 1924 to 1968 the college graduated 368 English majors; from 1953 to 1968 it graduated 480 elementary education majors.

8. Ruth Loving Higgins, review of *The Autobiography of a College* by Edward A. Fitzpatrick and S. Mary Dominic, in *Mississippi Valley Historical Review* 27 (September 1940): 328–29. Stable URL: http://www.jstor.org/stable/1896869. Accessed October 9, 2012.

9. Edward A. Fitzpatrick, "Financial Stewardship," in *Journal of Higher Education,* 2:8 (Nov. 1931), 441–45. Accessed Sept. 5, 2012 at http://www.jstor.org/stable/1974432. "Less Work Offered for College Group," *New York Times,* Nov. 22, 1931, p. 53.

10. S. Claire Lynch, Feb. 16, 1985.

11. *St. Benedict's Quarterly,* April 1934.

12. Eunice Fuller Barnard, "Our College for Women: Co-Ed or Not?" *New York Times,* March 26, 1933, p. SM4.

13. Sherrie A. Inness, *The Lesbian Menace: Ideology, Identity, and the Representation of Lesbian Life* (Amherst: University of Massachusetts Press, 1997), 38.

14. Lillian Faderman, *To Believe in Women: What Lesbians Have Done for America—A History* (New York: Houghton Mifflin, 1999), 235. Helen L. Horowitz, review of *Miss Marks and Miss Woolley,* in *History of Education Quarterly* 20 (Autumn 1980): 337–43, quote from p. 342.

So, Let Your Light Shine on 1957

1. In addition to Benedict, the saints included: Scholastica and Gertrude, Gregory, Bede, Boniface, Alcuin, Anselm, Augustine, Bernard and five others.

2. S. Grace McDonald's *With Lamps Burning,* her centennial history of the religious community in St. Joseph, used this same imagery, so did the college stationary in the 1950s.

3. Angeline Dufner, *So Let Your Light Shine* pamphlet, reprinted from Saint Benedict's Quarterly, June 1957.

4. Dufner, *So Let Your Light Shine.*

4. Everything Was So Clean

1. Lynn D. Gordon, "A Tale of Two 'Sisters'," in *Reviews in American History* 24 (1996), 63.

2. S. Hildegarde Marie, "Objectives of Higher Education for Women in the Light of Papal Teaching," *Bulletin, Catholic Educational Association,* 48 (May 1952).

3. Marie, "Objectives of Higher Education," 18, 21–22.

4. Jane C. Redmont, "Live Minds, Yearning Spirits: The Alumnae of Colleges and Universities Founded by Women Religious," in Tracy Schier and Cynthia Russett, eds., *Catholic Women's Colleges in America* (Baltimore: Johns Hopkins University Press, 2002).

5. Nina Fischer, *How to Help Your Husband Get Ahead,* pamphlet (Garden City, NY: Doubleday, 1964), 25, 28.

6. John Tracy Ellis, in *American Catholics and the Intellectual Life* (Chicago: Heritage Foundation, 1956), 46–47, criticized the habit in Catholic schools of overemphasizing "the school as an agency for moral development, with an insufficient stress on the role of the school as an instrument for fostering intellectual excellence." He continued: "No sensible person will . . . question that the inculcation of moral virtue is one of the principal reasons for having Catholic schools in any circumstances. But that goal should never be permitted to overshadow the fact that the school . . . must maintain a strong emphasis on the cultivation of intellectual excellence." Timothy J. Meagher, "'Never Take Shame in Your Mother Tongue . . . and Your Fatherland in America': Catholic Schools and Immigrants," in John Augenstein, Christopher J. Kauffman and Robert J. Wister, *One Hundred Years of Catholic Education: Historical Essays in Honor of the Centennial of the National Catholic Educational Association* (Washington, DC: NCEA, 2003), 284–85.

7. Redmont, "Live Minds, Yearning Spirits," 220.

8. *The Benet* 20 (October 1954): 1 and special supplement.

9. Stephanie Coontz, *A Strange Stirring: The Feminine Mystique and American Women at the Dawn of the 1960s* (New York: Basic Books, 2011), 59.

10. Tom Joyce '60 remembers that Fr. Eleutherius was found out when the student manager of the bookstore—"St. Michael's Shop"—ordered a copy of the book for himself.

11. Stephen J. Whitfield, "Cherished and Cursed: Toward a Social History of *The Catcher in the Rye," New England Quarterly* 70 (December 1997): 574. On the next page he noted: "No postwar American novel has been subjected to more—and more intense—efforts to prevent the young from reading it."

12. One outcome of the feud between Mother Benedicta Riepp and Abbot Boniface Wimmer in the 1850s was that sisters subsequently served under the jurisdiction of the local bishops. This uproar about *Catcher in the Rye* took place at the same time that the sisters were reorganizing their administrative structure, removing themselves from the bishop's jurisdiction.

13. In addition to his opposition to S. Mariella he fiercely opposed the "modernist" art produced by S. Thomas Carey. He especially disapproved of her crucifixes and got them removed and, fortunately for us, only stored away. Her work has since been resurrected and displayed, especially at the Haehn Museum run by the Saint Benedict's Monastery.

14. Full autobiography in Saint Benedict's Archives, excerpted at http://

www.csbsju.edu/CSB-Archives/CSBHistory/CSBAdministrators/Sister-Remberta-Westkaemper.htm. Accessed March 7, 2013.

15. Betty Friedan, *Feminine Mystique* (originally published 1963) republished with intro by Anna Quindlan (New York: Norton, 2001), p. 133.

Sister Formation Movement

1. Angelyn Dries, OSF, "Living in Ambiguity: A Paradigm Shift Experienced by the Sister Formation Movement," *The Catholic Historical Review,* 79 (July 1993), 478. Eby, Judith Ann, R.S.M., "The Sister Formation Conference, 1954–1971: An American Catholic Case Study in Authority and Obedience," Ph.D. dissertation, 2000, St. Louis University.

5. Merger from the Bottom Up, Part I

1. The sisters and the college remain metaphorically, then, in a position to need the monks, if only in the domain of the liturgy. The sisters—and other faculty and some students, too—are not immune to the frustrations of other women in the Catholic Church. At the college's centennial, however, the issue of who can serve as the celebrant at Mass doesn't cloud the relationship between the monastery and the abbey. The prioress, abbot, and their communities enjoy mutual respect and strong partnership.

2. Jim Marrin, "Coed Classes Capture Acclaim," *The Record,* September 27, 1963.

3. Within three years of the filing of this report—Connecticut College had gone coed (with Wesleyan); Vassar had turned down Yale's invitation to merge and itself gone coed. Barnard worked with Columbia but remained separate.

4. Lewis Mayhew, "Co-Institutional Study Report, July 1968," (generally called the "Mayhew Report,") in CSB Archives, Documents on CSB/SJU Cooperation, 1962–1972. For a guide to the cooperation documents, see http://www.csbsju.edu/csb-archives/csbhistory/cooperationwithsju/csbarchivesdocumentsoncooperation.htm. Accessed March 12, 2013.

5. The stated reasons for SJU's remaining part of the abbey included its interest in securing federal funding, which might be weakened by affiliation with the sisters. Other, perhaps more compelling explanations have to do with questions of liability for the hospitals spun off at the same time Saint John's Abbey and University formally separated in the summer of 2012.

6. This "subsidy" language was still alive and well when President Baenninger took office in 2004. Her decision to have CSB pay 52 percent of joint costs (reflecting CSB's larger size) helped eliminate this language—at least in public discourse.

7. Doug Ray, "Benny Slams and Hot Dogs," *The Record,* November 15, 1967.

8. Mayhew Report.

9. Sylvester F. Theisen to Staff and Faculty of CSB and SJU, August 25, 1971, CSB Archives.

10. See http://www.csbsju.edu/CSB-Archives/CSBHistory/CSBBuildings/BenedictaArtsCenter.htm. Accessed November 2, 2012.

Continuing Education and the Bahamas

1. See the extensive records for the Bahamas program in the CSB Archives, especially the several versions of "A Brief History." Some material is repeated from report to report, but changes in the program are revealed as well.

2. Trish Boeke, *Vitae,* April 11, 1975.

3. See Elizabeth Hoodecheck-Schow to Members of the Presidential Staff, "Concerns of Bahamian CSB Students," Oct. 30, 1987.

6. Cooperation from the Bottom Up, Part 2

1. "Idzerda file," in Colman Barry papers, SJU Archives.

2. Stanley J. Idzerda, "St. Ben's and St. John's: Why Should We Travel Together?" *Saint Benedict's* (Fall 1969): 8–11.

3. In the summer of 2012 the sisters declared Stanley Idzerda an honorary member of their order. Still living in St. Joseph he prays with them every morning he's in residence there, and he plans to be buried among them—next to his parents and his beloved Gerry, already in the sisters' cemetery.

4. The number of graduates doubled again in the 1980s; since then CSB has graduated nearly 400 women every year.

5. Saint John's was simply richer than Saint Ben's—its wealth was evident in the differences in physical plant, classroom space, and living space. The difference in wealth is a trope—or metaphor—for the disparity of wealth in the Catholic Church. The 2008 film *Doubt,* written and directed by John Patrick Shanley and set in 1964, contrasts a meal eaten in a convent with one

eaten in a rectory. The sisters are eating quietly and meagerly. The priests are enjoying a succulent and boisterous supper. CSB and SJU lived that metaphor before, during, and after the 1960s.

6. Historians of religious women cite the movement toward women's ordination as part of what weakened religious communities of women. Once the possibility of ordination was raised, the second-class status of convent was more poignantly painful.

7. Thomas M. Landy, "The Colleges in Context," in Shier and Russett, 95.

8. Through its department assessments, the report comments on the regard of SJU faculty for its CSB colleagues, but the reverse is not mentioned. Mayhew acknowledged SJU's strong sense of superiority; the report suggests he absorbed some of that, at least.

9. Sylvester Theisen to Jack Lange, November 2, 1971. Blecker Papers, SJU Archives.

10. [Sylvester Theisen], "Report on Meeting of CSB and SJU English Departments, November 15, 1971," SJU Archives.

11. Sylvester P. Theisen to Staff and Faculty of CSB and SJU, August 25, 1971, CSB Archives.

12. Stanley Idzerda to Fr. Michael Blecker, "Collegeville Nine," March 17, 1972.

13. Gervase J. Soukup, OSB, "Reflections Re: SJU and CSB Cooperation," December 15, 1967, CSB Archives.

14. Sy Theisen to Michael Blecker, October 13 (two memos of the same date), 1971, Blecker papers, SJU Archives.

15. Ibid., November 18, 1971.

16. Ibid., December 16, 1971.

17. Michael Blecker to Sy Theisen, December 17, 1971.

18. Ibid., April 10, 1972.

19. S. Alberta Huber to Stanley Idzerda, April 28, 1972. St. Kate's and St. Thomas exchanged about 2,500 courses; two-thirds were Tommies at St. Kate's.

20. Michael Blecker to Students, Faculty and Administration, October 28, 1971, Blecker Papers, SJU Archives.

21. Sy Theisen to S. Firmin Escher and J. Lange, December 29, 1971. SJU Archives.

22. "Recommendations Proposed and Accepted by the Governing Boards' Committee on Cooperation," April 4, 1972. CSB Archives.

23. Sy Theisen to Stanley Idzerda and Michael Blecker, Feb. 3, 1972, SJU Archives.

24. Sy Theisen to the Committee, June 5, 1972.

25. Moseley Report, John D. Moseley, Report to S. Emmanuel Renner and Fr. Michael Blecker, March 1, 1981, CSB Archives.

The Library

1. One architectural historian suggests that built-ins were increasingly attractive household features at the turn of the century because they were easy to clean (no moving or dusting beneath).

2. Michael D. Kathman, "Anatomy of a Merger," *Journal of Academic Librarianship* 9 (no. 4, 1983): 203–206. "Libraries to Merge," *Saint Ben's Today,* May 1980. Paul Webber, "Library Not a Social Center," *Record,* December 12, 1980, pp. 7, 14.

3. Patty Cousins, "It's Almost Impossible to End," *Independent,* May 16, 1989, p. 8.

Bella Abzug

1. CSB *Cable,* November 20, 1979, p. 1, December 17, *Record,* Dec. 7, 1979, p. 6.

7. The Embodied Bennie

1. The CSB volleyball team sponsored a naming contest, and first-year Bennie Mary Haffner submitted the winning name. A second contest asked for a Blazers logo. *Cable,* December 7, 1976.

2. Jon Roe, "St. Benedict Wins, Gets Final Four Berth," *Minneapolis Star Tribune,* March 14, 1993, p. 11C.

3. Senda Berenson, "Significance of Basket Ball for Women," in Senda Berenson, ed., *Basket Ball for Women* (New York: American Sports, 1903) at http://clio.five colleges.edu/smith. This book includes the photos of dozens of women's and girls' teams organized by 1903. Robin Bell Markels, "Bloomer Basketball and Its Suspender Suppression: Women's Intercollegiate Competition at Ohio State University, 1904–1907," *Journal of Sport History* 27 (2000): 31–49. Nancy G. Rosoff, "'A Glow of Pleasurable Excitement': Images of the New Athletic Woman in American Popular Culture, 1880–1920," in

Linda K. Fuller, ed., *Sport, Rhetoric, and Gender: Historical Perspectives and Media Representations* (New York: Palgrave Macmillan, 2006), 55–64.

4. Even this list of sports is partial—for which I apologize. So many women played so many different sports, and they all deserve mention.

5. Both the *Independent* and the *Record* were full of stories about this 1993 team. See the *Independent,* March 3, 1993, for postseason comments.

6. The unhealthy side of this body consciousness is the body hatred it has produced in many women. By some estimates, since at least the 1980s one in four college women has had some kind of eating disorder. Students and graduates have reported that figure is probably not far off at CSB. By 1982 the counseling center ran an eating disorders support group, and the counseling staff specialized in eating disorder treatment. In 1984 a self-identified bulimic student wrote a series of articles in the CSB student newspaper, in which she described what drove her to this issue and what treatments she found, as well as the relapses she suffered. The pieces are powerful and painful; the author did not sign her columns. These issues have remained stubbornly persistent for students (and for many American women). In a 2012 survey nearly 60 percent of CSB students identified as trying to lose weight; of those, 40 percent were dieting and nearly 10 percent were fasting. The Student Development Office has long run support groups for women who struggle with eating disorders. The health advocates work hard too to speak to issues of healthy weight and body image. Still, the problems persist. They're a difficult part of college life, because they're a difficult part of American life for women.

7. Shauna Smith, *Cable,* April 6, 1984.

8. See *Record,* February 24, 2000, special section "Scene on Sex"; also Feb. 10, 2000, and Oct. 9, 1997.

9. *Independent,* Apr. 21, 1994.

10. Not surprisingly, nothing in the college archives provides evidence of student sexual activity, especially not in CSB's first six or seven decades. This section is based, therefore, on stories that students and alumnae have passed on informally or without attribution. What they say, however, corresponds to what historians have written about women's experiences with having and talking about sex for much of the 20th century. See, for example, Beth L. Bailey, *From Front Porch to Back Seat: Courtship in Twentieth-Century America* (Baltimore: Johns Hopkins University Press, 1989) and Beth L. Bailey, *Sex in the Heartland* (Cambridge: Harvard University Press, 2002).

11. The college benefited from Jeanette's readmission. Her two daughters graduated from CSB, as did two of her granddaughters.

12. Anne K. Dotson, "Making Res Life Work With Your Child," *Independent*, April 26, 1901.

13. National figures on sexual activity among 18-to-21-year-olds would put the rate much higher.

14. *Record*, Feb. 12, 2004.

Bonnies and Jennies

1. Lois Gehr Livesey, review of *Beyond God the Father*, in *The Journal of Religion* 55 (October 1975): 478–79. Joanna Russ, review of *Gyn/Ecology* in *Frontiers* 4 (Spring 1979): 68–70.

Sources

Photos

Most of the photos used in the book are in the collections either of the Saint Benedict's Monastery or of the College of Saint Benedict.

Additional images from *Minneapolis Morning Tribune, Saint Cloud Daily Times, Princeton Union.*

Photos of S. Claire Lynch and Bishop Peter Bartholome from the collections of the Stearns History Museum and Research Center.

Online

The single most useful sources have been the online collections of the College of Saint Benedict Archives (created and maintained by college archivist Peggy Roske) at http://www.csbsju.edu/CSB-Archives.htm, and

Vivarium: Online Digital Collections of Saint John's University and the College of Saint Benedict hosted by the Hill Museum & Manuscript Library at http://hmml.org/vivarium.

See also the Saint Benedict's Monastery documents at "Minnesota Reflections," Minnesota Digital Library, at http://reflections.mndigital.org/cdm/landingpage/collection/stbm

Through the CSB/SJU library: *New York Times, Minneapolis Morning Tribune*

Through the Library of Congress: *Chronicling America* (digital newspapers)

The Minnesota Historical Society online collections at http://greatrivers network.org

Primary Sources

The records of the college are divided between the Saint Benedict's Monastery Archives and the CSB Archives. The break point is 1962—the year that the monastery and the college legally divided into separate corporations.

The collections in the monastery archives that were particularly helpful for this book were

> Annual Reports, 1932–1957
> *Catalog/Bulletin of Saint Benedict's College and Academy*
> College and High School ledgers
> *College Days*
> Correspondence of Sisters Inez Hilger, Remberta Westkaemper, Mariella
>   Gable, Grace McDonald, Nancy Hynes, the presidents and deans
> *Facula*
> Papers of the Deans
> Photo collections
> Records of the Board of Advisors
> Records of the Office of the Registrar, Dean, President
> *Saint Benedict's Quarterly*
> *Saint John's Record*
> Sisters List
> Student Directories
> *The Benet*
> *The Cable*
> *The Handshake*
> *The Independent*
> *The Torch*
> *The Vita*

Unpublished manuscripts

> Gable, Mariella, "In League with the Future," Spring 1964
> [Gable, Mariella], *Harvest: 1857–1957* (St. Joseph, 1958)
> Halligan, Marcia, "History of the College of Saint Benedict," 1968
> Kalinowski, Kathleen, Financial History of the Saint Benedict's Monastery

The Collections in the College of Saint Benedict Archives that were particularly helpful for this book were:

> *Saint Benedict's Today*

> "Institutional Cooperation, Policy Issues, and Organizational Options
> for the 1980s at the College of Saint Benedict and Saint John's University:
> A Preliminary Report, January 26, 1981."

"Co-Institutional Study Report," July 1968, the so-called "Mayhew Report."

Gervase Soukup, "Reflections Re: SJU and CSB Cooperation," 1967.

Marriott Agreement, S. Firmin Escher, Chairman of the Joint Study Committee on Cooperation, Feb. 7, 1973.

Moseley Report, January 26, 1981.

S. Emmuel Renner and Fr. Michael Blecker, "Memorandum," Nov. 27, 1981, in *Co-Campus News,* Dec. 16, 1981.

S. Linda Kulzer, "An Evolving Third Model," March 3, 1983.

Records of the Office of Continuing Education and of the Bahamas Program.

Collections in the Saint John's University Archives that were particularly helpful for this book were:

Papers of Sylvester P. Theisen, Institutional Coordinator, Presidents Colman Barry, Michael Blecker (in the manner of paper collections, these include mostly letters "to" these men, so these papers contain many letters from Stanley Idzerda and S. Firmin, and others at CSB).

Photo collections.

SJU and joint CSB/SJU catalogs.

Sisters, lay faculty members and administrators, alumnae have been exceptionally generous with their insights, their time, their memories. This book rests heavily on oral interviews—many formally conducted, recorded, transcribed and deposited in the College Archives.

Secondary Sources (selected)

Barry, Colman James OSB, *Worship and Work: Saint John's Abbey and University, 1856–1980* (Collegeville: Liturgical Press, 1980; 3rd edition, 1993).

Booth, W. James, *Communities of Memory: On Witness, Identity and Justice* (Ithaca: Cornell University Press, 2006).

Coborn, Carol K. and Martha Smith, *Spirited Lives: How Nuns Shaped Catholic Culture and American Life, 1836–1920* (2001).

Conway, Jill Ker, "Faith, Knowledge, and Gender," in Shier and Russett, *American Women's Colleges.*

Curran, Charles E., *Catholic Higher Education, Theology, and Academic Freedom* (Notre Dame: University of Notre Dame Press, 1990).

Dammann, Mother Grace RSCJ, "The American Catholic College for Women," in Roy Deferrari, ed., *Essays on Catholic Education in the United States* (Washington, DC: Catholic University of America, 1942).

Dries, Angelyn OSF, "Living in Ambiguity: A Paradigm Shift Experienced by the Sister Formation Movement," in *Catholic Historical Review*, 79:3 (July 1993).

Eisenmann, Linda, "Creating a Framework for Interpreting U.S. Women's Educational History" in *History of Education Quarterly*, 30 (2001).

———, "Educating the Female Citizen in a Post-War World: Competing Ideologies for American Women, 1945–1965," *Harvard Educational Review*, 54:2 (2002).

———, ed., *Historical Dictionary of Women's Education in the United States* (Westport: Greenwood Press, 1998).

———, *Higher Education for Women in Postwar America, 1945–1965* (Baltimore: Johns Hopkins University Press, 2006).

Ellis, John Tracy, "American Catholics and the Intellectual Life," *Thought*, 30 (Autumn, 1955).

Eschbach, Elizabeth Seymour, *The Higher Education of Women in England and America* (NY: Garland Press, 1993).

Fass, Paula S., *Outside In: Minorities and the Transformation of American Education* (1991).

Forster, Olivia, Emmanuel Renner, Evin Rademacher, Carol Berg, co-auth., *With Hearts Expanded: Transformation in the Lives of Benedictine Women, St. Joseph, Minnesota, 1957–2001* (St. Cloud: Northstar Press, 2001).

Gable, Mariella OSB, *The Literature of Spiritual Values and Catholic Fiction*, ed. with intro by Nancy Hynes, OSB (New York: University Press of America, Inc., 1996).

Ginzberg, Eli and Alice Yohalem, *Educated American Women* (1966).

Girgen, Sister M. Incarnata, OSB, *Behind the Beginnings: Benedictine Women in America* (St. Joseph: St. Benedict's Convent, 1981).

Gleason, Philip, "A Half-Century of Change in Catholic Higher Education," in *U.S. Catholic Historian*, 19:1 (2001).

———, "Baltimore III and Education," *U.S. Catholic Historian*, 4:3/4 (1985).

———, "From an Indefinite Homogeneity: Catholic Colleges in Antebellum America," *Catholic Historical Review*, 97:3 (2011).

———, *Contending with Modernity: Catholic Higher Education in the Twentieth Century* (NY: Oxford University Press, 1995).

Goldin, Claudia, "The Meaning of College in the Lives of American Women," Working Paper 4099, *National Bureau of Economic Research* (1992).

————, *Understanding the Gender Gap: An Economic History of American Women* (NY: Oxford University Press, 1992).

Gordon, Lynn D., "A Tale of Two Sisters," in *Reviews in American History*, 24:1 (1996).

————, *Gender and Higher Education in the Progressive Era* (New Haven: Yale University Press, 1990).

Gruber, Carol S., *Mars and Minerva: World War I and the Uses of Education in America* (1975).

Guttmann, *Women's Sports: A History* (NY: Columbia University Press, 1991).

Hansot, Elisabeth and David Tyack, *Learning Together: A History of Coeducation in American Public Schools* (New Haven: Yale University Press, 1991).

Harwath, Irene, Mindi Maine, Elizabeth DeBra, Executive Summary, "Women's Colleges in the United States: History, Issues, and Challenges," at ERIC (Education Resources Information Center) at http://eric.ed.gov.

Hellwig, Monika K., "College of Religious Women's Congregations: A Spiritual Heritage," in Schier and Russett, *Catholic Women's Colleges*.

Herbst, Jurgen, *And Sadly Teach: Teacher Education and Professionalization in American Culture* (Madison: UWP, 1989).

Horowitz, Helen, "Academic Women: Essay Review," in *History of Education Quarterly*, 20:3 (Autumn, 1980).

————, *Alma Mater: Design and Experience in the Women's Colleges from Their Nineteenth-Century Beginnings to the 1930s* (Boston: Beacon Press, 1984).

Jarchow, Merrill E., *Private Liberal Arts Colleges in Minnesota: Their History and Contributions* (St. Paul: MHS, 1973).

Kelly, Mary, *Learning to Stand and Speak: Women, Education, and Public Life in America's Republic* (Chapel Hill: UNC Press, 2006).

Kennelly, S. Karen CSJ, "Faculties and What They Taught," in Schier and Russett, *Catholic Women's Colleges*.

————, "Mary Malloy: Women's College Founder," in Barbara Stuhler and Gretchen Kreuter, eds., *Women of Minnesota* (St. Paul: MHS Press, 1977).

Kluge, P. F., *Alma Mater: A College Homecoming* (Reading, MA: Addison-Wesley, 1993).

Landy, Thomas M. "The Colleges in Context," in Shier and Russett, *Catholic Women's Colleges*.

Leahy, William P. SJ, *Adapting to America: Catholics, Jusuits, and Higher Education in the Twentieth Century* (Washington, DC: Georgetown University Press, 1991).

McDonald, S. M. Grace, *With Lamps Burning* (St. Joseph, Minn.: Saint Benedict's Priory, 1957).

McGuigan, Dorothy Gies, *A Dangerous Experiment: 100 Years of Women at the University of Michigan* (1970).

Meyerowitz, Joanne, ed., *Not June Cleaver: Women and Gender in Postwar America, 1945–1960* (1994).

Mihanovich, Clement, "Who's Who Among Catholic Sociologists," in *American Catholic Sociological Review,* 7:3 (1946).

Miller-Bernal, Leslie and Susan L. Poulson, *Challenged by Coeducation: Women's Colleges Since the 1960s* (2006).

Morey, Melanie M. and John J. Piderit, SJ, *Catholic Higher Education: A Culture in Crisis* (NY: Oxford University Press, 2006).

Moroney, Siobhan, "Widows and Orphans: Women's Education Beyond the Domestic Ideal," *Journal of Family History,* 25:1 (January 2000).

Mueller, Kate Hevner, *Educating Women for a Changing World* (1954).

Newcomer, Mabel, *A Century of Higher Education for American Women* (NY: Harper and Row, 1959).

O'Brien, David J., *From the Heart of the American Church: Catholic Higher Education and American Culture* (Maryknoll, NY: Orbis Books, 1994).

O'Connell, Marvin R., *John Ireland and the American Catholic Church* (St. Paul: MHS Press, 1988).

O'Connor, Thomas F., "The National Organization for Decent Literature: A Phase in American Catholic Censorship," *The Library Quarterly,* 65:4 (1995).

Oates, Mary J., "Sisterhoods and Catholic Higher Education, 1890–1960," in Shier and Russett, *Catholic Women's Colleges.*

Oates, Mary J., ed., *Higher Education for Catholic Women* (NY: Garland Press, 1987).

Quinonez, Lora Ann and Mary Daniel Turner, *The Transformation of the American Catholic Sister* (1993).

Rademacher, Evin OSB, "Internal Community Transformations," in *With Hearts Expanded.*

Redmont, Jane C., "Live Minds, Yearning Spirits: The Alumnae of College and Universities Founded by Women Religious," in Shier and Russett, *Catholic Women's Colleges.*

Reed, Cheryl L., *Unveiled: The Hidden Lives of Nuns* (New York: Berkley Books, 2004).

Robbins, Sarah, "Reading the History of Nineteenth Century Women's Higher Education," *Journal of Midwest History of Education Society* (1994).

Rossiter, Margaret, *Women Scientists in America: Forging a New World since 1972* (Baltimore: JHU Press, 2012).

Rossiter, Margaret, *Women's Scientists in America: Struggles and Strategies* (Baltimore: JHU Press, 1982).

Schier, Tracy and Cynthia Russett, eds., *Catholic Women's Colleges in America* (2002).

Schneider, Mary L., OSF, "American Sisters and the Roots of Change: The 1950s," in *U.S. Catholic Historian,* 7:1 (Winter, 1988).

Scholastica, S. Mary OSB, "A Composite of Freshman Self Portraits," *Catholic Educational Review,* 40 (October 1942).

Semper, I. J., "The Church and Higher Education for Girls [sic]," in *Catholic Education Review,* 29 (April 1931).

Smith, Lissa, *Nike is a Goddess: The History of Women in Sports* (NY: Atlantic Monthly Press, 1998).

Solomon, Barbara Miller, *In the Company of Educated Women: A History of Women and Higher Education in America* (New Haven: Yale University Press, 1986).

Taylor, James Monroe, *Before Vassar Opened: A Contribution to the History of the Higher Education of Women in America* (Boston: Houghton Mifflin, 1914).

Thelin, John R., *History of American Higher Education,* 2nd Edition (Baltimore: JHU Press, 2011).

Tidball, M. Elizabeth, Daryl G. Smith, Charles S. Tidball, Lisa E. Wolf-Wendel, *Taking Women Seriously: Lessons and Legacies for Educating the Majority,* (Oryx Press, 1999).

Van Kleck, Mary, "A Census of College Women," in *Journal of the Association of Collegiate Alumnae,* 11 (May, 1918).

Wells, Anna Mary, *Miss Marks and Miss Woolley* (Boston: Houghton Mifflin, 1978).

Whitfield, Stephen J., "Cherished and Cursed: Toward a Social History of *The Catcher in the Rye,*" in *New England Quarterly* 70:4 (1997).

Wolff, Sister M. Madaleva CSC, "Educating Our Daughters as Women," [1961] in "Mark Stephen Massa and Catherine Osborne, *American Catholic History: A Documentary Reader* (NY: NYU Press, 2008).

Index

Since arriving at CSB/SJU, **Annette Atkins** has attended more than 30 CSB graduation ceremonies. At each one she has taken enormous pride watching these amazing women students walk across the stage. She earned her own degrees at Southwest Minnesota State University and Indiana University. She's the author of numerous articles and books, including *Creating Minnesota: A History from the Inside Out*. She's currently a professor of history and the Saint John's University Edward P. and Loretta H. Flynn Professor serving the College of Saint Benedict and Saint John's University. She has strong and long ties with the Minnesota Historical Society, the Stearns History Museum and Research Center, and Minnesota Public Radio. She is married to Tom Joyce, SJU '61.